FUNDAMENTAL OF TRACK AND FIELD

DR. N.P. SHARMA

FUNDAMENTAL OF TRACK AND FIELD

DR. N.P. SHARMA
SENIOR READER AND HEAD
DEPARTMENT OF BEHAVIOURAL SCIENCE
IGIPESS (UNIVERSITY OF DELHI), DELHI

KHEL SAHITYA KENDRA
7/26, Ansari Road, Darya Ganj, New Delhi-110002

Published by:

KHEL SAHITYA KENDRA

7/26, Ansari Road, Darya Ganj, New Delhi-110002

Ph.: (O) 011-65190343, 43551324, 42564726
(M) 9811088729, (Fax) 42564726, (Res.) 47091605

E-mail: *khelsahitya1@rediffmail.com*

Web: *www.khelsahitya.com*

I.S.B.N. - 81-7524-290-6

PRINTED IN INDIA 2026

Laser Typeset by:
JAIN MEDIA GRAPHICS
Delhi-110035.

Printed by:
NEW GYAN OFFSET PRINTERS
Shahjada Bagh, Delhi-110035.

Price: Rs. 2000

Preface

It will be found that one of the basic assumptions of the present book entitled ***Fundamental of Track and Field*** is that best performances from track athletes and track coaches can be attained only after long, consistent strenuous, and intelligent work. There is no easy road to real achievement in this area any more than in any other area of human endeavour. A man gains in coaching knowledge in proportion to his willingness to pay for it in hard study and careful thought. Perusal of a few neatly drawn illustrations of good form such as might appear in a small book, may give one the illusion of knowing just how to do it. Or again, to present a single point of view or a one best way of performance in a few short paragraphs, neatly digested from the broad background and understanding of a writer may deceive the reader into believing that he too now has a similar background and understanding.

The book titled ***Fundamental of Track and Field*** is particularly well suited as a text book for different classes particularly B.P.Ed., M.P.Ed., D.P.Ed., etc. The growing body of knowledge and interest in Sports particularly Track and Field is perhaps best indicated by the several books published in the last decade. The contents and sequencing of chapters has been carefully co-ordinated to assure comprehensive coverage and progressive development of concepts. While eliminating undesirable overlap and inconsistency in terminology. Writing focus, styles and organisation have been standardized as much as possible. The rewards are many for those who choose to dedicate themselves to the pursuit of excellence and personal growth.

The basic assumption of this book is that the learning athlete as well as the coach needs certain background knowledge if he is to learn quickly and well. The validity of this assumption has been proved time and again in motor-learning experiments conducted for industry and education. In summary, then, this book is not intended for the half-hearted or half-way coach or athlete, although he will undoubtedly find sustenance here. It is no Ten Easy Steps to Success in Track and Field, although, again, a step-by-step approach is made for each event in Track and Field. Rather, it is a serious study of the great sport of track and field athletics, its history, its promotion, and its methods along with latest rules, measurements and illustrations.

Finally, and most inadequately, appreciation for endless encouragement and a thousand and one helpful suggestions from my family members particularly my wife Mrs. NAMITA SHARMA, my son ASHISH SHARMA and my daughter-in-law KASHISH SHARMA (Mona) and my grandson AYUSH SHARMA for their valuable assistance and help. The high acceptance given to this book is primarily due to their efforts. Words are inadequate to express my sincere thanks to them.

I am also indebted to the fine staff of Khel Sahita Kendra, New Delhi, most particularly Sh. Vivek Thani for his support and help in publishing this book in such a short time.

I hope that my this book too will be of great help to the students, sportspersons, prospective coaches, Physical Education teachers and other concerned people interested in studying Sports: Track and Field at various levels.

Suggestion on my this book will be highly appreciated.

—Dr. N.P. Sharma

Dedicated to
My
Dearest & Loving
Grandson

AYUSH SHARMA

Contents

1

Growth and Development of Track and Field Athletics

The high place of track and field athletics among the sports of the United States and of the world cannot be questioned and certainly needs no supporting argument here. However, two transcendent assets do need emphasis.

Competition in track and field permits many groups to be represented at a single time and place; and, secondly, primary emphasis is competition is against time and distance rather than against human rivals.

The first of these assets had repeatedly been the means of bringing representatives of widely different social groups together under the secure mantle of the rules of the game. Traditional group hatreds and even the enmities of war itself have given way to a single code of ethics giving each man full equality of opportunity.

The story of this remarkable phenomenon is found in the histories and mythologies of almost every people. Perhaps the most ancient of these records is that of the Tailtean games founded in Ireland about 3000 B.C. by Luguid the Strong in memory of his beautiful foster mother, Queen Tailte.

Others are related in the ancient myths of the

Egyptians, the Hebrews, the Arabians, the Germans, and best known of all, the Greeks.

Their influence upon the much admired Grecian character as well as upon Grecian art and philosophy can hardly be exaggerated.

A potentially similar situation exists in our own world. For example, in 1952, the peoples of 70 nations of the world concentrated their attention for two weeks·upon the Helsinki Olympic games.

Although competition occurred in many areas from art and music to boxing and wrestling, track and field was the major unifying activity. Track hold this major position justified by its very nature.

Sufficiently competitive and intriguing to catch the interest and imagination of all men, its primary competition, as just mentioned, is against time and distance and therefore does not lead to the intensely emotional crises between individuals and groups that tend to divide rather than unify.

Further, track and field is primarily an individual sport in which the team score, no matter how much emphasized, is a secondary issue.

It is entirely possible, if only the headline salesmen will co-operate relations without the unrestrained methods, bitter feelings, and all-our professionalism that are certain to accompany emphasis upon national team scores.

If the Olympic games are to survive, and the question is a serious one, they must somehow maintain the spirit of good fellowship that so marked them at Helsinki.

Without regard for the bitterness of feeling officially existing between many of the governments represented, with almost no signs of the rancour or enmity of the recent war, the athletes of rival countries ate together, talked together when language permitted, laughed together, and were often among the first to extend personal congratulations to one another after victory or unusual achievement.

Such conduct is an inherent and tremendously important part of track and field athletics. The over-all organization of track and field in the United States has three phases: high schools, colleges, and those groups affiliated with the National AAU.

Organization of College track

The organization of college track and field is, speaking generally, upon a conference basis with increasing emphasis upon a unified national supervision and a single code of rules for both competition and eligibility.

The great majority of colleges and conferences complete under the rules of the NCAA published annually in its official NCAA Track and Field Guide. Only the ICAAAA, with its honoured tradition of over 75 years of service, continues to fix its own rules and to print its own rules book.

For some years, now a joint committee has been making steady progress in an effort to combine the better aspects of each of these sets of rules and thus to unify all college competition.

Here, with the dates of their founding, are the major college conferences.

1875—The ICAAAA. As its name states, this is an association and not a true conference. A conference is, or should be, a grouping of colleges with natural ties and a common and equal basis for competition.

Ideally, the basis should rest not only on similar sports programs but also on common academic interest and extracurricular activities. In contrast, the ICAAAA provides competition a single-sport basis among over 65 schools having few common factors other than easy access to the location of the meet.

Of this number, only California, Marquette, and Michigan State are located outside the Eastern and Northeastern states. For many years, an indoor championship has been held on a board track in Madison Square Garden.

The outdoor meet has shifted between New York, Boston, and Philadelphia. In contrast to all other college track championships, control of meets and competition is not in the hands of the team coaches but is centralized in a small committee of directors of athletics.

The contribution of this great organization has been of tremendous weight and value in advancing true amateurism and sportsmanship both in and out of college in the United States.

1895—The Western "Big Ten" Conference. The little-known official title of this conference is the "Intercollegiate Conference of Faculty Representatives" and assumes a well-rounded relationship in many sports as well as in other aspects of student life.

Its present membership includes Illinois, Indiana, Iowa, Michigan, Michigan State, Minnesota, Northwestern, Ohio State, Purdue, and Wisconsin. All schools have either dirt or cinder indoor tracks, so that both indoor and outdoor track championships can be held.

The Universities of Michigan and Illinois have dominated the team championships, but all schools have had strong representation throughout the years.

1928—Missouri Valley "Big Seven" Conference. This conference is an off-shoot of the original Missouri Valley Conference formed in 1907 and now consists of

Colorado, Iowa State, Kansas, Kansas State, Missouri, Nebraska, and Washington. Both indoor and outdoor track championships are held each year.

1914—The Southwestern Conference. This group is composed of Arkansas, Baylor, Oklahoma, Rice, Texas, Christian, Texas, and Texas A. & M.

The latter two schools tend to dominate the team championship year after year. No indoor championship is held, but warm spring weather permits an early outdoor season with a team championship on the second week-end in May.

1915—The Pacific Coast Conference. Membership in 1952 included California, U.C.L.A., Oregon, Oregon State, Southern California, Stanford, Washington, Washington State, Idaho, and Montana State.

Although track has been one of the most successful sports in this great track area, the conference has been handicapped by the great distance between schools and the cost in time and money of travel.

It is over 1,200 miles between the most northerly and southerly schools. Southern California has dominated the win column in this conference, but California, Stanford, Washington, and U.C.L.A. have presented consistently strong teams. Only an outdoor championship is decided, climaxing a generally long season that, in the south, begins late in March.

Since 1938, a dual meet between the best men of this conference and those of the Big Ten has been alternated between the Far West and Middle West and has provided wonderful thrills for track fans and participants. Some of the biggest dual meets on the West Coast have drawn over 40,000 spectators, and special relay championships have done equally well.

Schedule Problems in High Schools and Colleges

A major problem facing those concerned with schedule making lies in estimating the relative value of dual meets, relay meets, championship meets, and special promotion meets.

The traditional dual meet is worth while in that it provides competition for many athletes from each squad, particularly those of lesser ability.

It thus furthers the true purpose of school sports, which is to encourage competitive experience for every interested and able student. This very fact tends to make such events of less interest to spectators.

Having fewer spectators means a lower squad morale, a tendency toward having men out for the sport, and certainly less money for trips and expansion of facilities.

Naturally, other more remunerative types of contests are being sought. Since track lends itself easily to multiple team participation at a single time and place, and since such larger meets afford better competition for the best athletes and more excitement for spectators, their number is constantly growing.

Newspapers, radio, and television are becoming more conscious of track as a spectator sport, crowds tend to increase, track fans are more enthusiastic; but all too often the individual of lesser ability has no chance to complete and the size of track squads dwindles.

The ultimate effect of this trend cannot be foreseen at this point, but the benefits of both the dual and the all-star meets need somehow to be maintained.

High School Organization

The conduct of track and field athletics, like that all of high school sports, is under the auspices of the state high school athletic associations.

In 1952 46 states had such associations and

conducted state track championships for the students of more than 9,000 high schools of the nation that now have organized track and field teams.

In general, competition occurs once a week during an outdoor season that varies in length, depending on the weather. Where distances between schools are short, as in large cities or the Eastern states as a whole there is a tendency of schedule two meets each week.

The one on the week end is usually a small championship or special relay meet; that on Tuesday or Wednesday, a ducal meet. This custom has the advantage of providing more competition and therefore increasing enthusiasm for as well as participation in the sport.

On the other hand, it places the study and practice of proper form at a minimum level, so that the athlete often develops a style that hinders future development.

Further, it holds the danger of excessive competition, which, ignoring the controversial issue of damage to mental and physical health, dulls enthusiasm, and takes unwarranted time away from studies. Indoor track in high schools is handicapped by lack of proper space and facilities.

These are gradually being improved with a wonderful effect upon participant as well as spectator interest in the sport.

Many large cities have indoor championships, despite small tracks requiring 20 or more laps to the mile and 30-yard straightways. But only four states had state indoor track championships in 1952.

On the national scale, the state association are banded together into the and supervises all high school sports in 46 states.

No national high school track championship is now

held. The one begun in 1901 by the University of Chicago under Amos Alonzo Stagg was abandoned in 1933 following the action of the National Federation, which strongly discouraged national championships in all high school sports.

Since 1904s, the National Amateur Athletic Union has sponsored a National Interscholastic Track Championship in Madison Square Garden. It is open to all comers, but state association restrictions limit competition to schools adjacent to New York plus a few individuals from Canada. Probably the earliest of all high school track competition occurred in 1896, at the Pennsylvania relays.

The number of participants in this great two-day carnival has steadily grown ever since, with over 2,500 school boys taking part in 1952.

Track enthusiasts and national magazines have each year selected national all-star teams and the National Federation has publicized annually a summary of state championship results.

Over a period of years, California has surpassed all other states in quality of high school performance, but in general the extent and quality of competition is evenly distributed throughout the county.

Organization of the National Amateur Athletic Union

The National AAU was formed at a time, 1888, when what little control there was over amateur athletics was in the hands of unscrupulous promoters and when at times it was difficult to distinguish between amateur and professional.

Its service was so great in these early years and its member clubs so widely distributed that in 1909 it finally split its nation-wide organizations into a number of district associations. In 1950, there were 43 such districts.

For many years the AAU placed much-resented restrictions upon colleges when they competed in AAU events. More crucial has been the struggle between college organizations and the National AAU for control of the American Olympic Committee, which only of late years has found a satisfactory solution.

In addition to the National AAU championships, one or more track meets are held each year in each of the districts. These are particularly numerous in the East, where most of the meets in which colleges compete during a long indoor season are held under the auspices of the AAU.

The most important function of the many athletic clubs affiliated with the National AAU is to provide opportunities for competition among older athletes.

America's greatest handicap in international competition and one of its weaknesses as a nation is the lack of a tradition of continued physical fitness and athletic competition beyond college years.

The average age of past American Olympic teams has been about five years younger than that of the teams of other countries, a tremendous disadvantage in endurance and skill events.

The athletic clubs of the United States, particularly in the Eastern states, have given great service of American track and field during the past 75 years, but the needs of the future call for greatly increased efforts and more nationwide promotion of the sport. Only by such club and National AAU activity can America maintain her present Olympic supremacy.

The Future of track and Field Athletics

The future of track and field does not lie entirely within the hands of those directly associated with it. On the contrary , it will inevitably follow the trends and attitudes developing within our society as a whole.

It could follow the same path toward professionalism and almost exclusive concern for the spectator that accompanied its breakdown in ancient Greek society. Or, to be more optimistic, mankind could discover a road to permanent international peace, and wisdom and balance in sports could then occur in an atmosphere of true wisdom in living as a whole.

Not that sports are ineffective in shaping the future, but they are only one part of larger whole and are more likely to be guided by the actions of the larger unit than to create their own exclusive means of progress.

Actually, sports can be an important factor in the creation of national ideals, as is clearly demonstrated in the history of ancient Greece or of modern England.

Sports and individual achievement in sports are not ends in themselves; they are the means for the development of many individuals to the betterment of mankind generally.

The cynic believes that such a statement is an impractical ideal, long devoid of meaning. He thinks that "Sports for All" sounds well but is too costly and requires too many facilities and too much teaching personnel.

In his mind, the value of such concepts as "growth" and "development" has been blotted out by his great admiration for achievement.

A nation's achievement in sports can best be judged by the performances of its great athletes; so long as they compare well with those of the champions of other nations, we can assume that the individual needs of the average man are being adequately met. Such cynics therefore recognize no reservations in time and energy for the champions, no more primary considerations, no limiting principles.

The champions has the right to put forth whatever how, society must justify and support his action. Either the definition of amateurism must be broadened to cover his special needs or society must learn to accept professionalism as an honourable way of life.

Such pessimists believe that the Olympic games will certainly drop the mask of "no team championship" about which De Coubertin was so adamant and will become a great rivalry for world supremacy.

They stable bluntly that the world has already moved a long way in this direction. America accused certain other nations, such as Nazi Germany during 1933-1936 or Russia in 1952, of all-out preparation of their best athletes from within the armed services.

Yet we have accepted without question our own system of highly paid professional coaching and, in 1952 permitted our own armed services to concentrate Olympic prospects in certain areas for special training. Such cynics argue that a similar pattern was followed in ancient Greece.

Although it was officially proclaimed that the laurel wreath was an adequate prize for an Olympic victory, the champion was actually greeted at home by having the walls of the city breached for his return entry and by being granted a home and a life pension, to say nothing of having statues created in his honour.

Yes, they say, such practices arc inherent in human nature and we shall never trudge our way out of the morass of promotion, publicity, and record breaking used to glorify our greatest athletes. But those who really believe in sports and in the contributions they can make to the proper education of modern youth take no such pessimistic point of view.

The oft-repeated words of the founder of the modern

Olympics, Baron De Coubertin, "The important thing in the Olympic games is not to win, but to take part," are the rallying cry of the great number of mean who believe in the future of democracy and in the value of sports in that future.

They believe that one of the great hopes of modern society is sports, with their spirit of keen competition but always the rules, of intense rivalry but only during the period of competition, and of doing one's best but always within the limitations of the amateur ideal.

They believe that such attitudes, if they can be made an integral part of the attitudes and action of the average man, will greatly influence the conduct of national and international affairs and will effectively further the permanent establishment of international peace.

We need our great performers in sports just as we need our great men in the fields of social progress and science as inspiration, as guides, and as means to a more widespread participation in the benefits they proclaim and develop.

One of the clearest examples of such benefits lies in the University of Pennsylvania relay carnival, which, in addition to its more than 3,000 participants, tries to procure the world's four best millers for a special Benjamin Franklin Mile. Some argue that such a race detracts from the more important collegiate and secondary school races, and it is true that newspaper headlines do support this contention.

However, meet sponsors protest that a single race of this kind is a natural adjunct of the meet. It not only serves as inspiration to the thousands of school boys who participate, but also increases the gate receipts, which are a necessary component of such an extensive and expensive promotion of sport.

To assume, as some do, that all such compromises

are only the beginning and that acceptance of a single such race will inevitably open the door to another and another until the present emphasis upon the average participant is shunted aside is to assume that man can neither control himself nor the forces that influence him. One must admit a certain tyrannical power of the doctrine of excellence, which as crept into all aspects of education.

Somehow we feel we must do more and more in less and less time. But such increased tension and loss of a sense of unhurried leisure are not out of control and can still be used to our advantage.

We must improve our teaching and budget our time and energy, not merely to accomplish more in our own field but to permit experience in other activities and thereby build the well rounded life which will make the "more" really worth while.

Sport, in general, and, to a significant degree, the sport of track and field in particular, must become an accepted and more integral part of Education as a whole. Somehow, levels of achievement must be established in terms of each student and of the time and energy he can properly devote to such achievement.

As science improves our knowledge of man, we realize more clearly that mind and body are not distinct entities that can be educated separately, and that only insofar as there is participation of the person as a whole does real education and growth occur.

A realistic book on modern track and field athletics must necessarily begin with the promotional aspects of the sport. Previous texts have repeatedly reviewed the techniques and teaching methods of track and field, but, strangely enough, have assumed that numerous candidates are already on the practice field, that they will continue to work consistently without special organization or special incentives, that the stadium seats are certain to be filled, or that, in any case, king Football will continue indefinitely to provide the wherewithal. Such assumptions never have been and certainly are not now valid. On the other hand, the word "promotion" must be interpreted from the point of view of the preceding Introduction.

Thus, school track and field athletics should promote many more participants, purely in terms of numbers, as well as the few individuals possessing superior athletic talents.

Unfortunately, at the college level, the latter goal has become predominant so that a realistic approach to the "successful" promotion of college track would entail instruction in methods of organizing alumni, raising funds for scholarships, making contacts with secondary-school boys not only in the United states, but anywhere in the world, and similar activities.

In that at least this respect, this book will not be realistic. In contrast it will seek to detail the many important aspects of promotion from within the school.

Track and field athletics is a wonderful sport to coach, but it is one that requires abundant energy and enthusiasm and a willingness to work endlessly at innumerable details and ever-present small problems.

Its first essential, therefore, is a leader who is many persons in one. He must first be an educator who understands the proper place of his sport in the educational system.

He must possess or acquire enough drawing power to secure good material. He must know the many aspects of track and field events and understand how they can best be taught. And, finally, he must know how to sell his product to this own institution to local business and social groups, and to the potential spectators who might support his efforts financially.

PROMOTION WITHIN THE SCHOOL

Wherever track has become pre-eminent, there has been a vigorous leader at the helm. At the university of Pennsylvania, it was Mike Murphy whose indomitable energies built a great track tradition.

At Illinois, there was Harry Gill at Southern California, Dean Cromwell; at Cornell, Dan Moakely. One could easily name 20 others whose names at their institutions are synonymous with energy and success.

Or, at a somewhat level but equally to the point, there is the account by Lloyd Skor of Plentywood High School, Montana, where neither late spring snows and cold north winds nor lack of a rack tradition and of a field on which to work to could cool the coach's devotion to his sport, to his school and team, and to the best interests of each individual. The track and field program that coaches like these men have organized from the regular student body is certain to have many angles and problems.

However, they can be summarized as follows:

1. Putting first things first;
2. Making preliminary preparations;
3. Getting the boys out;
4. Keeping the boys out;
5. Putting the right boy in the right event; and
6. Teaching efficiently and well.

Putting First Things First

The first step in any job should be to get the important things straight and clear in one's mind. What are the real purposes behind a track and field program in an educational institution? What means to achieving these ends are justified? Which are unjustified? What results are needed to prove to the community, to the school administration, and to the students that the program is successful?

The promotion of varsity athletics must be maintained at a level that is secondary to the intellectual and social aspects of school and college life.

The conducting of athletics in such fashion as to usurp the major portion of the interest and energies of students cannot be justified in the long run and will eventually lose friends and limit accomplishment.

Colleges and universities have been the worst offenders in this regard, but secondary schools also have been frequently guilty. The responsibility for the conduct of athletics must rest with the school faculty and the students, not with the outside groups.

Alumni organizations, interested parents and friends, local businessmen can be of tremendous help in furthering a sound program of sports, but all basic decisions and policies must rest within the school walls.

The siren demands of "Let's get it done now," "Compromise now while we're beginning, but when we're strong, we'll tread the straight and narrow," and "The other fellow's doing it, why shouldn't we"? are expedients the wise are farsighted coach will avoid.

Success lies in numbers. From every standpoint, the successful promotion of track and field athletics places major emphasis upon numbers. With numbers, many will benefit from the program.

With numbers, the best boys will be more plentiful, and success will follow in the big meets. With numbers, well-balanced teams will be forthcoming and a successful dual-meet program will result. With numbers, attention will be drawn to the needs of the sport and a stronger argument provided for filling those needs

Exclusive attention to the stars may pay temporary dividends but even in college, where this attitude is so prevalent, such a practice will eventually work to the detriment of the sport and of all those related to it. The sport exists for the body.

Obviously, benefit to the individuals who participate is the end; the sport and the sport program are but the means. True, the good of the team is sometimes more important than the immediate benefit to the individual, but team benefit should not be confused with a winning tradition or with a coach's pride.

Few dispute the statement that track and field athletics, properly conducted, is fundamentally sound, educationally and organically, as well as individually and socially. The only critical questions likely to arise are concerned with how much and how often. When in doubt, the answer will be found in another question, "If my own son were involved, what would my decision be?"

Making Preliminary Preparations

Unless careful preliminary preparations are made, attempts to get new prospects out for track may boomerang. When new candidates report back to their school associates that they are quitting because there were neither clothes to wear nor equipment to use and nobody seemed to know what to do, the program is already half-doomed. Proper preparations will include paying attention to the following suggestions:

Know your rule book. Each level of organization in track and field has its own rule book. High schools have their interscholastic edition of Track and Field Rules and Records; colleges have their National Collegiate Athletic Association Track and Field Guide.

Each of these books, as well as those of various

conferences and associations in the United States includes not only the rules governing the conduct of track and field meets, but extensive additional information that is essential to every coach, new or experienced.

It is impossible to do a good job of promotion, setting up equipment, and coaching without such knowledge. A complete list of such publications is given in the Appendix.

Subscribe to and read the publications in your field. The annotates list of periodicals in the Appendix will afford each month of the year new ides and new methods that every coach will do well to consider in connection with his own work.

As a matter of fact, the organizations of this chapter would obviously be impossible without he aid of innumerable suggestions taken from these very publications.

The better-written articles should be kept in files and made available to the track squad. Many coaches discourage such a practice for fear the boys will "get too many ideas," especially those inconsistent with what is being taught.

However, the values derived from thinking through these inconsistencies, especially if the boys is close enough to the coach to discuss them with him, will far outweight the possible dangers.

Without exceptions, the truly great track performers with whom the writer has been associated have been men who have thought for themselves and who have often had ideas that did not agree with those of their coach. In addition, to such magazines, there are the more permanent books on coaching track and field.

Each of these texts has its strong points as well as its

weaknesses. Only by being well acquainted with the more valuable aspects of each of these books can a man do his best job of coaching.

Attend track clinics. Track clinics are now being conducted by an increasing number of schools, colleges, and associations.

Personal attendance at these clinics and personal acquaintanceship both with those who head the clinics and with those who attend them will be of tremendous help in laying a groundwork of sound knowledge.

One of the most interesting and valuable examples of this type of promotion is described by Richard Larking of Upper Arlington High School, Columbus, Ohio.

The primary activity of the clinic is the evaluation of the form and style of high school track and field men. Times, distance, or height are given no consideration. Entries of not more than five men each are invited from local high schools.

Colleges and university track coaches serve as judges through the use of flash cards, as in the judging of diving at swimming meets.

Fifteen minutes only are allotted to any given event, at the conclusion of which the judges comment about the fundamentals on which they based their judgements, outstanding details of form by certain candidates, and so forth.

No team score is kept but naturally there develops a very friendly rivalry between coaches and schools as to the "form" merits of their candidates and their system of coaching, and this rivalry is extremely valuable. Occasionally this type of clinic is supplemented by the usual lecture and track movie.

Join your track and field coaches association. Within each area and at each level of education there usually exists an organization of coaches with the purpose of fostering and occasionally of administering track and field activities in that area and at that level.

Such organizations are of such tremendous value to the sport as well as to the individual members that one would suppose them to be universally successful.

Unfortunately, attitudes of "laissez faire" and just plain lethargy bring about a somewhat opposite effect. Where successful, they are closely tied to some regularly scheduled function to which attendance is almost mandatory.

Once together, the members are happy and get down to work with enthusiasm. Probably the best example in this country of such as association is that in the state of Ohio, which includes coaches from high schools, colleges, and universities.

See and how the champions. To be able to talk immediately of the champions of what they did it, is a tremendous assets in teaching generally as well as in instilling confidence in your knowledge and methods.

Have facilities ready. Adequate facilities given regular maintenance and care are essential to a well-organized program of sports.

Further, they should be under the supervision of a special greenkeepers and assisting crew of men. By keeping the tack, pits, and runways in excellent conditions, not only are the physical hazards reduced, but the respect and pride of the boys in their sport and their school are increased.

But, as in so often true, where these are financially impossible, other persons devoted to track should do the work before the new prospects report.

Perhaps certain coaches can make track enthusiasts out of pit diggers and track draggers, but for ordinary mortals it's a doubtful procedure. Safer by far is so get the returning veterans out before the first official practice and have them help get things in shape.

The newcomer, who usually reports with certain misgivings and reservations, is not likely to show up the next day if he is first asked, before running or jumping, to bring out the hurdles or to see whether there's a cross-bar in the shed. If he's a jumper, he wants to jump, and if he's a runner, he wants to run. First things should come first.

Have clean and well-kept clothing and shoes available. Whenever possible, track shoes should be given out to a large number of likely prospects. Few devices lift a newcomer's morale more than receiving a pair of spikes. Some how he feels he has made the team.

On the other hand, to have dirty or till, fitting track clothes and very poor or no track shoes is to reduce enthusiasm and confidence immediately. Yes, shoes are expensive, but with proper care they'll be less os, and in any case will be worth their cost.

Further, the practice of having good-looking, colourful meet suits and sweat clothes will be attractive to most boys. To be colourful is not to be loud or flashy but rather to attract reasonable and respectful attention.

Set up an attractive and prominent bulletin board. Such a board should be for track and field only but should be in a place where students of both sexes will pass it regularly.

Its effectiveness depends upon the continued care that is given to it. Track pictures of all kinds should be used but should include a large proportion of pictures of home team members and of local action shots.

It is important that material be changed often—every two or three days if possible. Otherwise, its attraction will soon be lost. Maintenance of a file of relevant material will prove most valuable.

Establish good public relations in the community and with the press and radio. The pleasure in seeing one's name in public print should be actively fostered.

An active interest by the coach in the selection of a newspaper representative from within the student body who is personally interested in track athletics will prove a most valuable procedure.

One of the better examples of such a promotion plan is that described by James Growney of West New York High School, New Jersey. By laying the foundation for his meet carefully and extensively, he assured its success long before the starter's first gun sounded.

Many groups co-operated: the department of health education, numerous civic clubs and groups, newspapers editors and reporters, storekeepers, the mayor, the board of education, the high school band, and even the town printer. At his first meet, all 5,000 seats were occupied.

Seek the co-operation and active help of school faculty members. A few of the faculty will be found to have had track experience and to be willing to give time to actual coaching.

Such coaching will be particularly helpful if confined to a particular event for which that person is the only coach. Divided coaching leads to confusion and sometimes of unfortunate and harmful disagreement.

Further, close co-operation with the coaches of football and basketball will pay dividends. Speed is essential to these sports and speed can be improved through track work.

Once students understand that the football and basketball stars are also on the track team, respect for the latter is immediately increased.

Encourage community, elementary, and junior high play days. These will usually include a few track events that are certain to create a desirable background in track knowledge and experience and an increase in track interest.

Provide an interesting and reasonably extensive schedule. Such a procedure should take the following points into consideration:

1. Trips are a great incentive to most boys, especially to large meets or attractive places.

2. Scheduling should be completed a year ahead of time. Track suffers from last-minute scheduling and inadequate preparation for meets. This is particularly true indoors when other sports monopolize the best "time" spots.

3. At lest six meets are needed. Many secondary schools in the East, where distances are short and competition plentiful, have a dual meet on Tuesday or Wednesday plus a relay or championship meet on Friday or Saturday. Restricted competition in all meets avoids undue hardships, according to the friends of the system.

4. Telegraphic or postal meets are a valuable supplement to all such scheduling. Meets can be arranged with teams at extreme distances, creating unusual interest. Early agreement between coaches concerning the exact date of telegraphing and the events and exact distances to be run is all that is necessary.

The fewer rules, the better. It should be mutually understood that each coach is free to use results as they best serve his particular situation. To have both schools win the same meet is not impossible and should occasion neither arguments nor accusations. It should be a teaching device, not another championship won or lost.

5. Relay meets are highly interesting and education to both contestants and spectators. One home relay meet each year is a minimum.

6. The first two meets should be "easy", permitting many men to score. Some schools agree to score as many as ten places and use the sum of the heights and distances in the field events to determine their score.

7. Larger meets probably mean fewer scorers within a given squad. The wise coach will limit the number of such meets if he hopes to maintain a large in the East lies in the weekly concentration of all teams at the big-time, big-city Gardens. They are fine meets in themselves but should never have been permitted to become the whole show.

8. Twilight or night meets may prove popular.

Promote interclass or other intramural meets. These should come well ahead of the first call for varsity practice and will thereby provide a background of interest as well as of talent. Varsity squad members should be ineligible so that the dub will be encouraged.

The more colourful and attractive such meets are, the more enthusiastic will be attitudes toward varsity track; if they are poorly organized or uninteresting, it will be assumed that varsity track is the same. Provide small, inexpensive medals or ribbons for event winners.

In addition, some school give participant credit toward a school intramural letter. Some coaches have scheduled these meets during the noon hour, when more students could be present.

If these meets are preceded by four or five weeks of instruction in the physical education classes, they will be more successful. Work toward recognition of track as a major sport.

Use various testing devices in the gymnasium classes. There are several of these in general use. The National AAU is more than willing to provide necessary materials for administering its physical fitness tests, most of which are directly related to track and field.

Similarly, age-grade achievement can be measured by use of Physical Education Achievement Scales for Boys in Secondary Schools, by Cozens, Tribe, and Nelson.

Organize a pentathlon competition. Such competition can be organized in many ways in physical education classes, between intramural groups, or within the track squad on either an individual or a team basis.

Complete information on the use of such a plan is described in the interscholastic track and field rule books. It provides three groups of activities from which five events are chosen by the individual, at least one from each of the three groups. This same scoring chart could be used, however, in other ways.

For example, set up a triathlon, in which one event would be the man's specially; a second event, either than 100 or 200 and the third event, one of the jumps. In this way, men gain in general co-ordination while discovering, in many cases, that they can make team contributions in other than their speciality.

Have many easy awards in addition to a few highly valued and more difficult awards. Freshman, junior varsity, intramural, and all such awards should be plentiful and easily won.

On the other hand, the varsity award should be a high honour and therefore more difficult to achieve.

Stage a spring cross-country run. Long before the cinder track is ready for use, boys can run over the golf or cross-country course. Such a race, perhaps on a handicap basis, will help to insure better physical condition for track and certainly will indicate those possessing unusual endurance.

If properly motivated throughout the physical education classes and intramural groups, a high percentage of the boys in school can compete. Be sure to make provision for the mass scoring at the finish line by setting up one of the approved "chute" methods, now commonly used in cross-country.

Keveren indicates that this idea is worth considerable special attention and recommends that a large number of prizes should be presented at an all-school assembly.

Have track facilities and equipment available. Place cross-bars, 12-pound shots, old but safe vaulting poles, and the like near areas where gym classes or city recreational groups are likely to gather. Few boys can resist such enticements to a little competition.

Stimulate the organization of multiple dual meets within the city or country schools. W. Harold O'Conner, track coach at Concord High School, Massachusetts, describes a system which the high schools of the Boston area have found most valuable.

In 1948, eight schools near Boston rented an armoury for four consecutive Saturday afternoons. On each Saturday four dual meets were held simultaneously. On the first occasion, school A met school B; C met D; E and F; and G and H. On succeeding days, the teams were rotated so that each team met each other team during the season.

Only finals were held, with not more than three men competing for each school. In the 60-yard dash or the mile run, for example, four separate final races were run.

Double groups of officials worked at the finish line so that there were no delays between races. In the field events, competition occurred as in a regular championship meet, except that performers dropped out as soon as their status within a given dual meet was decided.

In 1952 the number of schools competing under this system in the Boston area had increased to eighteen, so that nine dual meets were completed in a single armoury between 1 P.M. and 5 P.M. on any given Saturday afternoon. The potential value, for track athletics, of the extension of such a plan to similar areas throughout the United States is tremendous.

Keeping the Boys Out

All the preliminary preparations and promotional devices for getting the boys out will be the best possible assurance that they will stay out. However, a few additional procedures seem to have special value for this problems:

Set up some type of permanent individual record system. Such a record will require time and painstaking care but in many ways is invaluable. The writer has used individual record cards for many years.

Some oi the men neglect them, of courses, but others do an excellent and valuable job. By the use of both sides of a single 4" × 6" card, space is provided for the daily entries of an eight-week period.

Three or at most four cards a year for each man will sufficc. On these cards, each man records the specific distances that were timed in his workout and of course he results of trails and meets. On twelve well-kept cards will be recorded the story of progress of a given athlete during his entire school or college career.

Apart from his own pleasure in watching such progress, such a record is more valuable for others to review the development of a former champion and compare their own progress and hopes for their own future.

To summarize such careers requires a little paper and pencil work, of course, but as a motivating device it has few equals.

Install a well-arranged and lighted trophy case. Place it where all may see and include trophies and pictures that appeal to the viewer. It is better not to have the case overcrowded. Select a few permanent trophies, which will stay put, but rotate the remainder from time to time.

Give some attention to each individual every day. With several hundred boys reporting, this is difficult and requires efficient organization. Use team veterans to led practice wherever practicable.

Not only does such a method help the beginners, but it forces the veterans to analyse and understand their own events beyond normal needs.

Take the squad to big-time meets or track clinics. Such meets will serve not only as rewards for regular attendance or serious efforts but also as incentives and means of gaining insight toward better performance.

Use a "Who's Who in Track" board. Pelley also recommends this device as a means of increasing incentives. It provides on a series of small shields a sort of ladder arrangement listing the best school athletes and their performances in each event.

At least one day each week it provided during the early season for contesting and rearranging the names on the ladder. Later in the season, meets provide such a basis. Keen rivalries are stimulated by such an open display of comparative marks.

Never cut the squad. However, individuals should be cut when they fail to attend practice regularly, when they fail to make reasonable efforts toward maintaining progress, and when it is clear that a boy is wasting his time and would be gaining greater benefits in some other sports activity.

Make early workouts easy and fun. The main concern during the early season is to keep the boys out and working. Have something definite for them to do each day so they'll think they're getting special coaching but avoid tough assignments and trails of every kind.

The writer will never gorget a transfer quarter-miller who finally placed fourth in the National Collegiates. He had reported for track on one day only at his former college and had then turned in his equipment and gone out for football.

His only reason was that the coach had required the men to run many times to the top of the football stadium on the first day of practice. He decided immediately that if track required such effort so soon, it was not a sport for him.

Put up a record board. Such a board should be as colourful and attractive as possible and placed where not only the squad members may read it but where the students and perhaps even the public will constantly observe it. It will stimulate both new prospects and new records, for what has been done in always a challenge for someone else to do again and do better.

James Pelley describes in great detail not only the uses but also the construction of such a display board. It provides records at four levels: worlds, state high school, local school, and best squad records this year to date.

Small brass card holders, made in school, provide an easy change of record. Nicely printed white cards on a background of school colours are most attractive.

Be democratic and fair. Certainly religion, race, colour, social position, fraternity affiliation, and other irrelevant factors should not be permitted to influence decisions.

Every coach will have his personal likes and dislikes, but the boys should be as little aware of these as possible and certainly they should not influence squad selections.

Once trials begin during early season., see that no one boy is consistently winning or losing within a given group. Mix up the men in track events and run handicaps in field events so that no one gets too discouraged or lacks incentives.

Emphasize fundamentals. Only the usual athlete will be interested and profit from a multiplication of the details of performance. The athlete should respect the coach's knowledge but not be bored by it.

If a coach can lead an athlete to "discover" for himself a new insight or new emphasis in form, he has accomplished more than through a hundred lectures or comments.

Use encouraging and informal nicknames. This is seemingly a minor matter, but it is often an important means of establishing friendly relations between the coach and his boys. With Coach Cromwell of Southern California, "Hi champ" was a favourite expression, and somehow the name carried over into competition.

Use movies emphasizing track techniques. Such movies are worth endless words and even demonstrations. As a matter of comparison, take 8-mm. slow-motion movies of squad members. These are not expensive and will be very worth while.

Take them early in the year, completing the roll in two or three days, and show the film back to the boys just as soon as possible. Several weeks' delay may make the entire effort wasted.

A perfect example of the value of such movies occurred

in the case of Don Canham, now head track coach at the University of Michigan. In January of his junior year, a movie shot suddenly revealed to us that he was folding his left arm in close to his chest while jumping the straddle form in the high jump.

Obviously in that position it was likely to knock off the bar at higher heights later in the season. Somehow, although we had observer him closely for two years, that arm had never attracted our attention before.

He went to work immediately, of course, and by the outdoor season had succeeded in pulling the arm out of the way. In June of that same year, 1940, Don tied for the National Collegiate high jump title at 6' 7¼".

A picture taken of his winning jumps disclosed that his chest had just grazed the bar. Had his hand still been in close, he would never have won the co-championship.

Use a system of awarding letters that considers second and third places. Letters should be considered a high honour but they should not be shut off from the boy who works hard but is always second and never first. Total points for the season may be used as one criterion.

Try a modified "job sheet" system. Cromer writes of the success of Coach Joe Winchester of Pittsburgh, Kansas, High School in his construction of such a plan.

Coach Winshester worked out five job sheets or outlines for each of the thirteen track and field events, Monday through Friday, early season, mid-season, and late season. He placed these assignments on 4" × 6" cards.

By studying these cards, each boy knows the general nature of the day's workout. This is not a substitute for personal coaching, for each boy is expected to report to the coach for specific suggestions, but it does permit men to proceed with certain phases of their workouts when the coach is busy with other men.

Such a system holds the danger of mass assignments unsuited to individual needs, but properly used it should aid in the organization of a large and inexperienced squad.

Trophies won should be published. The fact that the coach has seen numerous trophies won by his teams in the past should not lessen his exuberance when new prizes are won. Present such trophies at the first school assembly and display them in downtown store window.

Make your important meets attractive to spectators. Certain meets should be primarily for the constants so that even the dub will have a chance to feel significant. But as the season progresses, a few meets should be well staged and well publicized.

Section II, entitled "The Promotion and Presentation of Meets," will give many helpful suggestions. To compete before a well-filled stadium is one of the great thrills of sports; to do so before empty stands will soon deflate both the contestants and the sport as a whole.

Track can be interesting but its reputation as a non-spectator sport may force extreme measures to restore its proper position. Either Lady Godiva or free peanuts have possibilities, and the end in view may justify trying both.

Organize practice so that no time is wasted and yet each man gets some individual attention. This is a very difficult assignment and requires careful planning and intelligent organization.

Complete efficiency may lose the individual; rigid individual attention may lose the group.

Organize a track club. Such a club can take several forms and prove valuable in all cases. Some prefer a rather exclusive organization, composed of lettermen only. It is them a distinct honour to be a member and becomes one more incentive to good performance.

Others take the point of view of the Spiked Shoe Club at the University of Pennsylvania, of which any interested undergraduate can become a member simply by paying small dues. This club is partially social, having three or four fine outdoor parties each year; but far more important is its assumption of full responsibility for the promotion and organization of six track meets each year.

Five of these are intramural; the sixth is a large secondary -school meet involving over 500 schoolboys. Every detail of these meets is the exclusive responsibility of this club.

To be its president is considered on a par with being captain of the track team itself, although in most cases the president has not been an outstanding athletes.

Teaching Efficiently and Well

To attempt to list here the elements and methods of doing a fine job of teaching, now that we have the boys on the field regularly and in their right events, would be unduly repetitions.

We would repeat much of the material already outlined in this chapter as well as what is to follow, for most of the remainder of this book will be concerned with just this problem of organizing teaching track and field athletics. Perhaps one comment may be justified.

The individual athlete is, or should be, but one part of a greater unit, the team; and the team, but one part of a greater whole, the school or college.

The morale of the individual is dependent, therefore, upon the morale of the team and of the institution itself. Where individuals seem to make a habit of outdoing themselves of coming through in tough competition time and time again, you will find a team organization and a team tradition that seep down through every phase of activity.

Where teams achieve unexpected victories year after year, you will find an institution sound in its educational program and rich in its traditions of service.

When boys enter such an institution and join such a team, they take of an added confidence and poise. Somehow they assume that they too cannot fail to carry on the high traditions and they too are men of valour.

A coach of track an field athletics is certain to gain greatly in teaching efficiency if he is associated with such a school or college, and to gain more than his share of victories if he can create or carry on such a team spirit.

A good team is equal to more than the sum of its individuals; and it is that "moreness" which is so often the vital difference between victory and defeat.

Getting the Boys Out

Track men, like all kinds of people, enjoy being members of the gang, especially when the gang seems to be popular and enjoying success. The first principle of getting the boys is to demonstrate numbers, even though such a demonstration includes a little "padding of the house".

If all or even most of the suggestions listed above have been carried out even reasonably well, there should be no concern on this score. But, for good measure, here are some suggestions that other coaches have found worth while:

Hold the "first call" meeting indoors. A meeting of all students interested in track, regardless of previous experience, should be held indoors at a place and time convenient to everyone.

Supplement such examinations by health and

training talks. Such talks distributed over the school year are essential to right attitudes by team members.

The fear, or even the uncertainly of damage to health is a very real deterrent to all-out efforts by some boys. On several occasions, the writer has discovered after the careers of certain boys were over that it was just such mistaken concerns that were behind their unwillingness to double in certain meets or to attempt certain tough assignments.

Complete assurance is even more essential to top performances than physical conditions itself. In addition, the need for a clear understanding of training rules and why they are important is obvious.

Organize an assembly of the entire student body. Both boys and girls should be present. Splurge a little on attention-getting banners or similar means.

One coach set up a public address system at the main school entrance and assigned a veritable side-show barker to the microphone.

State or national track leaders and former local stars attend. Show track movies having general appeal rather than coaching value. Salesmanship, and not always of the most modest kind, is needed.

Insist upon a complete physical examination. Where positive good health and vigorous organic fitness are present, the dangers of damage to the vital organs from over-work or over-competition are nonexistent.

A careful examination by a competent M.D. is therefore a must before, not during or after, the first workout. Of course, one should be constantly aware that even such an examination is inadequate and simply cannot detect certain deficiencies. Caution is always therefore the wiser course.

Such specific items as grip strength, body type or

build, and metabolic rate or pulse rate may be of particular interest and value.

However, always be prepared for some such experience as that of the writer when, in response to a special card inviting those having low pulse rates to report for cross-country, he was greeted by a giant 6' 4" tall and weighing over 250 pounds. Such incidents help to shorten the day.

Use of track and field films. No device is so likely to catch the interest of your prospective track men as he repeated use of various films on track and field.

Admitting the obstacles of cost, early scheduling of the films, immediate return, the need for the right type of projector, and the danger of torn film, this procedure will still pay heavy dividends.

Use available health and physical fitness records. Such records are more likely to be available in college than in the secondary school.

They may save much time and planning. Tom Jones made extensive use of such aids throughout his long and honoured coaching career at the University of Wisconsin.

Give many personal invitations. The rise in confidence that follows a personal invitation from the head coach is tremendous and will do more than anything else to encourage the boy who lacks the initiative or self-dependence to report for the first time.

Some coaches feel that such a practice is beneath their dignity or that the boy who lacks such courage is unlikely to display much competitive spirit in the meets. The absurdity of the first contention is obvious and probably exposes the coach's own sense of inadequacy.

As to the second, it should be clear that humans simply do not act in such patterns and that the apologetic, uncertain boy in one situation may be the toughest and most courageous in another.

Utilize every means for practice. Several coaches have written of encouraging boys to practice anywhere, anytime, when regular practice times are impossible.

Stories are common of boys who jump off the morning bus when it is a mile or two from school and run the rest of the way in. Backyard jumping standards and shop-put circles may be very helpful.

Make full use of the school or college newspaper. If full and sympathetic coverage is constantly present, the school paper can be a primary source of candidates and continued school interest.

Because of its emphasis upon the individual, there are always human interest stories in track. A reporter who is interested and knows track can always uncover a good story.

Above all, the coaches should be suggestive, helpful, and certainly publicly appreciative to the reporter foot his efforts, even though they are sometimes inadequate or even mistaken.

If a college coach, maintain close relations with high school coaches. Do this not for the usual purpose of gaining new prospects for the coming year, but rather to seek their advice in working with certain boys or their help in encouraging freshmen to report for track.

Such requests will be much appreciated by secondary-school coaches, especially since they are in contrast to the usual custom of ignoring the work of the high school coach and assuming 90 per cent of the credit for success in college.

Putting the Right Boy in the Right Event

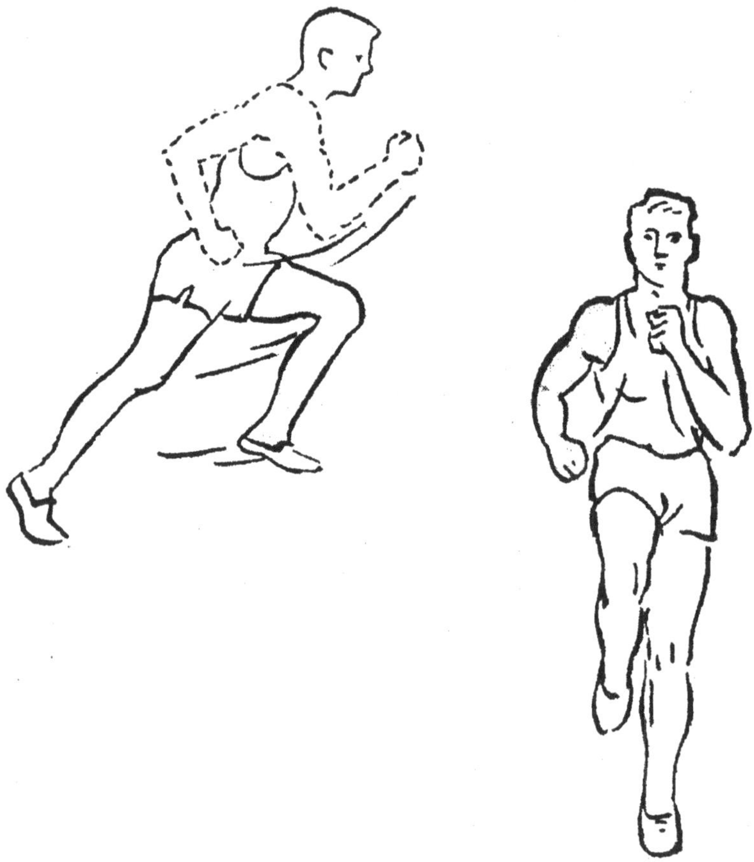

At the secondary-school level to a lesser extent at the college level, the problem of discovering that event for which each man has the greatest talent is often a serious one.

Interest is naturally of primary importance, but often the decision is made on a basis of interest alone and men become sidetracked from their best opportunities. Frequently hurdlers or high jumpers discover late in their careers that they are distance men, or sprinters find that they are better as javelin throwers.

Such losses of talent are particularly prevalent among sprinters, who stop looking for an event as soon as they discover they have speed.

Many times they have endurance as well and would have made great 440 men, filed event men, or even millers rather than remaining as mediocre sprinters. Every coach must discover his own methods for proper placement. However, a few suggestive principles may be of value:

1. The best test of ability in a specific event lies in performing that event. The first effort may. not be impressive in distance or time, but there are few good prospects that the eye of a discerning coach will miss.

Other devices are in extensive use because of their simplicity of administration with large groups, but, in general correlations are not highly significant or consistent. In the long run, unless very large number are involved, actual performance is the most efficient and productive criterion.

2. Start track practice early, in the fall if possible, so that you will have time to experiment.

3. Body types and structure may give hints about proper placement. Some coaches devote much time and energy to analysing body types and correlating them with abilities in the various track and field events.

Some of such efforts are worth while. Tall men do have an advantage in the numbs, hurdles weights, and 440. Usually they are at a disadvantage in the distance runs and 100-yard dash.

Heavy men are needed in the weights, and well-muscled men in the sprints and weights. But such attempts to classify in terms of types are likely to do more harm than good.

Put a shot in the man's hand and watch him try to put it a few times. You'll be closer to knowing his possibilities after that than by any other known means. The form may be frightful, but if something is trying to explode, you have a prospect. It he's too small, have him try the discus or javelin.

4. Urge every man to try other events during the pre and early season. Intrasquad competition, involving a triathlon or pentathlon, will stimulate such experimentation.

Further, every man will find certain events to be of value to his specially: springing, high jumping, hurdling, and shot putting will prove interesting and fun, with little danger of injury or undue muscle soreness.

5. In distance running, pole vaulting, and hurdling, psychological factors are of almost equal significance with physical factors and require careful consideration.

6. Various related testing devices have been developed in physical eduction and are described in textbooks on tests and measurement.

THE PROMOTION AND PRESENTATION OF MEETS

Certain basic facts confront every man who decides to promote a track meet:

1. Proper promotion of track is simply good salesmanship. It requires a sound product, attractively presented and well advertised.

The public will but only what it knows about and what it thinks is worth buying. Few communities are well enough acquainted with track and field athletics to know what it is or whether it has value.

2. Success requires "stick-to-activeness". Few meets are truly successful and almost none "pay off" the first

year. If they are on a really going basis after three years, the job of promotion has been very well done.

3. Track and field athletics, by its emphasis upon variety of events and numbers of participants, includes innumerable yet essential details that must be done exactly right and at exactly the right time if success is to follow one's effort.

4. Different types of meets have different purposes. Pick a meet that fits your needs, your facilities and the tastes and traditions of your buying public.

5. Preparation for the meet must begin at least six months ahead of time; a year is much better.

Pre-meet Considerations

The key to successful promotion of track and field meets lies in the Games Committee, whether it be composed of eight or ten men, as in the largest meets, or whether its functions are performed by a single Meet Director, as might occur in the ordinary dual meet. The functions of the Games Committee can be divided into six major jobs:

1. The Publicity Director, who promotes good will among press, radio, and television personnel and furnishes them with all desired information and materials related to the meet.

2. The Ticket Manager, who arranges all seating and the distribution and sale of tickets.

3. The Meet Director, who is chairman of the committee and responsible for all matters directly related to the conduct of the met. He is the co-ordinator, the gadfly, and the final authority where immediate decision are necessary.

4. The Program Editor, who gathers and organizes all material relevant to the program, arrange for its printing,

and supervises its sale.

5. The Public Relations Director, who is responsible for all activities that promote public interest and good will toward the meet, other than those directly related to the press, radio, and television.

Quite obviously, such a Committee must be well co-ordinated and capable of coming together often and at a moment's notice. Occasional attempts to stage large and important meets in a given city when some important members of the Games Committee live else whether have failed almost without exception.

Duties of the Meet Director

Fixing essential details related to the meet. Working with and through his Games Committee, the Director must establish the time, place, events, and time schedule of the meet.

Each of these factors requires careful consideration. Competition with other major amusements, athletic and other wise, may determine the extent of publicity and attendance as well, and thereby determine the choice of week, day, and hour.

Many big meets have moved in late years to the twilight and night hours, among them being the Compton relays, the Los Angeles Coliseum relays, the West Coast relays, the Big Ten—Pacific Coast meet, and the Beloit relays to Wisconsin. Choice of place is affected by considerations of population centres, transportation means and distance, parking facilities, spectator interest in track, seating capacity and arrangement, promotion and publicity possibilities, and other concerns that may determine success or failure.

Selection of the events and of the time schedule is usually predetermined by tradition and established rules. Where such factors are not present, the Director will do well to think through carefully the purposes of the planned meet and consider how he can improve upon schedules and events.

One aspect of this problem is determining how many events there will be and how many contestants will be invited.

One usually thinks of the short and simple all-star meet as being most interesting to spectators. In three years, Princeton University built up its invitational meet, with six events and the world's six best athletes in each, to a point where over 30,000 people travelled many miles and paid good prices to see it.

The Los Angles Coliseum relays are another example of such a successful outdoor meet. In complete contrast are the equally successful Pennsylvania and Drake relays, where the number of contestants and of events is the primary concern.

One of the most interesting experiments of late years has been the Pennsylvania attempt to stage a "meet within a meet" in its relays.

The traditional emphasis upon numbers is maintained throughout the schedule from Friday noon until Saturday at 3:00 P.M, but a two-and-one-half-hour session is reserved exclusively for finals and the events spectators have found most interesting.

A colourful ceremony opens this period and every effort is made to stage a dramatic production until its close at 5:30 P.M. This combined and well-co-ordinated emphasis upon the contestant and the spectator has proved both a sound and a successful venture.

Track athletic needs improvement; it has followed a set pattern of action too long. Do we need two sprint events? Two hurdle events? A mile and a two-mile distance race? Is the one-mile relay sufficient in our dual meets? Do we need ten minutes between events, or is this a device to facilitate a questionable doubling in certain events? Prizes present another important problem.

Either because of tradition or because it is a natural characteristic of track and field athletics, some type of prize has always accompanied victory.

Perhaps the custom goes back to old Pithecanthropus rectus, who, if he was fast and strong enough, ate the escaping animal for his dinner or won the fall for his bride.

Certainly the Greeks of Homer's day believed in prizes. As one legend has it, Hercules institute the ancient Olympic games after achieving the tremendous feat of cleansing the Augean stables and taking over the entire herds of cattle of his erstwhile employer as his prize.

In the Iliand, Homer relates that the winner of the chariot race at Patrocules' funeral games receive a large silver vase ad a beautiful bride endowed with all the domestic virtues.

In the ancient Olympic games, a growing concern over the problem of professionalism prompted the adoption of the simple but greatly honoured olive wreath to the Olympic victors.

Today, a similar serious concern over this same problem has led to an insistence upon prizes having little monetary or useful value.

Some well meaning but seriously mistaken and short-sighted friends of an Olympic winner feel he or she has legitimately earned a beautiful new car or a home for the family, or even a life pension.

Soon, if these efforts continue, athletes will consciously work toward perfection, not for the game's sake, but for the hope of winning the reward.

Such an outcome is already here in the case of schoolboys who deliberately work harder in order to win scholarships to some college or university.

One cannot blame and individual who do this. They are usually fine, intelligent, and deserving young men; but the growing number of those who follow such a procedure is a matter of serious concern, for with the practice will come all the evils off all-out professionalism.

The solution lies partly in maintaining the basic controls of our sports in the hands of such high and broad-minded men as the late Baron De Coubertin of France or Mr. Avery Brudage, long-time head of the American Olympic Committee.

Characterized as "old fogies" by many enthusiastic fans and press men, they are the bulwarks of defence of the amateur ideal and of a true "sports for all" program. But each promoter of track and field meets must share the responsibility by offering only amateur prizes.

The present-day tendency toward useful awards—luggage, watches, silverware—many seem innocent in its beginnings, but it contains the certainty of ultimate professionalism if allowed to grow.

Planning the track and field lay-out. Working closely with the Head Groundsman, the Meet Director should determine the placement of all field events and the starts and finishes of all races. If the crowd is likely to be small, there should all be concentrates around a focal point; if large, they might well be somewhat more separated.

In the usual football stadium, a crows of 10,000 can usually be seated within the space of a single straightaway of a quarter-mile track.

Events placed outside this zone or in which the start or finish occurs outside it are misplaced. At Minnesota it was found that not placing any spectators in the first four rows of the stadium enlarged the angle of vision greatly and made rising to see both the start and finish of a race unnecessary. One of the greatest handicaps track promotion faces is an almost universal oversupply of seats.

A smaller seating capacity is one of the best factors toward producing a sell-out. It is then a matter of social distinction to be able to get seats.

An advance gate sale is a wonderful asset from every standpoint, but it is only possible where spectator concern over getting a good seat, or better still, any seat at all forces early buying.

To concentrate the crowd, both reserved seat and general admission, is a wise practice. Nobody, likes the appearance or the effect of an almost empty house. Valste, the chief coach of the Finnish AAA, was very much impressed with this factor after making a tour of American colleges and track meets in 1950.

In addition, the Meet Director should instruct the Head Groundsman on the special facilities and equipment needed. Last-minute planning of these matters is impossible because of the multitude of details that accompany every track meet and require early, meticulous planning and construction.

At the University of Pennsylvania relays, it is almost startling to go to the field on Wednesday night before the meet on Friday and note that everything is already completed as though the meet were to be held the next day.

The official's stand are in place, the track lines are drawn, the pits are dug and covered. Nothing to do all day Thursday and Friday morning!

Yet there never seems to be time enough to finish the last roll of javelin runway or to find straighter bars for the high jump. The motto here is well taken: a time for everything and everything on time.

The details of meet management are too numerous and extensive to permit full coverage here. Excellent summaries can be secured, however, from the National Federation of State High School Athletic Associations Track and Field Rules and Record Book, and the National Collegiate Athletic Association Track and Field Guide.

The Meet Director will feel the over-all responsibility for such matters, but he will necessarily delegate many of these duties to the Head Groundsman and almost all the others to the track manager and his assistants.

Planning for pageantry and drama. The degree to which this type of planning is carried out depends upon what the Games Committee considers to be appropriate and dignified. Dignity is a relative matter and in showmanship is determined by the mood and the setting established.

Ordinarily the release of a few hundred pigeons might be thought of as a silly and cheap publicity stunt, but when it is staged at the Olympic games, 100,000 people are awed by its splendour and moved by its symbolism.

Actually, showmanship is natural to track, for each performance is deliberately as impressive as the athlete can make it. He not only wins the events but continues on to establish a new record. The added pageant or parade is merely another somewhat more spectacular event on the program.

One of the more obvious methods of building interest and drama is entirely neglected in track, that of placing the student body in a special honour section with cheer leaders and organised cheering.

Such a practice is ordinarily not consistent with track atmosphere, but in many cases it is most effective.

The writer will never forget the Finnish contingent at the Amsterdam Olympic games with their "Hoo-ee-

ee, hoo-ee-ee, hoyah; hoo-ee-ee, hoo-ee-ee, hoyah; hoo-ee-ee, hoo-ee-ee hoyah; NURMI, NURMI, NURMI."

Or the organized cheering of the University of Pennsylvania student section as the 1950 Penn distance medley and four-mile relay teams kept the gold watches at home after a long distance.

When the first fireworks bomb was used to begin the Drake relays back in the 1930's and when the first Queen of Beauty was introduced, many shook their heads in disapproval, but others shook with a certain thrill and liked it and came again.

Of the college indoor meets, the first to place real emphasis on true colour and rams was the now abandoned Butler relays under the very able directorship of Hermon Phillips. His use of brightly coloured red and green sawdust over the entire arena, his bevy of gorgeously gowned Queens on their large flower-bedecked thrones, his insistence upon formally attired officials, his use of the famous announcer Ted Canty, who scorned a public-address system and had a dynamic voice that justified his doing so—all these and other innovations made the Butler relays a marked success for years.

Their successor, the Purdue relays, supplemented these precedents with moonlighted high jump and pole vault standards and track curb.

Before proceeding blindly to accept or reject in toto all such tactics designed to attract the crowd and build up the gate receipts, a few basic principles should be considered:

1. All stunts and devices should be indigenous. Such naturalness should be related to three factors:

(a) The sport itself. In this sense, the marathon might be called as indigenous stunt based upon the heroic running of Phidippides from the battle field of Marathon to Athens to tell his beloved city of its victory over the Persians. Similarly the thrilling sight of a runner bearing a torch relayed from Athens through many countries to the Olympic games, circling the huge stadium, and ascending the great steps to light the Olympic flame is a natural symbol of the Greek origin of the games and of their modern internationalism.

In contrast, the use of spectacular fireworks, of Queens of Love and Beauty, or of circus clowns and stunts has no track background and no natural place, in the writer's opinion, in track athletics.

(b) The particular school or conference staging the meet. Early established traditions or natural environmental features will serve as guides.

The Navy goat or Army mule are examples of what might be the centre of a five- or ten-minute stunt and be accepted as dignified and respectable. Again, Outing Club activities at Dartmouth or Indian ceremonies at Illinois are sufficiently famous to serve as natural themes there.

(c) The customs and traditions of the local people and of the area in which the meet is stage. Many natural stimuli are present in this category. The Quakers and Independence Day at the University of Pennsylvania, the cowboy and his "wide, open spaces" in Texas, and the Mormon customs of Salt Lake City are a few well-known examples of an almost inexhaustible list.

2. All pageantry should serve its purpose of being interesting and even spectacular but should be short and subservient to the main show, the track and field events themselves.

A gorgeous fireworks display, in addition to being unrelated to track or local traditions, might become the main features, to which the track meet could easily play second fiddle.

In view of these considerations, it will be clearly realized that the entire matter of pageantry and dramatics is a big undertaking requiring careful management and organization.

If he wants to undertake them on such a scale, the Meet Director should have one or more assistants whose specific duties are in this area only. It should be noted that the Darke relays had a chairman and full committee assigned to showmanship.

Informing schools and coaches. It is also a major duty of the Meet Director to see that all interested schools and coaches are well informed of all relevant matters. It is good diplomacy to send duplicate information to the school principal or athletic director as well as to the track coach:

1. Date and place of the meet should come at least a full year ahead of time.

2. Events, time schedule, are preliminary information having to do with making entries or securing hotel accommodations should be mailed some months before the competitive season so that coaches can make necessary plans.

3. Final entries should be accepted from competing schools post-marked not later than Saturday midnight preceding the meet on Saturday.

4. Lists of final and actual starters should be secured from each school, summarized, and relayed back to the coaches for their final planning.

At the Purdue relays, the names of final starters are sent by air mail and special delivery to the Games Committee, which arranges heats and lanes and presents the results on mammographed sheets to the assembled coaches for their final approval and correction.

In the Eastern states a tradition has been well established whereby the Games Committee, after accepting scratches and recommendations concerning heats from the coaches, proceeds without further advice to make up the final slate.

This method is much faster and more efficient, but it neglects the personal element and leaves the competitor as well as the coach in the dark about his actual opponents until the last possible moment. In other section, however, a "drawings" meeting of all coaches is held, at which the following is the order of procedure:

(a) Scratches of entries as well as added entries are made in each event. Such decisions should not be subject to change.

(b) The number of preliminary heats is determined on the basis of the number of actual competitors, the number of lanes available, and the number of contestants desire in the semifinal or final races.

The practice of picking only two qualifiers in each preliminary places too great an emphasis upon the judgement of the committee and is often unfair to the contestants.

(c) Heat leaders are agreed upon and assigned by lot to the various heats.

(d) A second, a third, and perhaps even a fourth round of evenly matched men of demonstrated ability are selected and assigned to the heats by lot. Where extensive knowledge of men's abilities is had, the ICAAAA practice of listing the top 12 to 15 men in their order of past performance has certain advantages. Such a method is likely to assure even heats. However, it does permit differences of opinion and occasional wrangling over comparative abilities.

(e) Competitors from teams having several entries are next assigned by lot. Coaches have the right to separate their best men if they have more contestants than the number of heats.

(f) The remaining entries are placed in heats by lot.

The make-up of semifinal and final heats is usually determined by the referee and a committee selected at the meeting for drawing.

Men winning heats or making best time are separated in order to make the heats as equal as possible. Men who ran in the same preliminary heat are separated whenever possible, and this practice is also followed with members of the same team.

Other qualifiers are then assigned by lot. Lames in preliminaries are usually determined by lot, although in dual meets a courteous practice gives the visiting team its choice of lanes in each event.

In semifinal and finals, a growing custom involves placing heat winners in the centre lanes, second-place men in the next outer lanes, and third-place men in the outside lanes. This practice is helpful to both officials and spectators. In field events the order of competition must be determined by lot, with the order in the finals reversed in terms of performance.

Selecting and instructing officials. This is a most complex and important problem. Track officials are seldom paid for their efforts. Only the starter, referee, and perhaps the check of course are paid, and often they are given expenses only.

Further, to be chosen at a large meet is generally considered a distinct honour and there is pressure to select those whom the Games Committee would like to honour.

Unfortunately, these are not always the same people who will do the best job as officials. For them the meet becomes an opportunity to meet old friends and recall dear memories; yet the officials' first duty is to run off the meet properly and exactly on time. Attempting at accomplish both purposes simultaneously is often unsatisfactory.

Certain rather obvious but sometimes ignored considerations apply in making these selections:

1. The officials should be actively interested in track and especially in their assigned job. Every job has its intriguing, aspects in which a man can take grate pride.

Even the thankless marshal's task of clearing the field courteously yet decisively has been considered a privilege by a few men who take as great delight in enforcing the rule that everyone must have a badge as the athletes themselves may do in breaking a record.

2. Officials should have had personal experience in the event in which they are working. They are likely to have not only greater interest but also sounder and more certain knowledge of its problems.

3. Officials should be selected whose backgrounds will suggest no possibility of bias toward the contestants. Many men, sincerely loyal to one team, can yet give decisions without prejudice.

However, the seed of bias often grows into the whole tree and bitter differences occur. Avoid the appearance of unfairness as well—what it is surely unnecessary to state—its actual presence.

At the same time, it is common and desirable practice to select faculty men as officials as a means of promoting closer relations with them. In such cases, select those sincerely interested in track and preferably those who have graduated from other schools.

4. The clerk or clerks of course and the referee can be helpful in arranging meet details and will be more familiar with possible difficulties if they have had this

experience. They should therefore be carefully selected from nearby communities and be available for pre-meet meetings. A competent clerk of course is one key to a successfully run meet.

Proper instruction of officials is often neglected, perhaps through carelessness, perhaps through concern over the implication of inadequate knowledge. But rules do change from year to year, and memories are often short and in need of annual refreshing.

The mailing of relevant sections from this year's rule book is a worth while practice. The specific delegations of duties for each official varies in different rule books and should always be learned from that particular source.

It is not therefore within the scope of this volume to furnish complete or exact information on this matter.

Welcoming teams and coaches. Undoubtedly the most important public relations duty of all is that of helping and making welcome the incoming athletes and their coaches.

Because of its importance and its complexity, an assistant to the Meet Director should be given full responsibility for this job. Under him should function such groups as the Blue Key or Kite and Key service societies that serve so well at some colleges in this general capacity.

The Darke relays have been outstanding for many years on this point, primarily because the University as a whole and the town of Des Moines, Iowa, have together and individually, assumed that the incoming groups were their personal guests at the delays.

Cars are placed at their disposal, along with taxi and show tickets, information booths, and occasionally escorts to a party after the meet.

The athletes really enjoy going to Drake and are inclined to vote to return the coming year. One of the finest and most legitimate means of performing this pleasant duty is stimulating the local alumni of each of the competing institutions to assume the role of hosts for their own team and to arrange a special welcoming committee, a tour of the city or surrounding country, and a banquet or party after the meet, all subject of course of the written approval of the respective coaches.

Duties of the Public Relations Director

The Public Relations Director is responsible for the promotion of all activities that further public interest and good will toward the meet, other than those directly related to the press, radio, and television. The extent of his efforts within this area are limited only by his own ingenuity and energy and by what the Games Committee might consider appropriate and dignified. Previously attempted projects and stunts are almost endless in number and variety:

1. Many make a special effort to get into contact which luncheon and service clubs, as well as local school and neighbourhood groups, showing movies of previous meets or of competing athletes, giving talks, and even selling tickets. In large meets the promotional uses of colour movies are almost inexhaustible. Everyone is anxious to use them if they are made easily available. The New Orleans Mid-Winter Sports Association annually appropriates $5,000 for the cost and maintenance of movies of the Sugar Bowl events. There are sent free of charge to many groups all over the world so that each year millions of persons see them. The direct return in terms of meet spectators may be questioned; the value for municipal promotion cannot.

2. Drake, Minnesota, Texas and many others have

organized pre-meet parades involving no athletes but other groups, floats, bands, and stunts related to track.

3. Many of the big meets go in for paid advertising in newspapers, in street cars, on posters and in periodicals devoted to local goings-on. The Fresno relays use billboards and matchbooks.

4. First Drake and later Minnesota staged downtown relay events in which hotel bellboys ran down the main street of the town using suitcases for batons.

5. Pennsylvania has encouraged downtown stores to feature track pictures, trophies, and mementoes in their window displays.

6. Ted Carpenter, athletic publicity director at Marquette University, suggests that pole vault or high jump standards might be erected in a prominent downtown place with the bar at, say, 14'6" and that a sign might be hung from it stating that this is the record height made by Harry Mickle-flips of Siwash College.

7. At many meets, certain social organizations or groups have made the meet a focal point around which they could stage a week-end party or over all celebration. If the meet is an evening affair, especially indoors, formal attire by such groups adds tremendously to general prestige and interest. Fresno State College has gone a step further in this direction in its promotion of the Fresno relays by working through the society editor of the local papers.

8. In secondary schools and sometimes colleges, contests between organizations over the sale of pre-game tickets have often proved successful. What better salesmen could one get to sell to local businessmen and local families?

9. The Pennsylvania relays were successful in securing a proclamation from Philadelphia's mayor

declaring the last Saturday in April to be that city's official University of Pennsylvania Relays Day.

Such a list of projects is merely suggestive of means that have been tried and, in at least certain down-to-earth thinking will provide many other, perhaps better ways. Throughout such planning it should be kept in mind that people are primarily interested in other people as individuals and have a lesser interest in statistics or events, or facilities.

Duties of the Publicity Director

Probably the finest article written on the subject of publicity in relation to the press and radio is that by Bill Read in the National Collegiate Athletic Association Track and field Guide for 1947. As Director of the Big Ten Service Bureau, Reed had outstanding success, much of which was based upon the methods outlined here.

The principal mediums for promotion are the press and radio and they will be treated alike in this discussion to the extent that the same material, despite its different uses, may be provided both agencies. This is not to say, however, that the slight effort involved in transposing news matter for publication into material for the radio news announcer will not be well repaid. Nor is it to overtook full exploitation of the most distinctive and perhaps the most valuable services that each can provide, by furnishing outstanding pictures or mats to the press and by arranging interviews with competitors, coaches and dircctors or other informed and interesting commentators on the radio. By reason of the very fact that track and field lacks so many enthusiasts and thorough students the work of the publicist in its behalf is less difficult, for he will find invariably that e sports writer or editor will welcome all help that he can receive in coverage of a meet, including the advance notices that are the promotor's major concern. He will use the promoter's material in his news columns, is the signed columns, in his news broadcasts or mommentaries.

The single qualification is that the material he is provided must have legitimate news or feature value. He may be so ignorant of the sport as to miss a phony feature or a patently inaccurate story the first time but he won't a second time, whereas he will go along even with the "planted" story provided it has a legitimate basis. Therein lies the promoter's principal task, one that involves indefatigable effort in ferreting out items of worth that will provide a steady and prolonged flow of material to the promotional agencies. A well-planned program of preparation and release is a paramount demand. The story cannot be told with full worth upon announcement of the meet, nor can it be delayed until immediately before the event. A considerable volume of releases must be organized with a view to timing them so that interest can be sustained and gradually heightened in the ten days or so before the meet takes places. One of the most valuable of all promotional features is the "form sheet", compilations of which involves considerable research and properly should begin with the start of the season and should include a consultation with Guides and other records references to provide performances of previous seasons.

The "form sheet" should include all local, meet, collegiate or scholastic, national and world's records and a listing of best performances for the year and for past seasons by outstanding entries in the meet. This sheet has almost limitless possibilities for news and features stories and should be prepared in carbon or preferably in mimeographed form for distribution to all the possible publicity sources for the meet. The "form sheet" may be the basis of the "dope" stories that are always of peculiar interest in track and field as they conjecture upon prospective performances in the way of team and individual competition and the possibility of records being broken.

The coach or a local fan can also be the source of such stories in the same manner that Prof. Phil Diamond has lent much assistance to the promotion of Big Ten track meets for many years with the stories from Ann Arbor, Mich., based on his "dope sheet" of anticipated performances. Here are a number of other possible stories of news or features value that may be exploited in advance of the meet:

The entries. In a Conference or closed meet the entries were known immediately but the number of entries with a listing of outstanding performers included is always a good story. If the meet is open or such that entries trickle is gradually a continuing volume of stories is assured. The announcement of the meet itself, with dates and places and the championships involved. A recapitulation of past team and individual champions. Defending champions entered, with conjectures based on season's performances as to whether they can repeat. A full listing of record performances, local meet, national, world's performances as to whether they can repeat. A full listing of record performances, local meet, national, world's, dwelling upon possible association of any of the marks with the meet or performers at hand and the possibility of breaking any of the records. Competition for the team title.

Events in which keenest competition looms. The program, stressing any pageantry or colour being employed. Features on outstanding athletes entered, either on their past performance or on colourful or noteworthy accomplishments to their credit. Features on the coaches, on their past personal or team performances or on their predictions for the particular meet. Announcement and features on any special match races or field events scheduled. A roundup story immediately prior to the meet employing highlights from the above. The mechanics of distributing this publicity material will vary with the community and the area which it is desired to cover.

Much will have its greatest value when distributed in person to the sports writer or editor; announcements of general intense undoubtedly should be duplicated and distributed in advance of a specified release date to assure all of getting a fair shot at the news. Wire services will contribute much in overall coverage and the building up of general interest. But since it quite certainly is local interest and local attendance that is the immediate goal, it should be borne in mind that no local outlet is so small that it does not have a following among whom are potential fans for the meet at hand. The responsibilities of the press steward are not to be overlooked in the functions of the promoter, for the publicity director generally will act in that capacity and the character of his efforts at the time of the meet will have untold influence on future promotional efforts which begin with the colour of the actual coverage of the meet.

The press and radio men attending the meet should be furnished with a complete set of entries for each event, including numbers, first names and school or club affiliation; and complete records for each event together with performances, place winners and winners of the previous year. To these facilities should be added an assurance of suitable writing conditions with pre-arranged telegraphic service, and a means of direct communication with the field, by phone or by runners, so that results and other important information such as lap times can be relayed promptly and accurately to the press box. Unfortunately even assuming an excellent job of releasing news material to the press, the limited space of present-day sports pages and the tremendous hold of professional sports upon this limited space remove all assurance of a satisfactory advertising outlet there.

Consequently, the situation often calls for special measures and special incentives for securing space. This is particularly true in the highly papers. Other towns of lesser size or where the professional sports influence has not gained a strangle hold afford a more cheerful prospect. Although in no way related to a single meet or even a series of meets, one of the most effective organizations in terms of track promotion is the New York City Track Writers' Association. During the track season it holds weekly lichenous, to which are invited those track personalities who hold the centre of the stage of the moment: coaches, meet directors and promoters, visiting stars, and the like. Despite the difficulties presented by professional sports in our biggest city, this group of men has played a vigorous and vital part in the development and maintenance of track athletics in the East and particularly in the New York City area. The role of television in sports promotion is as yet not clear.

Undoubtedly this medium holds excellent possibilities for pre-meet publicity. The usual radio interview with sports figures and athletes is greatly enhance by the visual image. But far more cogent in its television possibilities is the track and field movie. Shots of action in the preceding year's met are to interest as well as those of this year's competitions who appeared elsewhere the week or the month before.

A further important use lies in films that educate the fans on the finer points of track and field: action shots of methods of baton passing, of starting procedures, of high jumping styles. These are sufficiently interesting in themselves to warrant their use, but at the same time will serve as a splendid means of creating and educating track fans.

Duties of the Head Groundsman

The Head Groundsman may well be the least important member of the Games Committee, but if he is in any way shirks or is unable to fulfil his responsibilities, the meet will fail. Only a man who knows all aspects of his very difficult job, who is happy in his work, and who takes personal pride in having a field and a track exactly right can adequate carry out the full duties of the Head Groundsman. To detail his efforts here would be out of place, but to praise this usually unsung hero is very much in point.

In the 1951 ICAAAA championships, the five best broad-jumpers were well beyond their usual marks and the two top men, Groundine of Cornell and Stanfield of Seton Hall, had three jumps, each better than their previous best, ending up with 25'9¾" and 25'9" respectively. Everyone, particularly the press, lauded these outstanding performances. Yet no one publicly mentioned that the Head Groundsman, Jack Eveland, had personally supervised the watering, brushing, raking, rebrushing, and repeated rolling that very morning. He should have had part of the gold medal and of the newspaper accolade. Of course, he never thought of such a thing, after all, he was just doing his job; but, nevertheless, he took a quite but very real pride in the entire affair.

The National Collegiate Athletic Association Track and Field Guide lists fifty-four separate items or tasks for which the Head Groundsman must take responsibility. Most of these break down into from two to ten parts. If the Meet Director is the head and the brains of a meet, the Head Groundsman is its feet and its foundation.

Duties of the Ticket Manager

The primary duty of the Ticket Manager is to device

means by which an advance sale may be successful. He has to assume the presence of such obvious assets as an attractive track show, a colourful and well-planned field and program, and a co-operative press and radio. The stimulation of ticket-sales competition among campus groups, service club groups, or local stores is his task. Several schools have used the football fan mailing lists and have solicited early ticket buying as a special privilege in return for their past patronage. Choice seats or a special price are both effective.

In a conference or association meet, mailing lists of alumni of related schools have proven effective. At the Kansas relays, Bill Easton has used such a system of direct ticket sales.

Duties of the Program Editor

The Editor and Manager of the meet program also faces a difficult task if the meet in a large one. The program must be accurate and complete. It usually is cross-referenced in terms of teams, individual names, and numbers. It is the official reference for all records for this meet and other relevant performances and must therefore be exactly right. It must be organized so that the fan can find whatever he may wish to see at a single glance, without the hurried turning of pages. It usually contains not only complete factual material but also articles, pictures, and stories connected with the meet or with track in general. And finally it must be attractively enough presented to insure its sale at a profit to the meet management. One attempt to increase interest in track meets that the writer has thought over but never had the opportunity to try in using the official dopster's scoring in the program itself. It the meet score is to the close and therefore one of the main points of interests, there should be great speculation about what the dopsters think. For example, in such a meet what reaction should that Podunk has scored eight points and

Siwash one.

Perhaps Podunk should be cheering because they've picked up a second place they never counted on; but, on the other hand, perhaps that one unexpected point

by Siwash in the first event is the real break that will decide the entire meet. Only the informed track fan can have the thrill of such knowledge. Why not inform him, then? On the official program score card, why not insert the dopster's score on one half of the square for each team's score? Every real track fan does this for himself anyway.

Give the less well educated a hint of the dopster's craze for track athletics. In fact, do we dare go a step further? If the dopster's final meet score was 62½ to 61½ in favour of Podunk and Siwash picked up a point in the very first event, is there a serious objection to announcing, 'The meet score is now Podunk eight, Siwash one. However, the final dopster's score has now been changed to Podunk 61½, Siwash 62½"? Every coach who is on his toes does exactly this for very meet and it is the source of his own excitement and his own strategy in the use of his men. Perhaps the fans might like to have a similar knowledge and do their own strategic planning. If the official program should not attempt to predetermine and thereby influence the meet score, perhaps an unofficial dopster's score on a separate sheet could be inserted in the program or simply handed out free at the gate.

During the Meet

If all the seemingly innumerable details given above have been carried out adequately, one might feel that the running of the meet itself would be an anticlimax. Actually, the pressure increase and no one can relax until the last fan and the last athlete have left the stadium. First of all, the officials must report at least thirty minutes before the meet begins, a most important custom that cannot be overstressed. To insure it success, most big meets set up a luncheon for their officials, at which, in addition to a little fun, last minute details can be emphasized. Each man should already have been informed of his exact duties, one of the greatest of which is that of keeping out of the spectator's sight as much as possible. An official should act, and in some cases even be heard; but to the seen unnecessarily is to fail his duty. The practice of swinging up a group of officials indiscriminately and then delegating their assignments after they arrive on the field is inexcusable and a definite causes of delayed meets and poor spectator attendance. Official's duties are detailed carefully in each of the rule books and should be learned from that source.

However, their basic work can be summarized as follows:

1. Rule books vary concerning the degree of authority of the referee. However, in most cases the referee's general responsibility is interpreting and enforcing the rules and deciding all questions relating to the conduct of the meet for which settlement is not already provided in the track and field rule book under which he is operating.

2. The starter has sole jurisdiction over the problem of getting the boys away together at the start. To do this properly, he will need to be a man of both ability and experience, and will do well to follow the National Collegiate rule of allowing at least two full seconds between the command, "Get set," and the firing of the gun.

3. The inspectors and head inspector report whatever they may see in the way of rule infractions to the referee for his decision and resulting enforcement of the rules. He alone can make these decisions.

4. The number of timers is traditionally four, all of whom time the winner only. Three watches are official, with the fourth watch to be used in case of any failure by the others. The official time is that of the middle watch or of the two identical watches. The most common error

in timing is in stopping the watch too soon at the finish line. The same time interval should elapse between the actual finish and the stopping of the watch as took place between the flash of the gun and the starting of the watch. That is, the timer should first see the winner reach the finish line and then press the watch control. For the information of coaches, the press, and the runners, additional timers are now being used to catch second, third, and even fourth positions.

5. The judges of the finish, one more than the number of places in the meet, select all place winners in accordance with their preferred pattern of working together. All rule books suggest workable methods.

6. The clerk of course is the most important of all officials from the standpoint of running events on schedule. Assuming that a proper length of time between events has been allowed, he should feel it his personal duty to start the last event one minute ahead of time.

7. Similarly, the chief judge of field events is responsible for the correct and rapid completion of all fields events. That every contestant should have a reasonable opportunity to do his best is unquestioned; yet such consideration has undoubtedly been overstressed and should be balanced with a demand for getting the job done on time.

8. The judges of field events, under the chief judge's supervision, are delegated the responsibility for running off their assigned events in accordance with the rules and on time.

9. The marshal must take on increasing responsibility as emphasis upon the spectator increases. He should be adamant in his insistence that every person on the field have an official's badge be. If such badges are handed out indiscriminately by the Meet Director or the Press Relations department, they are the culprits, not he, and they should be penalized.

2

Construction and Care of Facilities and Equipments

Whenever one finds strong track and field teams, one will also discover, almost invariably, soundly constructed facilities, well-maintained for both practice and meets; adequate and well-organized equipment; and, basic to it all, groundkeepers and equipment men who are well-paid and interested in their jobs. Many are the record achievements that might properly have been credited to the construction engineer, or to the groundsman who gave the track "just one more brush and roll", then raked and brushed and rolled it once again. The most important essential in constructing track and field facilities is a sound plan based upon the wide experiences of many other persons and institutions as well as upon a careful analysis of local conditions and local needs.

The latter condition is just as important as the former. One might feel safe in adopting the recommendations of a recent survey based upon the opinions of 177 track coaches. Yet actually such a recommendation is merely an average opinion that might be entirely out of place considering local conditions and needs. Ralph Young, Director of Athletics at Michigan State College, mentioned in a talk before the National Track Coaches Association that he had spent two years in planning their outdoor track, had personally visited most of the best tracks in the country, and had secured detailed plans from 60 different coaches and colleges, including four foreign countries and the International Olympic Committee.

In addition, he used the college's Agricultural Department in making soil analyses and selection its climatologists for information about prevailing winds and their effect on direction of runways and so forth, and of course its engineers for all aspects of actual construction.

How many, many times in discussing track facilities the writer has heard the complaint, "If only they had planned a little better and built the thing right in the first place."

The needs of both spectators and participants, local soil beds and available soils, rainfall during the months of competitions, prevailing winds, presence of other athletic facilities or parking areas, the extent and kind of use to which the facility will he put during its many years of service—each of these and many other details demand the most careful consideration.

For example, in order to meet the increasing needs of its great Relay Carnival, the University of Pennsylvania rebuilt its track in 1951 to provide 12 lanes of 38 inches each all the way round. On its Friday program, in which there are innumerable 440-yard relay heats, this meant a saving of 45 minutes and a great increase in spectator appeal. Few track programs would require so many lanes or such width of track.

Track Construction

Track dimensions. All outstanding tracks in the Far West, the Middle West, and the East are 440 yards in length but vary in the radius of their curves from 97'6" at Ohio State to 127 feet at Stanford.

There is a growing tendency in track presentation to start and finish all races as much as possible in front of

the spectators. This leads to more frequent running around the curves and to greater need for increased radii and widths of track on the curves.

The best hurdle lane is 50 inches wide, and thus a total track width of 25 feet is required for 6 lanes of hurdles. This point of view explains the request, in the Athletic Journal's 1952 survey, for a track 5 feet wider than that requested in Henry Schulte's 1930 survey.

Coaches agree that best conditions for participants occur in the 220; 440-, and 220-yard low hurdles when 250-yard straightway is provided.

Consequently, they are loath to eliminate this feature even though increasingly concerned about better vision for spectators.

Drainage. The nature and extent of the problem of drainage is dependent alm'ost entirely upon local conditions of soil and weather during the track season.

At the University of Nebraska, for example, the track bed is almost pure sand and therefore required a minimum of excavation and rough fill. On such a track, the more it rains, the faster the track is likely to be.

Other tracks, in contrast, have been laid on low marshy ground where there is much rainfall in the spring. Full timing and use of storm sewers would therefore be necessary.

Normally, however, full excavation of from 21 to 24 inches with rough and medium filling, as indicated later, will take care of all requirements. Where drainage tile is required, only an engineer can decide just how much and where to put it.

At Drake University, 48 lines of 4-inch tile were laid laterally to the track in coarse cinder ditches so that they passed beneath the track curbing and empties into the track infield. Since the track is built 4 feet above the infield, bot the subsoil and surface layers are pitched to the inside.

At Michigam State, catch basins were located every 35 feet both inside and outside the track. On the infield side of the curb, a path 2 feet wide and 13½ inches deep was excavated all around the track.

After 6-inch tiles were loosely laid, they were covered by 10½ inches of coarse gravel and cinders, with 3 inches of fine gravel on the surface. Later, this path was found to be usable for practice purposes even during the rainy season. Each locale has its own problems, which require specific planning.

Rough fill. There is general agreement throughout the country on the use of either heavy clinkers or 3-to-4 inch stone, either or in the forms of gravel, for the initial coarse layer.

Local conditions will determine its depth, although about 20 inches is usually considered adequate. To hurry settling and provide an early top surface, this layer is usually rolled thoroughly. However, such rolling is dangerous to tile and sometimes crushes coarse cinders.

Middle layer. On top of the rough fill, it is common practice to place about 6 inches of coarse cinders such as would be retained on a ¾" mesh screen.

Top dressing. Tradition in the United States suggests a mixture of 1 part clay or clay loam to 2 parts "front" or "head-end" cinders.

These latter were the hard little cinder pellets that were caught by the locomotive stack screen and dropped back into the head-end of the fire box to be shovelled out at the roundhouse.

Unfortunately, the use of softer coals and the expense of saving such material has made good head-end cinders almost unavailable. Ordinary boiler cinders crush easily and either turn to dust and blow away or, worse, remain in the track to form an impervious hard pan when dry and mud when wet.

Much care should therefore be taken in selecting cinders, for they can easily negate much of the expense and care of building the track. Without doubt, American coaches should be turning to science and research for the discovery of better materials for top dressing on their running tracks.

Actually, our knowledge of what is best for fast running as well as best for maintenance is quite uncertain and based almost entirely upon opinion. One the one hand, for example, we hear respected coaches speaking of tracks that have "life" or "bounce" or "resiliency". Yet they also praise the fast clay tracks of the West Coast or the University of Chicago fieldshouse, which have no "give" or "bounce" whatsoever.

In writing of Stanford's new track, the engineer, J.H. McDonald, stated that "every track in order to have a 'jarless,' yet firm surface must be cushioned." The builders therefore very carefully placed 1½ inches of redwood bark 12 inches below the surface, under cinders, clay, and crushed rock, to provide a "cushion" against too solid a foundation.

How really effective was this procedure? One of the virtues for cinder tracks generally is that they are easier on the legs in both practice and meets than harder and less buoyant surface.

Yet teams working on indoor wooden tracks or on the clay surfaces at the Chicago, Michigan State, or Purdue fieldhouses certainly have no more "shin splints" or sore muscles, and possibly fewer, than where tracks are softer and tend to give with each sprinting stride.

It seems clear that we actually know very little in this and related subjects and that careful research in the future is needed to establish the facts of the case and the best materials to use for both track and field facilities. Greater differences of opinion concerning the right materials and right proportions for top dressing were found by the 1952 Athletic Journal survey than on any other subject.

The average opinions was given as 3 parts of cinders

to 1 to clay, but at least a dozen alternatives were suggested, several of which had many adherents.

Proportions of 4:1, 3:1, 2:1, 1:1, 1:2 and 1:3 of cinders and clay all had their advocates. Brick dust and clay was suggested by five coaches. The addition of peat moss and sawdust was mentioned as helping to hold moisture in the track.

In the West, where oil-burning makes cinders almost nonexistent, experiments with "decomposed" granite and clay, sifted carbon with clay, decomposed lava ash, or crushed limestone have been tried and have their supporters.

The Crub. Opinion is almost unanimous that concrete curbing provides the best and most permanent material. Present rules suggest a curb that rises 4 inches above the track, and common practice makes it 4 inches wide.

Its depth in the ground is determined by the frost line and should be established so that no heaving during the winter months can possibly occur.

Wood that has been well creosoted has often been used, but at least it provides only a dozen years of use. Old railroad rails have also been used, but one would have difficulty in finding such material available today.

Undoubtedly the most unique and spectacular of all curbing was a hollow plastic tube, with fluorescent lighting, which was used at the indoor Purdue relays.

Track grading. Accepted practice in the construction of tracks is to make the top surface exactly level. Excess surface water will run to the surface drains on either or both the inside and outside of the track while the porous track materials absorb the remainder.

However, constant use of the inside lane tends to lower this part of the track, and groundsmen all too frequently fail to maintain its height.

On nine-tenths of the tracks of the country, inspection following a heavy rain will discover water standing around the inside 2 or 3 lanes of the track, just where it is least wanted in either practice or meet competition. All plans for both construction and maintenance should keep this serious problem in mind.

Field Lay-outs

An ideal plan for track and field facilities requires careful consideration of many factors. Foremost among these are (1) the requirements of best athletic competition,

(2) the needs of spectators,

(3) the costs of construction, and

(4) the cost and ease of maintenance.

Michigan State's outdoor track probably accomplishes the first two of these considerations more completely than any other track in the world.

On the other hand, both its original cost and the tremendous daily care required for such extensive facilities make their adoption at other schools very difficult.

Note that the pole vault and broad jump use the same runways. Since wind directions determine the direction of run in both instances, no interference can result.

In such case, groundsmen will maintain both runways equally well. Where there are separate places for these two events with two runways for each, there is an almost universal tendency to neglect the runway opposed to the prevailing winds. Then, when an emergency forces their use, poorer competitive conditions almost always result.

In the writers's judgement, it is easier and even

cheaper to maintain a single runway are likely to be more consistently maintained.

However, each of these plans assumes a field that is used exclusively for track and field athletics, an all-off-infrequent occurrence. The requirements of football and other sports using the field force the placement of field events outside the gridiron.

As a matter of interest, such requirements undoubtedly influenced the decision early in the history of track and field as to the length of running track.

From a spectator's standpoint, a smaller track—220 yards for example—with wide curves would have provided a much more interesting prospect. Undoubtedly this is one of the great reasons for the popularity of indoor track in the East and Middle West.

Everything occurs directly in front of everyone and the athletes become clearly viewed personalities rather than distant blurs with arms and legs.

The fertile brain of the man who was probably track's greatest innovator, Bem Ogden, of Temple University, has proposed an outdoor horseshoe stadium around a 220-yard track.

The 100 and high hurdles would be down the centre of the field, the 220 and low hurdles around one curve. This would be a little rough on these latter contestants but wonderful for the spectator.

A fair cored would seem large and encourage pre-game ticket buying whereas even a good track crowd in a football stadium seems lost and disappointing. Regardless of the merit of such a field, the fact remains that in the great majority of cases, the lay-out of track facilities must allow for an inner field that cannot be unaided.

Construction of Field Event Facilities

In general, the plan for excavation, drainage, and choice of materials will be consistent with that followed in constructing the track itself. However, because runways and circles can be raised as well as covered by waterproof materials, there is a lesser tendency to provide special and costly drainage systems.

These two reasons, added to the need for a running surface that is more firm and resistant to concentrated use, also produce a tendency to use a higher proportion of clay or clay loam in the top dressing mixture.

Pole vault. The runway in the pole vault should be from 120 to 140 feet in length. Where a single runway is used with two pits or where the pole vault and broad jump are combined , a length of 150 feet is best.

The runway width should, in general, be 4 feet but should be determined by maintenance considerations—the width of the brushes and rollers that will be used, for example. In most cases, it will be found best to raise the level of the runway at least 3 inches above that of the surrounding ground, and thus prepare for unusually heavy rainfall.

On innumerable occasions, the success or failure of an entire year's preparation for the big championship meet has been determined by facilities rather than by the ability or the perfection of preparation of the athletes. Simply to laugh off a soggily runway with.

"That's the breaks of the game" is infuriating to one who knows that it was actually laziness or lack of interest that created the "break", rather than the untouchable gods of chance. The pole vault pit is now misnamed. The terms is undoubtedly derived from the outmoded custom of digging into the ground to form a softer surface for landing.

Today, such a practice is, or should be, unthinkable and should call down the wrath of other coaches, contestants, and spectators alike.

If a coach wishes to discourage vaulting, he could think of no more certain methods. The more modern term should be a "pole vault mound," for the landing area should always be a mound of thin shavings and sawdust at least 2 and preferably 3 feet high.

One of the greatest deterrents to best performances in the pole vault is the feat of injury in making a landing. Such a mound, if at least 16 feet wide by 12 feet deep as demanded by National Collegiate rules, is the best means of removing such feat. Its expense is not great, although rain, wind, and the neighbourhood kids to require that it be covered by canvas at all times when not in actual use.

Extra bags of shavings should be placed completely around the mound to hold the loose shavings in place, and also against any protruding boards or pole vault standards that might prove injurious to the vaulter.

Such assurance of freedom from injury is almost guaranteed to add 6 inches or even a foot to the average vaulter's performance. Materials other than shavings have been and are being tried, of course. Sawdust, shavings and sand, tanbark, a foam rubber mattress on top of be springs and cotton-seed hulls all have their advocates.

Ben ogden, of Temple University, has invented a kind of circus not held up to a 6-or 8-foot height be weights and pulleys, which wafts the vaulter as gently as a feather to the ground.

Out of such concern for increased safety and comfort will eventually come ever greater world's records. Indoors, it is occasionally or even regularly necessary to move the pole vault pit to make room for bleachers or other sports events.

In the Chicago fieldhouse, shavings and sawdust used to be dumped wherever the event was to be held, sometimes along the wall, other times in the centre.

By erecting the pit 3 feet high and taking special precautions to stamp down the shavings a little before anyone vaulted, no injuries occurred from the hard clay surface underneath. A different device was erected in Yost Field at the University of Michigam.

A strong wooden box 16' × 12' in size and 24 inches deep was raised from the hard ground on 5 steel dollies. Shavings were heaped in the box to a height of 3½ to 4 feet from the ground.

The runway side of the box was low, with bags of shavings holding the pit material in place. All wooden edges were covered with mats and shavings bags. Vaulters could run up into the box and even through if necessary.

Visiting vaulters cleared heights that were consistent with their effort elsewhere. The great advantage of this device was that it could be run into an out-of-the-way corner in just a few minutes and back again when needed.

Broad jump. The runway for the broad jump can properly be identical to that of the pole vault. Broad-jumpers, on the average run farther than pole vaulters, and allowance must be made for the placement of the take-off board; but a length of 150 feet should prove adequate. Its width could be as great as 5 feet, for, it the take-off board is equally wide and the landing pit 6 feet wide as the rules require, runners can move to either side of the centre of the runway in their search for better footing.

The take-off board should be placed from 8 to 12 feet

from the landing pit and should, according to National Collegiate rules, be a "joist 8 inches wide and at least 4 feet long, which shall be set firmly in and on the same level as the ground."

Opinion that this broad should be widened to prevent the very prevalent heel bruises that come from hitting the near edge of the broad is gaining ground in college track circles, and the National Federation of State High School Associations now accepts records made on boards up to 24 inches in width.

A solid take-off is essential to both safety and good jumping and therefore it is common practice to use an 8" × 8" timber as a foundation under the 2-inch-thick take-off board. This permits quick change of the board when badly chewed by drawing spikes and insures a level and firm base from which to jump.

Any future change to a wider take-off board will necessitate a similar increase in the width of this timber. The pit should be at least 15 feet long, exactly level with the take-off board, and should extend at least 4 feet beyond the best possible jump by any competitor.

It is usually filled with sand mixed with sawdust and/ or sandy loam. This should be soft enough to prevent scratches and undue jarring, yet cohesive enough to provide accurate measurement.

This latter point is very important and often neglected. Many a record jump has been reduced by the use of materials that fall away as the heels of the jumper dig into the pit. Dry sand is very poor in this respect.

As in so many other instances, experimentation in the selection of the mixture is all-important.

High jump. If one can assume dry conditions, as is the case during indoors meets, clay is the best material for a high jump take-off. It requires an exact knowledge of just how much water is needed and when to apply it, but once this is attained, a clay take-off is simple to maintain and will take an endless amount of jumping.

The University of Chicago, for example brushed enough sawdust into its clay surface to maintain consistent moisture conditions. Their groundsmen know that a given temperature in the field house called for just so much sprinkling each week.

During the many years in which the Big Ten championships were held there, the writer never noticed other than ideal conditions for both track and field event.

Outdoors, however, the spring rains complicate the problem considerably. Clay is dangerously slippery when wet, and, although canvas can be used to cover the practice area at all other times, rain during a meet makes jumping almost impossible.

Where spring rains are common, adequate drainage is provided and cinders are usually mixed with the clay. In the Athletic Journal study, 58 percent of Eastern coaches, 40 percent of Middle Western coaches, and 25 per cent of Western coaches used a clay and cinder mixture.

Experimentation with all-weather materials is occurring, for 6 per cent of the coaches in the East and South stated they were using an asphalt take-off.

It seems cleat that, for outdoors uses, better materials should and probably can be found. In 1952, an excellent clay surface was constructed for the high jump at the University of Pennsylvania.

The area was kept constantly under cover when not in use and water was applied exactly as needed. The danger of rain during a meet was realized, but the benefits of a clay surface were considered to offset such a possibility. That same year, it rained for four days straight just before the big Relay Carnial. The canvas was in place, but water flowed around and under it in such quantity as to make jumping at any height almost impossible.

In desperation, the groundskeeper, Mr. Jack Eveland, spread off a full inch of clay mud, then brought in large quantities of dry unmixed cinders. These were ranked down into the clay and lightly rolled.

The result was truly amazing and provided a surface from which 4 men cleared 6'2" and one the winning height of 6'5". It now seems probable that a cinder mixture will be maintained at the high jump on Franklin Field.

The all-too-common practice of cutting in directly to the high jump standard, forming an area resembling a truncated triangle, is unfair to the jumpers who approach from the extent left or right.

The entire area should be built up at least an inch above the surrounding ground and sloped so that water will run off toward either natural or artificial drainage system.

Constant rolling, which is so important to good high-jumping, will gradually lower this so that each year new materials must be added.

The pit must, according to National Collegiate and High School rules, be at least 16 feet long and 12 feet wide. Height is not essential, but accepted practice calls for a mound of sawdust or thin shavings and sand that is about 12 inches above the ground.

All boards used to hold the dirt walls of the pit in place should be covered with bags of sawdust. In rainy areas, especially before meets, canvas covers for both the pit and the take-off area will prove invaluable.

Shot, discus, and hammer circles. Best practice in those institutions that take pride in maintaining excellent field facilities is to set aside an area about 10' × 24' in size for each weight event. This permits iron circles to be moved in practice as use may suggest.

National Collegiate and High School rules state that the circumference of weight circles shall be marked by an iron or wooden band, sunk flush with the ground; but for practice purposes they can be moved from place to place on the ground surface.

Having areas of this size also makes possible easier maintenance, for the entire area can be brushed and rolled with the same machines as in the other field events.

An usual, the type of surface varies with climatic conditions. When these are ideal, clay is considered best; when poor, a cinder-loam mixture will be most satisfactory.

It is always best to raise the surface above the surrounding ground level and to provide both drainage and run-off means. In the Northeastern states, where spring is late and often wet, concrete circles for shot, discus, and hammer throwing are rapidly gaining favour.

They provide consistently level and non-slippery surfaces that are identical at all institutions. They are somewhat more costly to construct but require almost no care. Further, they can be used throughout the entire year whenever temperatures or snowfall conditions permit.

Javelin. One of the greatest deterrents to excellent javelin throwing in the United States is the grass runways that are still considered adequate in both high schools and colleges. Their use is excused on the grounds that lack of space does not permit a special and permanent runways for the javelin.

And this can actually be the case. But if record distances are expected, a firm footing not ordinarily provided by turf must be assured. National rules have recently been changed to conform with international standards.

At the present time, the run-up for the javelin shall be marked by 2 parallel lines 13' 1½" apart and the throw shall be from behind an arc of a circle drawn with a radius of 26' 3". Such are shall consist of a band made of wood or metal 2¾ inches in width sunk flush with the ground.

In Europe, this run-up is constructed like that of the pole vault and broad jump, with a curb enclosing a raised runway made of clay or a clay-cinder mixture. This permits the firm footing that is so necessary to the fast momentum and great distances achieved in European styles of throw.

Track Maintenance

First concern during the pre-season period is to gain every possible assurance that both drainage and seepage are adequate.

Early spring rains will bring into clear evidence the low areas in the track, and additional top dressing should be applied to produce the grading level desired.

However, seepage is equally important and needs special consideration. In cold climates, where the frost line goes well under the surface, the upper inches of cinders and clay are well loosened and seepage occurs naturally.

Where winter freezing is not so deep, and certainly with indoor cinder tracks, annual dicing or harrowing to a depth of from 2 to 4 inches will prove beneficial. The hard pan produced by repeated watering and rolling will be thus broken up and the top layer renewed.

The depth of this dicing must be governed by the depth, of the track's top dressing, so that larger cinders are not brought to the surface.

Some groundsmen resort to deep manual raking to produce this result, but this is not likely to be deep enough to break through the hard pan. In any case, no heavy machinery should be used on the track until it has been thoroughly brushed and dragged to a level and consistent surface. Each groundskeeper usually has his favourite device for this smoothing process.

Most use push or pull brushes that are from 4 to 6 feet wide. Some like first to drag the track with a heavy steel bar or I-beam.

Others use a large steel door mat with added bags of sand to weight it down. Brushing after the use of such drags is always worth while. If needed, watering should always follow this levelling work, never precede it.

Using the exact amount of water is an important and tedious task. Hand sprinkling is time consuming and almost never consistent in its application of water.

One spot gets too much, and another too little. Sprinkling tanks similar to but smaller than ordinary street-sprinkling wagons have been used and provide a consistent a nuisance to fill and use.

At Stanford and other Western and Southern schools, where the climate during the track season is generally dry, permanent sprinkling pipes and sprayers have been installed around the track so that a single turn of a valve will water a large section exactly as needed.

The question of rolling can be answered only in terms of the type of construction and local conditions.

In many cases, the top surface of the track is hard enough. In others, rolling merely produces a surface firmness, which quickly gives way under the flying spikes of track men.

In many instances, where drainage and seepage and adequate, the best means of securing surface firmness is to give the track a thorough soaking.

Many a great record has been made on tracks where rain with its myriad hammers has just tapped out a durable and spike-gripping surface. With few exceptions, heavy rolling is not recommended, for it hardens the upper layers and destroys the value of the early dicing.

If the binding qualities in the track are not effective with light rolling, heavier will probably also be of little use. In summary, a running track is a mirror of the personal interest and energy of its groundskeeper.

His pride in the perfection of all details of construction and maintenance should equal that of the coach in all aspects of the track team and its program.

Care of Equipment

As with the problem of maintenance, proper care of equipment depends upon possessing adequate space, a proper place for everything, and an equipment man who knows and takes a personal pride in his job.

He must be a handy man who can do any thing and everything. He should be a carpenter, a seamstress, a shoe repairman, a gunsmith, a record clerk, and, perhaps above all, a patient and likeable personally who gets his fun out of life by helping others.

Such a man will ask and plead and demand until finally he has enough shelves and drawers for every item of equipment in all sports. He will smilingly accept one or twenty pairs of track shoes at night and somehow have them cleaned or repaired and ready for use the next day.

He will take a coach's idea for a new piece of practice equipment and delightedly produce the finished product with his own improvements. He can take a sheet of aluminium and make a protective device for a hurdler's ankle or knee bone.

He can construct a method of hanging javelins so they will not warp and will store them where they will not dry out. He's usually one of the least-honoured men on the departmental staff, but he's certainly one of the most valuable. At least the team members know his worth, even though the salary dispenser usually does not.

Starting Blocks

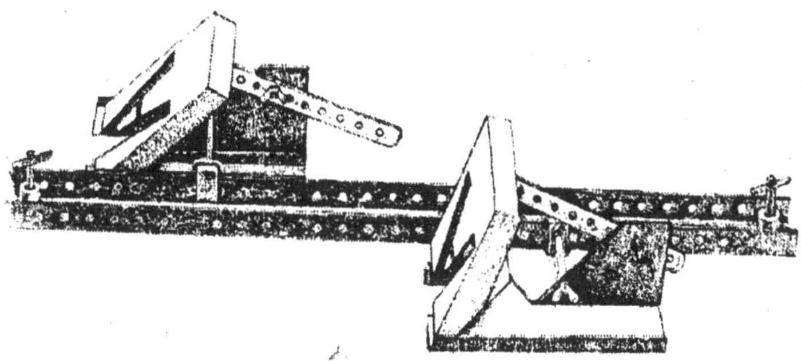

In various kinds of races, runners can use starting blocks, which should be constructed of rigid material. They should be constructed in such a manner that can be altered according to need.

The equipment room. The first essential of the equipment room is adequate space; the second maximum use of space. There never can be shelves enough or bins enough or drawers enough. Reserving an area for working space at least 10' × 10' in size, one can begin by installing as many shelves as possible.

Their width and height is very important if space is to be best utilized. A complete list of all equipment should furnish a guide in this matter. In general, an adequate equipment room for track and field athletics will include:

1. Shelves for practice sweat clothes, divided into small, medium and larger sizes.

2. Shelves for new shoes; indoor, outdoor, and rubber-soled.

3. Shelves for practice shorts and shirts, divided by sizes.

4. Shelves, two sets divided into either 6 to 12 compartments, for old shoes by sizes.

5. Closet, cedar-lined, for hanging and storing wool meet suits and sweat shirts. A large cedar-lined box may suffice.

6. Shelves divided into 24 compartments 12 inches wide by 10 inches high, for keeping meet clothes and shoes separate and ready for each man.

7. Locked drawer for guns, shells, and stop watches.

8. Work bench and full set of carpenter's tools.

9. Floor bin for shots weights, discuses, and so forth.

10. Small stall cabinet with many small drawers and compartments for various sizes of track spikes, nails, screws, bolts, and so forth.

11. Storage space for scales and various measuring devices for javelin, discus, and so forth.

12. Sewing machine for cloth and heavier fabrics.

13. Horizontal pipes for hanging and drying sweat clothes, meet suits, and so on.

14. Shoe repair equipment, including stretching devices.

15. Device for hanging a dozen javelins for everyday use.

16. Steel filing cabinet for records of equipment issued, inventories, equipment catalogues, and so forth.

3

Fundamentals of Coaching Field Events

Organisation. There are at least five different field events and seven different places where a track coach ought to be at any given moment of an afternoon during the winter or spring. His legs may be long and active, his eyes sharp, and his voice loud and far-carrying; but even a coach with the magical powers of Houdini finds it impossible to fulfil the requirements of such a situation.

Wise coaches will recognize their personal limitations, will do what they can to organize the practice lay-out of events, and, equally important, will establish a realistic coaching method. First consideration in the lay-out of field events should be given to meets and to be the best interests of both contestants and spectators.

However, it is only slightly less important to have a lay-out that provides good organization in practice. Ideally, a coach should be able to work with his sprinters and hurdlers and still be within easy seeing as well as calling distance of the shot-put, high-jump, pole vault, and perhaps other events as well.

The shot circle is easily laid out. Modern jumping pits can be set almost anywhere, since they do not need to be dug but can be built above ground level with sawdust-filled burlap bags and shavings.

Runways require care, of course, but the time and effort involved will pay excellent dividends. Of the hundreds of fields visited by the writer, few indicate that planning has been done along these lines.

Yet a little planning would save numberless steps by the coach and help to lessen that sense of frustration which is the bedfellow of every track coach. Secondly, a coach should seriously consider and organize some system of event captains.

Every track and field situation has a captain, whether the coach likes it or not. Any time three men work together in a given event, one will assume leadership in advising the others.

The question is whether this is done willy-nilly, without planning, or whether a carefully worked out method grasps all the values that are there. One successful high school coach uses the following plan: A captain for each event, track as well as field, is selected by a committee. The coach spend special time and uses special materials in educating this captain.

The captain works with and coaches all the men in his event. A period of time is agreed upon during which there is competition on a basis of improvement within each event-group. Performances at the beginning and at the end of this period are scored on the regular international Decathlon Score Charts.

The problem of having different numbers of men in each event is solved by taking an average improvement score.

The members of the winning group are rewarded by a scrumptious Sunday dinner at the coach's house, and the event captain is given a very nice small cup.

Other equally effective methods can be worked out, but planning in this area is essential to effective organization and coaching.

Other aspects of this matter of organizations should be read and studied in the paragraphs dealing with getting and keeping the boys out.

Personal experience in field events. Personal experience is absolutely essential to a sound knowledge and to effective coaching in the field events.

Actual competitive experience is desirable. Certainly the writer found that his efforts in national and Olympic decathlon championships provided an invaluable background for understanding and efficient coaching.

Few coaches can have this privilege, but all good coaches must handle the implements and gain a feeling, both mental and muscular, for every event.

Good coaching presupposes a true understanding of and insight into the fundamentals of an event as contrasted with its nonessentials. Such insight can occur only through thoughtful direct contact.

Coaching fundamentals of form. In every field there are certain fundamentals of form and action that govern the range within which every athlete who is achieving his maximum must perform.

For example, one such fundamental in the weight events is that all body positions and action that directly affect the impetus of an implement should be along a single plane in the direction of the throw; another, in the jumps, is that a man should use to the fullest extent all the momentum that is potentially available is the run.

It is such fundamentals as these about which the coach should do this hardest thinking and on which he should do his hardest in his coaching work. To spend time and wear out the patience of both coach and athlete in teaching nonessentials is wasted effort.

Every time a coach calls the attention of the athlete to a "defect" in any detail of form, the learner suffers a temporary loss of over-all co-ordination and confidence.

One of the leading advocates of this emphasis upon "fundamentals only" is Frank Ryan, assistant coach at Yale University in charge of field events. Ryan calmly accepts the minor idiosyncrasies his men naturally develop in their actions, but he is adamant in his emphasis upon the essentials of form.

Fuchs could shake his head just before starting across the circle as much as he pleased, so far as Ryan was concerned; but let his head get out of line or balance with the action as a whole, and he'd hear about it in a hurry.

A corollary of this whole idea is distinguishing between symptoms and causes in correcting errors in form. Certain aspects of form errors are readily apparent and therefore are likely to be called to the attention of the athlete.

Actually, however, these errors are merely symptoms and the real cause must be sought further back in the action. For example, a coach quickly notices that the throwing hand of a shot-putter or javelin thrower carries off to the left after the implement leaves the hand.

Often the coach will then emphasize a proper follow-through and suggest that the hand should continue in the exact direction of the throw. Actually this action is at a symptom; the true cause of the fault probably lies in the position of the feet or in the action of the right hip.

Or again, in the high jump, an easily apparent dive over the bar might suggestions from the coach about use of the head and arms while over the bar. Yet the true cause of the dive undoubtedly goes back to the angle of take-off and the method of foot placement.

To deal with causes is to teach efficiently, to coach symptoms is, reminding us again of the bit of verse, to distract the centipede unnecessarily.

Practice alone does not make perfect. Only correct and thoughtful practice can produce best results. Modern psychologists are agreed that learning does not occur by experience alone, but by experience and the insight that accompanies it.

It is entirely conceivable that a correct action can be taught by coercing a man to follow exact instructions again and again , thus wearing a pathway through the neuro-muscular system much as a river deepens its channel and eliminates loss of water into other streams.

But intelligent practice, in which the performer is stimulated to think through the how and the why of his event and his practice, will produce a better result more quickly. In his 25 years of coaching, the writer has always found that those men who make greatest use of the their abilities are not yes men.

Rather, they tend to consider seriously what the coach passes out to them and then to make up their own minds in terms of what feel right and what works for them.

Often their decision have not been considered correct by the coach, but it is more important that they should maintain their interest and independent thinking about their events than that the coach's ideas should be blindly and exactly followed.

The man who combines enthusiasm and thought with limited practice on the field will go further than the man who, without thought, spends only many hours on the field.

Deciding which form to teach. The proper answer to this problem can be given only in terms of the particular event concerned and of the interests, plans, and abilities of the individual athlete.

In general, interest and plans for the future take precedence over ability in this matter. Where determination, intelligence, and adequate time for practice, both in hours per day and in months per year, are present, a potentially "best" form can be selected.

When these are lacking, that form which produces quick results most easily will be most worth while. Assuming the former conditions it is one of the basic premises of this book that the essentials of correct form are approximately the same for all individuals.

Often in coaching clinics coaches slight the question of why a certain man performs in a certain way by pleading "individual differences".

One sometimes wonders whether it is not their own uncertainty or, worse, their own carelessness of thinking and coaching that produces their answers. It is true that there is a range of deviation from what might be called "perfect" form within which great performances may result. For example both Fuchs and Fonville put the shot about the same distance, over 58 feet.

If force can be assumed to result from a combination of power and momentum and 58 feet is assumed to equal 10 units of force, it can be logically stated that Fuchs accumulated his 10 units through combining 6 units of power with 4 units of momentum, whereas Fonville totalled 10 by combining 4 units of power with 6 units of momentum.

In similar fashion, there can be a certain deviation from all aspects of correct form, yet always within the range of tolerance.

To state another example, the toe of the left foot can be placed against the toe-board exactly in line with the centre line of the circle, where it provides maximum bracing effect and maximum power, or it can land about 15 inches to the left of the centre line, where it permits the hip to come through with maximum speed.

It is entirely conceivable that new world's records in the shot can be made in which the left foot it any point within this range of tolerance. If far to the left, momentum will be a major factor; if on the centre line, power will be the major factor.

As stated above, both 6 plus 4 and 4 plus 6 are equal to 10. To argue, as some coaches do, against the establishment of correct form on the basis of individual differences is to indicate a misunderstanding of these considerations as well as the basic similarity of all human beings.

Relaxation and co-ordination. These two words express almost the same meaning, although with a slightly different emphasis.

Co-ordination is more generally understood than relaxation. It is the harmonious and efficient working of muscles to produce a given action.

The flow or timing of muscular contraction, the degree of contraction of each muscle group, the exactly timed relaxation of opposing muscle, the complete relaxation of unrelated muscles are all essentials to a well-co-ordinated movement.

Similarly, a relaxed action in sports involves these same essentials but emphasizes the last two, the relaxation of opposing and unrelated muscles.

Certainly relaxation does not in any way imply a less forceful effort. On the contrary, force can only be created at a maximum level when complete relaxation of appropriate muscles is present.

To relax is to concentrate action within those muscle

groups that produce the wanted movement. It is a channelling of effort rather than a lessening of effort.

Perhaps the simplest illustration lies in the biceps and triceps of the arm, the actions of which are opposed to each other. The biceps pull object toward the body; the triceps push away.

If, in attempting a chinning exercise, both muscle contract equally, no action can occur. If an effort to pull up as quickly as possible includes any contraction of the triceps or, incidentally, of the facial or neck muscles, a tense action results that is relatively slow and fatiguing.

In contrast, a relaxed all-out chinning effort involves complete and immediate contraction of the biceps and complete relaxation or inaction of the triceps and all unrelated muscles. Only relaxed efforts are best efforts.

For an athlete to understand these matters verbally or mentally will not insure his understanding them originally or muscularly, but in almost all cases it will help. Attempts at clearer understanding will pay dividends.

Teaching momentum. Until an athlete has gained a little skill in the basic co-ordination of his event, the momentum with which he performs should be either ignored or restrained.

For example in the javelin throw, until a man knows how to hold the shaft, or to pull it straight through over the shoulder so that its flight is high and smooth and ends in a one-point landing, the momentum of the run preceding these actions is entirely secondary.

On the other hand, the teaching of momentum during the early phases of the form should not wait the various parts of the action have been perfected.

An athlete may perfect the co-ordination of an event

while moving slowly and then discover, when he speeds thighs up, that his balance and skill are upset and that he must learn things over again.

In the discus, for example, balance is os precarious that coaches and athletes tend to cut down momentum whenever it seems to interfere with balance.

From the standpoint of immediate results, this practice is usually effective. But when greater performances are needed and greater momentum in the turn is attempted, balance again is lost and must be learned all over again.

Each time a new level of performance is sought, each time a faster turn is attempted the same difficulty is encountered. It is writer's carefully considered opinion, which gains in certainty with each year of coaching experience, that momentum should either be allowed to take its natural course or should be deliberately introduced into the learning process as early as possible.

That is to say, once the basic co-ordinations are reasonably well established movement with momentum should be a regular part of the daily practice schedule. Best possible performances will thereby be achieved most efficiently and most rapidly.

This point of view is consistent with the findings of time and motion studies in industry and psychology.

Practising for form versus practising for distance or height. Every recognized authority on this question agrees that the emphasis is practice work should be placed upon form rather than upon height or distance. Cromwell, for example, believes that "in training for the event the athlete should work for a long time on form only, letting distance come gradually as technique is perfected'.

Nor does the writer wish to disagree basically with

this point of view. On the contrary athletes and other coaches have accused him many times of harping on form to the exclusion of distance and even gold medals.

"Do it right and the gold medals will take care to themselves" is a reasonably safe point of view in coaching.

Until a fair mastery has been gained of the basic co-ordinations of field events, the speed with which they are excused should not be emphasized.

But this is not to say that momentum and distance should be considerably reduced. On the contrary, they are an essential part of good form and as such should be encouraged along with right position and right balance. The important elements in all such questions is attitude and attention.

As long as the athlete's attention is upon learning, upon method and position, and upon the how of performance, the distance to which the implement may go in practice is a matter of secondary concern.

The emphasis then should never be upon holding back distance but rather upon keeping the mind on form. It may be argued that we have run around the question rather than answering it; but the difference indicated here is an important one.

It places a positive emphasis upon form where it is needed, but it removes the negative approach to distance, which is the best of all incentives to practice.

The difference in approach will permit pegs to be placed in the landing spots in practice and a steel tape to be present at all times.

The athlete will bc aware of how far the throws or puts are going, but it will be what might be called in psychology an associate and secondary awareness, whereas consciousness of form and method will be primary. "Put it as far as you can, as long as your mind is on putting it right" combines sound learning and good fun.

However, approached realistically, proper form includes both momentum and explosive force and cannot be separated from them.

In the weighing of emphasis upon whole versus part learning methods, part learning must form the basis for understanding and development, but only actions of the whole event and the whole body can be considered true learning.

Both body momentum and explosive force require practice just as much as position itself, it not more. The value to a 50-foot shot-putter of a practice put under 47 feet is limited. To practice on so-called form—that is, right position of all body parts—on Monday, Tuesday, Wednesday, and Thursday, and then to expect competitive spirit to pull momentum and explosiveness out of nowhere is completely to misunderstand the elements of motor learning.

The final answer, then, does not lie in a negative approach to throwing for distance, but rather in a continuous and positive emphasis upon form, with distance simply taken for granted.

Work. The related problems of how much work is excessive of how many throws of any kind can be productively taken in practice, or how many throws for distance are possible day after day increasingly coming to the attention of athletes and coaches today.

One athlete is reported to be working longer and harder then ever before.

Somehow the others can't let him outdo them, so they work even harder and longer than he does. Many wise and well-balanced coaches believe there are limitations on both time and work established by the demands of more important factors, those of academic studies and preparation for a life-work. They insist that a high school or college student has neither the time nor the energy to do justice to his schoolwork and still practice on a maximum basis.

Further, they believe that amateurism is not merely a matter of not being paid for one's efforts but also of keeping sports in their appropriate place, a place that is secondary to mental achievement and to service to one's associates and society.

For them—and the writer would be honoured to be included in their number—the problem of work is not so much one of physical capacity as one of relative social and personal values. In the writer's opinion, this, and not the question of subsidization and scholarship, is the crucial problem in college athletics today.

However, in extra-academic circles and, unfortunately, in those educational institutions that have lost their sense of values, the pros and cons of physical capacity will be uppermost.

Entirely apart from what should or should not be, the writer is convinced that we have only begun to work. The demand for an ever greater degree of excellence is a primary one in human affairs and it has certainly not run its course. That we can work harder and longer seems self-evident.

The modern dance, for instance, which involves intricate and rapid movements, demands from 30 to 40 hours of rehearsal each week for many weeks.

Professional gymnasts and acrobats often work twice a day for several hours each time in perfecting their acts, many of which involve strength and fatiguing exercises.

How, then can we assume there is danger that we are

over-working, or that we may become muscle-bound? In every event on the track and field program, one can conceive of improvements in either form or momentum in even our greatest champions.

As long as that is true, better records are possible and will be achieved through longer hours of more intense work. Obviously, relatively poor physical condition places limitations upon both intensity any length of effort, but the final answer lies not so much in doing little work as in gradually improving body conditions and being able to do more work.

The statement has been made here that increased emphasis upon momentum is the greatest reason for present-day improvement in the weights.

But proper use of momentum, so that it includes balance and smooth integration of all movements, presupposes regular practice on an eight- or ten-months basis.

Only by such practice can a man gain the exactness of form and the perfect consistency of action that are absolutely essential to best effort.

Only where consistency in all the phases of action has been established with a minimum of deviation; only when the right foot always comes out of the back of the circle in exactly the same way or when the left foot always hits the toe-board at exactly the same spot and in exactly the same position can a shot-putter concentrate his explosive energies on maximum distance.

As long as the emphasis is upon fast action and explosive power rather than slow strength, there is no danger of becoming muscle-bound in the weight events or of losing one's spring permanently in the jump events, any more than there is danger of losing one's speed through ten months of "speed-play" in the case of distance running.

Further, as long as the athlete keeps his mind on his objective clearly and certainly, there is no danger of going stale. Some coaches will accuse the writer of taking all the fun out of track and of overemphasizing its values.

Yet the drive toward excellence knows few if any reservations or limitations. More than that, enthusiasm and fun are not the exclusive possession of the dilettante of the "take it easy" specialists. There's no fun like work if you enjoy the work. This is written in the full knowledge that few writers and coaches take so positive an attitude toward work.

The tendency for weight men to play football means that the shot is likely to be done on a minimum basis. Coaches have therefore assumed toward the weight men attitude quite different from their attitude the distance runners. Yet the problem is basically the same.

In a very real sense, the important question is not, "How hard should I work in the field events?" but rather, "How much does excellence in performance mean to me?" Coaches, therefore, should devote at least as much attention to establishing incentives and motivating practice as they do to form itself.

For example, the following methods have been used with good results in creating proper incentives:

1. See that men in field events get as many chances for trips and for competition as do the runners—that, is that not merely the one best man but two or three or more be included if they have a chance to place.

2. Work actively toward the inclusion of all field events in all meets and toward the placement of such events directly in front of the spectators. Thirty minutes spent filing the holes made by the shot in the football

field in May or June will completely hide them in September.

3. Encourage the scheduling of dual meets in which the combined distances of three or even four mean in each field event decide the team score.

4. Place a special "Progress Chart" for each field event on the team bulletin board or even on the general school record board. Select improvement records of appropriate local stars for comparison.

5. Set up special medals for the most improvement or for outstanding performance in all field events.

In creating fun in practice the following measures have proved effective:

1. Be enthusiastic about each event yourself. As a rule, wherever one finds a series of outstanding performers in any given field event, one also finds a coach who is especially enthusiastic about this event. Enthusiasm, of course, must be based upon sound knowledge and a certain personal experience with the event.

2. Permit as much trying for distance as the demands of good form will permit. Only the very exceptional athlete will be happy when forced to work on form only. As a matter of fact, there is a serious question, in the light of present-day emphasis upon momentum, whether any such restriction on distance is desirable.

3. Encourage competition in practice between shot-putters, on a handicap basis where necessary. Have a 48- or 50- foot are drawn they arrive on the field.

Keep a chart of wine and losses for the season and then have a little celebration for fun—a party, with special pair or cake or ice cream for the winner. Betting should be kept out of the picture entirely, but a special prize "for fun" will work wonders.

4. Keep the men working together. Not only will they have more fun but they will get more done as well.

5. Have the men work in spurts. "Work fast and hard for a while, make as many jumps or throws as you can; then rest for a while and start in again". This is particularly applicable to shot putting.

6. Have a workout plan each day, as you would for distance runners. There is much to be done and little times in which to do it.

Therefore, there is no reason for standing around, watching other performers, or wondering what to do next. Such practices are always a sign of poor motivation and probably of poor coaching.

The Weight Events

A proper understanding of the weight events must be based upon five fundamental aspects of form:

(1) the building of greatest usable body momentum,

(2) the co-ordination of this momentum with

(3) the greatest possible body force acting through

(4) a maximum time-distance, and at

(5) the most productive trajectory.

In addition, coaches and athletes must understand certain matters common to all weights events, such as how much and what kind of work is desirable, the meaning of explosive power in human action, or the significance of individual differences in form. It is the intent of this section to further such understanding.

Body momentum. The accumulating of body momentum occurs during the early stages of a weight event. It occurs during the run in the javelin, during the glide in the shot, and during the turn in the discus.

Its importance cannot be overestimated in achieving best performance, even in an event like the shot, where a tiny 7-foot circles places body momentum at rather minimum levels.

In the javelin, achieving momentum is no problem at all; the difficulty here is in making proper use of it. It is the writer's carefully considered opinion that the great progress that has been made in weight events during the past quarter century has occurred primarily through increased momentum and its more efficient use, and that future progress will occur along similar lines.

Momentum is not something to be added to good form after balance and co-ordination have been fully achieved; it is essential part of it.

Good form in the field events can be considered only in terms of the correct actions with momentum. It is not a series of proper positions such as one sees in sequence pictures of form. It cannot be demonstrated by doing all the phases of form "perfectly", although at slow speed. Correct form implies "form-with-speed" as single indivisible concept

The co-ordination of body momentum with body force. For convenience of understanding and discussion, we may think of body force as beginning from a stationary position, and equalling that speed-power or explosive power which the muscle of the body, acting with maximum efficiency, can generate.

The problem of co-ordinating body momentum with such force is fundamentally the same in all weight events, subject of course to their particular limitations and elements.

Basically, it is a matter of stopping momentum of the lower parts of the body so that their accumulated power can be concentrated toward the upper extremities and the implement involved. The whip concept is valuable to understanding. The velocity of the tip of the whip is dependent upon four factors:

(1) the forward momentum of the stock or handle,

(2) the shortness of time and space within which this momentum is stopped,

(3) the length of the whip, and

(4) its flexibility.

Similarly, these four factors are active in each of the weight events. In the javelin, the basic advantage of the Finnish cross-step style lis in the shortness of space and time within which body momentum is stopped.

It occurs within the short length of a single stride, a simple placement of right and left feet, and a throw. In contrast, the stopping of forward momentum in the now discarded back-cross-step style involved the space of three full strides, thereby making momentum almost useless.

In the shot put, the traditional emphasis upon a somewhat closed stance, with the left foot hard against the toe-board and stopping the forward motion of the lower body, is an effective device. This same device is present in the discus despite its use of a turn.

In all three events, body height is an aid to implement velocity, and of course flexibility of the throwing arm, wrist and fingers is an important factor. The whip concept is only partially in point, for the body has forces within itself by which to accelerate velocity.

In general, early attempts to learn right form emphasized this factor. Proper placement of the feet, right use of the hip, back, and abdominal muscles, and a full follow-through were of almost exclusive concern.

Exercises that produced an increase in muscle power were stressed, and body momentum across the circle was seldom permitted to interfere with good balance and co-ordination. The problem today is different.

Performances is nearly all meets are now at such a high level that only a combination of both maximum momentum and maximum force will prove effective.

Maximum time-distance. The velocity of a shot or other implement is determined by the acting force multiplied by the time-distance through which its acts, divided by the mass of the subject.

The factor of time-distance in which force can be applied and thereby made to accelerate a given implement is therefore extremely important. Hence the development of a straight-forward action and a full follow-through.

Hence the great value of the form of Jim Fuchs in the shot put, with his extreme backward lean and very low position.

As compared with other putters, he thereby increased by at least a foot the distance within which force could be applied.

Again, this is the advantage that the American hop style in the javelin possesses. The hop permits a greater turn of the body to the right as well as a greater backward reach with the javelin. The problem here is whether this advantage is not more than offset by the resulting loss in body momentum.

Trajectory. In general, the science of ballistics states that 45 per cent is the most effective angle for propelling an object such as the shot or javelin.

The shape of a discus, however, introduces the problem of wind resistance and the difficulty of obtaining such an angle of release without meeting such resistance.

For many years, coaches and athletes have assumed that 45 degrees was too high an angle for the human body to use effectively. The construction of our joints and tendons did not make such a high put or throw of practical use.

Yet, today, the greatest champions are throwing at exactly 45 degrees in both the shot and the javelin, and, when wind conditions are right, in the discus as well.

Further, in all three events, it is agreed that acceleration occurs best when applied along a single line or plane of action. There are no longer any dips, crouches, or lifts that are out of line with the throw.

The Jump Events

Although the jump events are more diverse in their fundamentals of action than are the weight events, there are sufficient common fundamentals to warrant a short general discussion at this point. The jumps can be summarized as having four basic aspects of form:

(1) the establishment of momentum,

(2) the conversion of this horizontal momentum to a vertical direction,

(3) the co-ordination of this accumulated force of momentum with body force through whatever means are available at the take-off, and

(4) the efficient use of the resulting impetus to achieve either height or distance as desired.

Detailed discussion of just what this means for each of the four jumps—the high jump, the pole vault, the broad jump, and the hop, step, and jump—can be deferred to those particular sections later. But the following points are important to understand and use in coaching work:

1. The take-off leg in the high jump, the broad jump, and the hop, step, and jump can be compared with the

vaulting pole, which braces against forward momentum and permits the conversion of force vertically.

This use of the pole is readily apparent. A similar use of the take-off leg in the other events is not so easily understood but is just as important.

In the broad jump, a man should secure as much higher as possible without a disproportionate loss in horizontal momentum. Here the emphasis is upon distance.

In the high jump, a man should secure as much speed in the run as possible provided that it can be converted into a vertical direction. Here the emphasis is upon height. Yet, despite the difference in degree, momentum is important to both.

2. Momentum is a supplementary force to muscular spring and power, which should be used to the fullest extent. It has its important uses even in the high jump.

It is interesting to note that Mikio Oda, the great Japanese hop, step, and jump champion and coach, praised the form of Brazil's de Silva by emphasizing his maximum use of momentum and his knack of keeping the body weight well forward throughout the three jumps, with a minimum jar at each landing.

4

Considerations in Conditioning Athletes

More champions are married than made in the days of adolescence through the enthusiasm of parents, the ignorance of games masters or the eagerness of the young athlete himself, who trains and trains, striving always after maximum results, if he is left to his own devices, until he is tired out, both mentally and physically, and becomes utterly stale.

In time this type of so-called training, which is really straying, produces a definite mental lethargy, induces wrong outlook towards athletics, so that functions of the muscles becomes adversely affected, and the boy loses that indescribable something, call it his "snap" if you will, which is a characteristic of all great champions.

The average boy, of course, likes to be athletic, it in his ambition to possess a strong, well-developed body, and subconsciously he longs to gain that social approval which is the reward of success in sport. Without social approval there can be no major success for either man or boy, and just because it is so important and because athletics among juveniles are almost daily achieving a greater degree of important in the eyes of the public, there may well arise the danger that young boys will show a tendency to overdo things, by demanding too much of their immature strength.

Even without the incentive of competition and its complementary part, which is social approval, boys may still strive too hard after immediate success. It is so nice to run just a little faster, to jump higher or to throw things farther than one has ever done before, and so, all too often effect is sought and cause is forgotten.

And this is just where the wise parent or games master should step in. This statement is as true where men are concerned. The endless striving to achieve better performances by sheer brute strength at every training session seems to be a peculiar attribute of British athletes, and must be held accountable for many of our field events failures in international contests.

So much, then, for the natural inclinations of the adolescent athlete. Where parents are concerned, the case is different, and it is a fact that there was a time when the evil practice of fathers perambulating promising sons all over the country on pothunting expeditions became so general that the A.A.A. passed a rule that "open races for boys shall be confined to boys who are over 10 and under 15 years of age at the date of the competitions, and have for three calendar months immediately preceding the race resides within a radius of eight miles of the sports ground."

The rule, of course, was not made applicable to school sports and inter-schools contests and the meetings of special organizations with which a boy might be concerned. Regarding games masters: Their sings, in the past, have been rather those of omission than the reverse, and ignorance of athletic lore and fundamental principles has led to the boys being left largely to their own training devices, with the inevitable unsatisfactory results.

On the other hand, the circumstance is still far from being unknown of masters wilfully putting too great a strain upon immature athletes, both in training and competition, for the sake of gaining points in some wretched inter-house contest. Some people asked the question, "How much training should be done by a growing lad, and how much competition should be allowed?"

Those questions can be answered, in almost every instance, upon the merits and in accordance with the circumstances of each individual case alone. Some youngsters thrive on a sensibly balanced amount of hard work, others eat up much of their nervous force in the brief space of a single contest.

It is not safe to be dogmatic. The two things to remember are these. A boy overtrained and given too great an opinion of the importance of athletic success is likely not only to lose his fire, but will become nervy, anxious and unhappy, and all the joy will be banished from the game for him.

On the other hand, too great care, taken obviously, may well create in his mind the impression that he is taking risks with his health, and in that case the creation of a namby-pamby sort of youth is well on the way.

Speaking generally, the ideal scheme is to get boys under 16 years of age to regard athletics as play. Boys at this stage of their lives should not be allowed to train seriously for any athletic contest, as the word "training" is understood in its generally accepted meaning.

In the years between 1924 and 1927, when we spent our summer holidays at the little Norfolk fishing village of Bacton, that late W.E.B. Henderson, an old Oxford Blue, and we used to collect dozens of children each day, on the sands, or in the field at the top of the cliffs.

We would organize for their amusement games in jumping, throwing a very tiny discus, putting the stone, pole vaulting, and so on. The inevitable outcome of those games was the holding of a children's sports meeting in a kindly farmer's field towards the end of each summer holiday.

The form some of those children produced was nothing less than remarkable, merely because they had learned correct technique by playing at athletics during the most impressionable physical period of their lives.

Subsequent results are even more interesting. Of the children who took part in the Bacton games, T.P. Moll gained a high jump blue at Cambridge, his brothers, G.M. and J.S. Moll, were awarded Country colours while still in their teens and both won Public Schools Championships, as did R.F. Walker, while F.R. Webster was a Country colour at 14, and an English International at 17, besides holding the English Junior Pole vault and Discus Throwing records.

In 1935 he won the Pole Vault for Cambridge against Oxford with a new English record of 12 ft. 6½ inch, and also the first English Indoor Championship with a record vault of 12 ft. 3 ins., which he equalled when successfully defending his title in 1936, has represented England at the Empire Games, Great Britain versus Germany and France, and Oxford and Cambridge in South Africa, where he made five new records in the course of seven matches.

Joan Webster gained her Country and Southern Counties colours at 15 and a year later won the Southern Discus title with a new record, and in 1935 was third in the English open Championship.

The youngest sister, Peggy, at 15 was runner-up in the Bedgordshire High Jump, Discus Throw and Shot Put, and third in the Southern Counties Championship Discus event.

A year later she won the Country Javelin and was second in the High Jump and Discus events. In no instance did any of these children train seriously, but what they did do was to acquire correct technique in the years when their minds were impressionable and their bodies most plastic.

As to how much a child should do, and we are speaking now mainly of the twelve-year-olds and under, one might almost say "as much as they like". The point is that a very young child will play just as long as it pleases.

In other words, it will play until it is tired, and then it packs up. It may not play long at any one event, but that does not matter; let it move along from one physical amusement to another at its own sweet will.

The harm is done when the person in charge of the play insists upon the youngster sticking to one type of event until it has mastered some particular physical skill.

One can direct, of course, but the main thing is to allow the physical skills to develop naturally at that particular age. What has been said so far concerns mainly throwing and jumping, which postulates plentiful rest periods for each child while other children are doing things.

Where running comes into question we do not think that a boy under 12 should be allowed to run more than a furlong and that not often, and some think it is far better to keep him down to 100 yards.

All these matters, however, that have dealt with far more fully in Athletic Training for Men and Boys and in The Games mater Handbook than it should proposing to do in the present volume. Where the work and play problem in relation to children is concerned, the great thing to remember is that they must always be encouraged to regard athletics.

The main motive for taking part in athletic, or, for that matter, any other form of sport, should be for the fun we get out of it. That is important from the scientific point of view and the health point of view, if we define health in terms of mental hygiene, since enjoyment is a necessary attribute to both physical and mental well-being.

Perhaps we might examine that proposition a little more carefully, since it has a very definite and important bearing upon the problem we are considering. Many people think there are two sorts of fun to be got out of athletics; the first in the sort of "kick" we get quite naturally from instinctive activity and the sheer pleasure of doing a thing.

The second pleasure is that of doing a thing rather well, of winning and of acquiring merit. There is enough in that dual fun-motive to keep people interested in athletics indefinitely, but the fun-motive must be maintained, and that can only be done by the athlete being taught to regard his athletics as play, and by giving him an entirely different sort of play-period later on to balance the real hard work which characterizes the training of the matured contestant.

So far the work and play problem has been comparatively easy to handle, because we have stuck to the theory that children should only play at athletics in the years when they are, almost unconsciously, building up certain requisite physical skills.

Where the fully grown athlete is concerned, the situation assumes an entirely different aspect. To succeed in modern athletics a man must train hard and sensibly; to reach the very top of the tree he has got to give pretty well everything there is in him to the game; he must be prepared to punish himself in training when his coach calls upon him to do so, or else he will never face the punishment that comes sooner or later in competition.

In addition he must learn to use his brains as well as his body. All of which postulates a fairly prolonged and a fairly severe mental and physical strain. Neither of these strains need be, or should be, harmful.

One can, in fact, point out certain definite physical debits and credits. In the first place, the practice of athletics improve growth. That can be proved by taking any two groups of men at a university, the one group definitely following athletics and the other group not doing so, and it will be found that in a period of three years the men in the athletic group will gain more pounds and inches in development than do the others.

They will show, also, improvement in appetite and an increase in the circulatory reserve, and, as Dr. Dean Smiley, the American authority, has pointed out, "an athlete can better withstand an attack of pneumonia, where the pulse is going at 100 to 120 beats a minute for five days, than a non-athlete."

Other benefits to be derived from athletics are the correction of postural deformities, the improvement of muscle-tone and control, and the stimulation of the activity of the internal organs. On the other side of the ledger we have got to face the facts that athletic sport loses much of its value if there is undue concentration upon the performances of a few stars and if the competitive spirit so dominates training and competition that the instinctive pleasure of doing a thing for the sheer joy of doing it is killed.

In both cases there is the danger, also, of working the willing horse too hard and even of aggravating existing disease or disability by using a man on the team who is, at the moment, not really fit to compete. In relation to the present argument, however, the greatest evil is to be found when athletics are allowed to become no sport at all, when over-eagerness to achieve results turns training into sheer drudgery, with no recreation in it, and everyone heaves a tired sigh of relief, and probably breaks out into an imperial beano, when the competition season is over.

From all of which it follows that a person's main motive in taking up athletics should be for the health-giving fun which he anticipates getting out of the sport, and that, while training must certainly be undertaken seriously, it is equally important that the training work should be balanced by due periods of rest, play and recreation, of a suitable nature not to interfere with training, which will act both as anodyne and antidote.

It has been briefly indicated already that the strain imposed by training for athletic contests is both mental and physical. It is obvious that this must be so, for no matter how instinctive our actions may be, nor how much pleasure we may derive from any voluntary, spontaneous performance, it still remains the fact that muscles do not function unless they receive orders to do so.

As we shall see later on, the training of the sympathetic nervous system plays a big part in this connection. Meantime, it will suffice for our present purpose if it is pointed out that messages are continuously passing from the brain to different parts of the body in order that various purposes may be fulfilled and if, also, we bear in mind the circumstance that the nervous system is in two parts.

There is the central nervous system and the sympathetic nervous system. The former is under the control of a person's own will, the desired movements of the muscles being actuated by will transmission from brain to muscle by way of the motor-nerves. That is why conventional form exercises, such as are set out in Exercises for Athletes play such an important part in the training of the athletic.

Perfection and practice of the proper movements

involved in the performance of a physical skill, widen and wear smooth by much traffic the paths of the nerve impulses travelling from brain to muscle-substance.

The sympathetic nervous system, however, does not come under the control of one's own will; but this system does control the action of that important involuntary muscle, the heart; and having mentioned the part of the heart plays in the athletic success, it at once becomes apparent that the way in which training affects the sympathetic nervous system is a matter for primary consideration.

Formerly trainers, or coaches, had two objects every in view: one was to create endurance, the other was the development of muscular power. Like the Greeks of old, these trainers knew that certain methods generally produced certain results. They saw the effect, but remain in ignorance of the cause. Then came the discovery that the skeletal or locomotor muscles are controlled by the central nervous system; and, since it is no bad thing to let the athlete know as much about himself as is good for him, boys in particular are recommended to indulge in a small experiment in biology.

With the aid of a microscope and the body of a dead frog, the athlete can examine a nerve for himself. He will find that it is made up of hundreds of long and very fine fibres, not one of them more than a tenth of the thickness of a human hair.

The nerve with which we fell and those that carry the impulses from the brain to the muscles have each a separate fibre with a cover and on inside, in the same way as electric wires are insulated. If the dead frog is skinned and its leg tissues are separated the sciatic nerve may be identified as a small white thread leading from the spinal column to the calf muscle.

This nerve and the muscle to which it is attached can be removed, since the frog is dead, and the nerve itself will remain sufficiently alive to serve for experimental purposes for several hours. Below mentioned figure represent this:

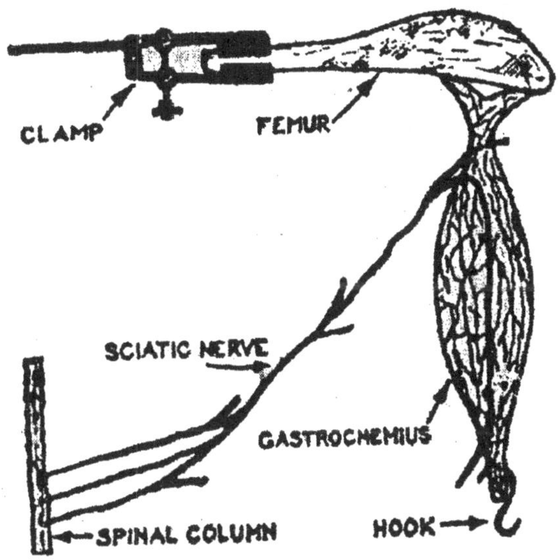

The sciatic nerve as shown, should be dissected right out from the spinal column to its entry into the muscle, and the branches which do not actuate the gastrocnemius should be served.

The muscle depends from the bone, with a hook placed through the tendon at the lower end for the purpose of recording and measuring movements. It is, broadly speaking, the motor nerve-cells of the spinal column which transmit orders to the muscles; the higher parts of the nervous system are contained within the skull.

The discovery of how muscular movement was brought about did not, however, take the athletic research scientist nearly far enough. The trained muscle showed longer amplitude of contraction, better blood supply and quicker response to nerve impulses, while the untrained muscle produced an altogether poorer efficiency.

It then became apparent that the blood supply is the all-important factor, and that very gradual training of the central nervous system produces the best type of that quick muscular contraction which is so important in sport. The system by, and the speed at which messages pass to the muscles varies in accordance with the urgency, or otherwise, of existing circumstances.

Exertion causes the creation of carbonic acid and lactic acid in the muscle substance, a man becomes short of breath, and the poisonous substances passing through the blood-stream cause the nervous system to notify the respiratory muscles that deeper breathing is needed to supply more oxygen for the culmination of the poisons.

That is the slower of the two methods. In the other, where quicker action is called for, the message, or impulse, passes more rapidly along the unbroken living length of a nerve. A wave, as it were, passes along the nerve, but it is a wave of change, and not of anything material. If the back of a man's head and the back of his spinal column were removed you would find the brain laid bare.

At the top of the spinal column are the cerebrum and the cerebellum, each divided into right and left halves. In the spinal column itself would be seen the roots of the nerves, having inner portions of grey matter, which act as "exchanges", and outer portions of white matter, which constitute the nerve-fibres along which messages are transmitted.

It is by the gradual development and improvement of the "exchanges", and outer portions of white matter, which constitute the nerve-fibres along which messages are transmitted.

It is by the gradual development and improvement of the "exchanges" that the human brain and nervous system have been built up, until what was mainly automatic at first has developed consciousness, understanding and liberty of action.

The speed at which messages are transmitted to the muscles can be roughly reckoned, either by actuating the muscle of our frog by an electric current applied at two different points on the nerve; or—but this is not so accurate—an electric shock can be applied at two different parts of a living body and the time taken for the appropriate reaction to ensue can be noted.

In the case of man, nerve impulses pass at a speed of 400 ft. per second, at our temperature of 37 degrees Centigrade, whereas light passes at a speed of 186,000 miles per second, all of which shows the importance of the correlation of brain and body, because if training, or any other form of development can be utilized to accelerate the speed at which human nerve impulses travel, it is obvious that the athletic records of today will soon be flung into the limbo of the past.

In these circumstances, it seems that further improvement in athletic records is likely to eventuate, not from any muscular development, but rather from methods which scientists may evolve for the training of the human nervous system.

Meanwhile, even club coaches can do a lot by training those committed to their care to be more mentally alert, by getting them to realize with their brains the fundamental principles of technique and the nature of the demands they are making upon their bodies.

There is yet one other point in this connection, and it will be referred to again, which we think that all athletes should be made to understand, and that is the relationship between body temperature and the speed of nerve-impulses.

For example, the south African Schoolboy record-breaker, W. Betts, produced wonderful times in

Johannesburg, but at the Olympic Games of 1924, held in the colder European climate, he quite failed to reproduce his home form.

Or again, it is known that in the case of frogs, with the temperature at 18 degrees Centigrade, the nerve impulses pass at 95 ft. per second, but if that temperature is lowered by 10 degrees the speed of transmission falls to 53 ft. per second. It is, of course, this circumstance that supplies one of the main reasons for limbering-up before a contest of any kind.

Apart from the fact that preliminary action increases the depth of tidal breathing and does various other things, it certainly raises the body temperature and serves the purpose already indicated.

Again, this question of maintaining the body temperature at a high level supplies a very good reason why the athlete should keep his track bags and sweater on until the last moment and should always resume his outer garments when not actually in action.

This is particularly important in the case of field events men, who should never hang about between jumps, or throws, with only their shorts and singlets on. Directly an attempt has been made, or a turn taken, the track suit should be resumed and worn until the next turn comes round.

Without going too deeply into the matter, it may be added that the oxygenation of the blood through the process of limbering up has also something to do with mental or "nerve-impulse" alertness, since a nerve breathes, like any other living things, and therefore requires oxygen.

We know that the oxygenation of the blood turns the harmful lactic acid in the blood stream back into beneficial glycogen, and since the rise in temperature of perhaps a millionth of a degree, due to the passing of a nerve impulse, postulates a chemical change in the nerve in question which transmits a message, it may be that the "recovery " change that follows is also benefited by oxygen.

One important consideration in the conditioning of athletes is to be found in the family and medical history of each individual who is to be put into training. Especially is this the case in relation to schoolboy athletes. They come to one in all sorts of shapes and sizes and from all classes of society, and if one acquire a knowledge of their antecedents it is often a big help towards determining the particular type of event to which they are most likely to be suited.

It do not mean to suggest that because a boy's father has been a high jumper, the son must necessarily follow in the footsteps of his sire; we do not deny that some have known more than one champion who, so far as could be ascertained, had no ancestors who were in the least degree interested in any form of sport at all.

Conversely, it is known the sons of great athletes, with long histories in athletics on both sides of the family, who have shown no aptitude and less liking for the game. What we have in mind is rather this: if you know that a boy's family has a tubercular history, to take the most obvious case, you would certainly keep a pretty close eye on that youngster, with a view to building him up to resist any hereditary weakness, and you certainly would not take the risks with him that you might be willing to run with other youngsters.

But you must have knowledge of the medical history of that boy and of his people, before you can use athletic training to make him into a fine man. That, however, you may regard as just common sense precaution, rather than anything to do with the science of athletics.

Suppose a tall, likely-looking lad comes along and

wants to take up athletics, but has not the faintest idea to which particular event he would like to concentrate upon when he gets through his play-period and also the subsequent stage, in which he will still go on practising a number of events for the sake of his balance and general development.

The probability is that he will want to take up running; most of them do, because it looks easier than the field events and, apparently requires less concentration and does not involve the taking of so much trouble to master the mysteries of technique. But if the boy is tall for his age and shows signs of developing into a big man of heavy build, the probability is that he will never make a first rate runner; none the less, running, and particularly sprinting, is an excellent adjunct to field events training.

You may decide that the boy in question has some of the makings of an excellent shot putter, in which case a few standing long jumps will serve to test his spring for the drivel across the circle. But you have no guarantee that he will go on growing. He may have shot up suddenly and he may stop growing abnormally early.

This is where a knowledge of his family history will prove helpful. If he has tall parents and tall brothers and sisters, the balance of probability is that he will go on growing. Physical education plays no small part in the proper conditioning of athletes for competition nowadays, and modern P.E. is something very different to the old-time P.T.

In America, for example, they speak now of "total body activity", using that term to cover the whole range of both mental and physical activities which previously were spoken of separately. Working upon the theory that all life rests upon the power in physical organism, which is not entirely synonymous with the word "health" alone, the modern physical educationalists hold that organic power has a triple foundation, in that it is a fundamental biological law that well-balanced and properly controlled exercise develops and strengthens the human organs, so that the body gains power through exercise.

The building up of this power begins in the human organisms during childhood and continues on into late adolescence. The cells of the human body contain this power and burn food material as fuel, but oxygen is required for the elimination of certain elements, such as carbon dioxide, nitric and lactic acids.

In this connection, the blood stream conveys nourishment to the cells and carries away the waste products which must be eliminated. The human body has its own mechanisms for digestion, circulation, respiration and elimination; it is able to adjust, repair and maintain those mechanisms and should be capable of adjusting itself to most conditions, and it is the degree of its adaptability that represents its power.

The degree of adaptability, and, therefore, the "power", is contingent upon training. Actual experiment has determined the rate and the amount of increase in crest-load that can be brought about by such means.

One of these experiments was carried out with a man who started with the very low crest-load of 2,000 foot-pounds and played tennis, or handball, or took what the Americans call setting up exercises for one hour a day over a period of nine weeks.

At the end of one week the crest-load had risen to 4,000 foot-pounds, to 6,000 foot-pounds at the end of the second week, and then did not increase any more during the next three weeks, but later advanced to 7,000 foot-pounds by the end of the sixth week.

Further experiments in the gas analysis of the air the man exhaled showed that, as the result of training, he absorbed a greater proportion of oxygen and that the quantity consumed was materially affected by training.

This increase was due, in all probability to an improvement in the blood circulation.

The main results of the experiment were the obtaining of proof that training produces a gain in strength, accompanied by a better supply of oxygen to the active muscles, so that lactic acid was more readily converted into glycogen and the respiration was moderated under strain.

5

Human Mechanism

To be a good athlete a man must have a good brain. It is not suggested that even a nit-wit cannot be taught to perform certain athletic feats with a satisfactory degree of mechanical precision. This applies particularly perhaps to the more conventionally formal technique of some of the field events.

But, even so, such a man is entirely dependent upon his coach. He may have outstanding natural athletic ability; by practice, precept and imitation he may become perfect in technique, and so may enjoy a marked degree of athletic success, but he will never have the broader vision that is needed for the exploration of the greater possibilities in developments of style which should ensue logically upon his personal natural ability.

A man of no particular brain-power, but who possesses great natural speed and stamina, may even win flat races in good company, but the task of planning most of those races for him generally falls to the lot of the coach. Great athletes as a rule, are extremely clever people, as witness the careers and the personal characteristics of such men as the late Lord Alverstone, the late Sir Montague Shearman, Professor Philip Noel Baker, M.P., Drs. Rex Wood, Arthur Garrett and Henry Stallard, and those eminent barristers, H.M. Abrahams and D.G. A. Lowe. To be a really great athlete in the most intimate sense of the term, a man must be able to study form, to think out points of technique for himself, to root out scientific explanations of both physiological and psychological phenomena, and to interpret the implication of things that happen in his pleasurable pursuit of athletics.

What has been said applies to all forms of athletics; but where racing, in particular, is concerned, a very high order of mentality is called for if continued success is to be assured.

Men of the type instanced above have planned not only their races but their training with the same meticulous care and forethought that they have brought to their careers when running days were over. To take Douglas Lowe as an outstanding example.

All the world knows how cleverly he won his two epic 800 metres Olympic titles, and one feels sure that every phase of the manner in which those two races were to be run was fully planned well in advance.

Lowe, think has a peculiar genius for summing up both the possibilities and the potentialities of his opponents, and one can well believe in the case of his second Olympic Championship in 1928, that he had studied and summed up all the previous performances of the American, Lloyd Hahn, who was generally regarded as the most dangerous challenger for the title Lowe had won in 1924.

Further than that, some convinced that, before the games began, Lowe had a good working knowledge of the form of Bylehn, Sweden; Englehardt, Germany; Edwards, Canada, and his old rival, the Frenchman, Sera Martin, who also reached the final.

The reason to believe, moreover, that in the period which elapsed between the decision of the eliminating heats on Sunday, July 29th, and the running of the final on Tuesday, July 31st, Lowe considered every phase of each heat in order that he might assess in his own mind the easy the men would run and what would be the best strategy for him to adopt in the final.

In the foregoing connection we will remember certain happening at the World's Student Championships at Farmstadt in 1930. Lowe was there as President of the Universities Athletic Union and British delegate to the C.I.F. Conference, while R.F. Kerslake was manager of the British Universities team, to which was acting as Honorary Chief Coach.

On August 7th J.G. Helps, Birmingham, who was captain of the British Universities team, and J.M. Ross, Edinburgh, both came successfully through the eliminating heats of the 1500 metres.

Lowe made no remark, beyond congratulating the British runners upon their success. On Friday evening, however, he came round to the Marienhoe, where we were living, and the five of us settled down round a table in a corner of the dinning-room. Then Lowe, in his own inimitably quiet fashion, gave a summing up of the way the 1500 metres heats had been run.

This was followed by a masterly piece of deductive reasoning as to the capabilities of the various runners who would be concerned in the final next day. Then came Lowe's considered opinion as to how the race would be run, just what times would be returned for each lap and who would be leading at various stages, if the foreigners were allowed to dictate the strategy.

Working from that data, backed up by our knowledge of just what Helps and Ross could do, Lowe proceeded to outline the way the race ought to be run, if Helps was going to win it. Ross, incidentally, was to be offered up as a very game sacrifice; he was also to act as buffer-state in what we anticipated would be a race not free from bumping and boring.

Among the finalists were Krause, the German champion, with Surjatta and another German to cover him, and the international middle-distance runners Cerati, Italy; Le Due, France; Dahlstrom, Sweden; and

Johanssen, Norway; while neither Helps nor Ross had yet been chosen for England or Scotland. Saturday afternoon came, and not only were Lowe's predictions fulfilled to the very letter, but the race was run just exactly as he had planned if for the benefit of the Britishers.

Directly the race was on, Ross piloted Helps to the front round the first bend; then, according to prearranged plan, they let Surjatta and Cerati take the lead in the back stretch, being careful themselves to drop in behind the Italian, so that it was not feasible for the Germans to form a running phalanx, which Lowe had said would be fatal to our chances.

By the half-distance Ross had taken a good deal of jockeying, in sheltering Helps; he had, moreover, set the shattering pace which Lowe had advised, and was just about all in. Helps, however, was quite ready to look after himself from that stage of the race, and at once put out a feeler, which livened up the pace considerably.

Helps then shot away from the surprised Germans, who were beginning to hedge him in, and was still in the lead when he came to the last bend. Le Duc, on the outside, came up to the leader and it looked as though Helps was going on to the grass, in fact the Englishman eased to avoid fouling and the spectators gasped, but so exactly had the scheduled been planned to suit Helps capabilities that, although Dahlstrom had now joined Le Duc, Helps raced round them and came right away down the home-stretch to win a grand race comfortably in 4 min. 1.7 secs.

Ross that day showed that he had the heart of a lion, Helps proved his courage and produced his speed, but it was the wide experience and the admirable judgement of Douglas Lowe that lay behind the victory. Men who are going to be athletes must be taught to think clearly and concisely, they must learn to reason things out of themselves, for even the ability to take infinite pains in all their undertakings is not the whole genius of athletic success. As to how the brain functions, in relation to the rest of the body, that will appear from time to time as we discuss other problems.

Not long ago a famous Finnish athletic official and former champion told me that he knew most there was to know about athletics and felt himself competent to lecture upon any branch or phase of the game, "but." he added, "Had never venture to try to coach field events athletes, simply because we have not got the 'coaching eye.' "

Now what did that sportsman mean by the "coaching-eye"? Everyone who is neither blind nor woefully short-sighted can see things that are happening; some people see things more quickly than do others, some people are able to take in a far greater proportion of the details of the things they see; but it is only a very, very few who completely comprehend the whole significance of a series of actions which are performed rapidly.

From this it follows that it is absolute essential that there should be the closest co-operation between eye and brain. In training boys, often give them tests in visual training which we think will tend to sharpen their alertness. Apart from the fact that it is undoubtedly a very great asset when one is competing against a champion in the field events, and so has the chance of watching him closely, it is also of inestimable value to be able to observe his every action and to sum up exactly what each action means and its utility as applied to one's own technique.

It is even more valuable to train one's mentality by constant practice, so that one can tell almost to the fraction of a second the pace at which one is travelling and at which a race is being run. It is equally important to train one's eyes and brain, acting in concert to assess both speeds, heights and distances. The low-hurdler for example seldom finds it possible to maintain the same number of strides between flights when he is approaching the end of a gruelling 440 yards race run over 3 ft. fences; nor will blind courage and determination carry him cleanly over the last three flights. It is for this reason that men who have become first class in this event have trained themselves to take care of the rest of the race, have worked and worked, running at one hurdle from varying distances, until they have built up the ability by mental and visual training to estimate the take off correctly. That estimate must be made several strides before there arises the necessity to chop the stride to fit in the take off step.

It is believed that a man with good eyesight and a good brain ought to train himself to estimate his take-off without having to rely upon the very doubtful aid of glancing at check-marks placed on the track as he tears down the runway. The visual height training of pole vaulters and high jumpers is much more intricate, because a man aiming to raise his body over extreme heights, no matter whether he relies upon spring alone, or has the pull of his arms upon a bamboo pole to help him, has got to learn to assess the height of something that is non-existent.

The whole object of both types of athlete should be to arrange the spring, or swing-up, so that the foot, or feet, will reach maximum elevation at a point beyond and higher than the bar on which they wish to raise the centre of gravity of the body. Some men do this purely instinctively, but for ninty per cent athletes, the sort of the judgment that is needed can be acquired only by long practice and the closest training in visual appreciation. The care of eyes and their training is important in another connection, for it must be remembered that the head is the athlete's rudder.

Normally speaking, the position of the head dictates the angle of the body, and the set of the head is often unconsciously controlled by the direction of the eyes. In this way, we know that the habit of fixing the eyes on an imaginary moving spot located on the track some 12 to 15 yards ahead of the runner will automatically adjust his body balance to the correct angle. Similarly, if the hurdler when taking one flight will fix his eyes upon the top-rail of the hurdle next beyond it, he is less likely to take a toss by rapping the top of the hurdle he is then clearing.

For athletes it is advisable that not merely be content to let your coach teach you to use your eyes, to go an oculist now and then and let him test your sight, and by an oculist. There are some cases of athlete's performances being very materially affected by his eyesight. One of such a case is of a high jumper who apparently had all the spring in the world, coupled with the most dour determination to succeed. It did not matter, however, how much one tried to help that boy. You could put down check-marks and take-off spots as often as you liked, he would never hit them, you could rig up all sorts of gadgets to help him to get the elevation of his centre of gravity at the right point in relation to the bar, but it did not make the slightest different, he went bang into the lath every time, or else jumped so short that he came down right on top of it. At last he went to an ophthalmic surgeon, who prescribed the right sort of spectacles and that youth developed into an exceedingly fine higher jumper.

Another case of such kind was of a man who had got his glasses from a quack who had fitted him for astigmatism. The man was a long jumper, but he just could not get the take-off board, so he too went along, to a qualified doctor, who diagnosed his trouble and prescribed glasses that corrected the fault in his vision to the great improvement of his athletic performances.

The eye is set in a mass of loose, fatty tissue filled with delicate vessels which are easily suffused by any rise in blood-pressure, such as inseparable from violent effort. Violent laughter, or violent weeping, cause a person to close the lids instinctively for the protection of the delicate vessels of the orbit and the eyeball, and still more, and for the same purpose, does a person about to sneeze, or seized with a severe fit of coughing, shut his eyes tightly. This instinctive shutting of the eyes tightly is nature's means of protecting the blood vessels in the eyes, by supplying counter-pressure against the eyeballs, which have a tendency to protrude from the bony cup which constitutes the orbit when they become swollen and congested. They are held back in place by the constrictor muscle of the eye. Looked at from another angle, we shall be considering presently, it may be argued that additional work is put on the heart in this way, which is true.

None the less it is a question of values, the additional strain on the heart can at the worst be but very small, and meantime the vessels of the eye are extremely delicate, and so it is a mistake to tell the athlete not to shut his eyes, unless he is a runner and therefore almost bound to keep them open in duty to himself. If one of theses vessels does burst there is bleeding into the retina and the eye becomes seriously injured. Again, if an athlete is constantly showing even slight engorgement of the eyes after effort, he should be sent to a doctor, for in some forms of high blood pressure, you get a rupture in the vessels of the eye with subsequent loss of sight.

In the same time, coach should not be led away into the theory that because an athlete shows a smiling face under alleged strain, and is therefore not risking his eyes or putting unnecessary pressure on his heart, all is going well, because it is a fact that the athlete whose expression does not denote violent effort, cannot be making a violent effort.

It is found that even when a man is at rest, his blood circulates at nearly a gallon a minute, which is about equal to the total amount of blood in his body and represents nearly 500,000 gallons a year. Under the stress of violent exertion, the output may be eight times as great, and even a man doing normal work would produce the equivalent of raising almost a ton of water from sea level to the top of the Mount Everest. The heart will work for us in the most exacting and what often appear to be unfair conditions. It is, in fact, comparatively hard for a really fit man to give his heart too much work to do.

Violent effort imposes a big strain upon the blood vessels and the blood-vessel walls, and if the heart is not sound or if the muscles are old or are inelastic, there is a danger of rupture. But if the muscles are young and fully elastic, as they are in the case of a well and sensibly trained athlete, then the danger of such a rupture has not been shown to exist. One hears, occasionally, of instances of erstwhile great athletes dropping dead, when they have reached the forties, and inevitable question is asked, would that have happened to them if they had not followed athletic sport so keenly in their young. Quite frankly, there never can be a proper answer to that question, simply because each such case can be judged only on its own individual history. Should is to happen that the man in question has fallen dead while taking part in a veterans' race, then the answer is that if a man is fool enough to join a suicide club, no one but he himself can be blamed for the consequences.

Players will be served and Anno Domini cannot be denied. The governing body of athletics should make it a hard and fast rule that no veterans' races should be run in connection with any sports meeting held under A.A.A. laws. In the field events, the case is different. Apart from man who go on competing long after they should have the good sense to hang up their spiked shoes, it often happens that a man who has given to athletics pretty well everything there is in him, until he is, say, five and twenty, suddenly decides that it is about time he began to think about settling down to earn his living.

Then, he brings to his work that unbounded vigour and enthusiasm that previously he has given to athletics. So knee on his job does such a man become that he takes little or no exercise, overworks and possibly over eats. He over-eats, because in the later years of his athletic career, he has been accustomed to doing himself pretty well, for the sake of making up muscular wastage.

Going from an active to a sedentary life is the very deuce, anyhow, and if you add to that the worry of establishing a business, you get a pretty good idea of why that type of man soon begins to suffer from indigestion and nervous dyspepsia. In such circumstances, one cannot blame his early demise on to his athletic career, for a man similarly circumstances who never had been an athlete would be just as likely to pass out.

There are different opinions concerning the heart of athlete. Some say that it is not proper to believe that in a healthy person even the most violent exercise can produce strain or disease of the heart. Some says that an athletic heart is a large heart, and a large heart is very much like any other large muscle, it is developed to supply the definite need. If you are living a very active athletic life, you require a large and well-developed heart. The man who has not got, it is not able to stand the fatigue. It will go down as the necessity decreases, that is, if a man leads a less active life, the heart will grow smaller. It is, of course, sometimes called soldier's heart, among soldiers marching. It is called athlete's heart and it is called miner's heart among men who have heavy work to do. It implies the same thing. It means an increase in the size of the heart to supply the necessary amount of force for increased muscular work.

Reduction of size is accompanied by a softening of the heat, but in that connection, the only danger associated with such softening, which is like the softening of any other muscle that is allowed to go out of training is the really great danger that there is in a man of trying to do what he used to do suddenly without training.

By one school of thought it is maintained that it is impossible to strain the heart of a perfect sound individual by hard exercise. When cardiac lesion followed excessive exertion, it was held to be toxic, and the blame was laid at the door of some laten focus of sepsis, such as diseases tonsils, a chronic appendix, intestinal stasis, sinusitis, or some similar cause. Further, experience now leads to believe that a primary strain may occur in the hearts of hitherto perfectly sceptics individuals.

When an athlete strains his heart, such primary cardiac over-strain is a cardiac disorder which is the immediate result of excessive physical exertion in an individual whose heart has been sound. It is questioned by some whether the affection can occur in persons with previously sound heart who have been properly trained. In this context it can be said that during growth, each organ develops in greater or less proportion in different phases, and it is known that the heart achieves its biggest innings of growth in the period of general development. Hence, it follows that the heart of a boy of 15 is smaller in proportion to the size of his body than will be the case when he has reached 20 years. This is a sufficient answer to those who advocate exhausting cross-country runs for young schoolboys.

One of an Irish-American U.S.A. Olympic Coach declared that of all the athletes he had known and trained, he had not been able to trace the death of one of them to the so called athlete's heart. Constant exercise enlarges the heart, gradually in proportion to the development of the other organs of the body, and said that the larger and stronger the heart, the slower will be its beats.

In other words, a heart with a pulse-beat of 60 to the minute will do the same amount of work as another heart with a pulse beat of 72. But why should one be concerned if his heart, beating 60 times to the minute, sends the same amount of blood through his arteries as his comrade's heart, beating 72 to the minutes. Relating to this fact, many experiments have been conducted in America. The investigators were doctor who was a well-known heart and lung specialist and an equally famous athletic coach, who had as their purpose the determination of the immediate effects of vigorous athletic exercise upon trained and untrained subjects. The first subject was a trained champion walker. A diagram of the man's own heart was drawn on his chest, and he then walked a mile in 7 mins. The subsequent immediate medical examination of this man showed that his heart had expanded 3/8 of an inch. A man entirely untrained then walked half a mile in 6 mins., and showed a heart expansion of 1½ ins. He had walked half the distance at approximately half of the speed of the trained champion, but the heart expansion was more than doubled.

Another experiment of such kind was done with a trained runner covering a mile in 5 mins., and an untrained runner going half a mile in three mins., produced an almost identical result, in relation to the proportionate heart expansion of trained and untrained subjects. In the foregoing experiments, the fatigue coefficient was present to some small degree. It is still remained to investigate cases of violent effort. Here the difference between the trained and the untrained runner was very much more pronounced.

The first subject was a man who had been in steady training and leading a regular life for two years. He ran a fast 150 yards and his heart remained virtually unaffected. On the other hand, the untrained man, who ran that distance at but ¾ of the speeds was completely exhausted. The experiments were then carried a stage farther and it was clearly proved that, even in the case of two runners neither of whom had trained, or was in training, the effect of brief, violent exercise was far greater in the case of the smoker than in the case of non-smoker.

Very careful records have been kept of the effects which athletic training and competition have upon the average boy; and from these statistics, it would appear that the youth who trains conscientiously, who neither smokes nor drinks, and who is content to participate in actual competitions to no more than a reasonable degree during adolescence, has no need to fear that he will contract that somewhat mysterious and quite possibly mythical complain called athlete's heart. On the other hand, there is an almost overwhelming consensus of authoritative opinion that a sane system of athletic training not only strengthens the heart, but also renders that organ better able to withstand the sudden strain of violent effort, to sustain better the demands imposed by athletic fatigue and to resist any sudden form of shock.

The thing to avoid at all costs is any sudden change in one's mode of life. Even at the end of an athletic season, the athlete should go out of training gradually. When he hangs up his spikes for the last time, he should find some milder form of physical sport, in any case, he must moderate his eating and he must go on taking a reasonable amount of exercise. Now question arises that what does the heart do and what are its functions in relation to the athlete. In the first place, an increase in muscular activity calls for a corresponding increase in blood supply, first to make a greater volume of oxygen available and secondly to remove the waste products which induce fatigue. It is by proper training that the necessary adjustments in the human system are brought about.

When a man is in normal health and functioning normally, his heart does not get tired and no amount of exercise is likely to strain it, unless there has been some previous cardiac defect, but the heart can become dilated by excessive exertion and thereby the seeds of future disease may be sown.

Thus, it can be said that training is of vital importance because, by training, the vasco-motor centres which direct the supply of blood to the body can be accustomed to concentrate more and more upon the muscular system, while the heart also is being trained to develop a correspondingly more rapid and more forceful action. The violent athletic exercise brings into action muscle-fibres which otherwise would lie virtually dormant, and tiny blood channels, the capillaries, which otherwise might remain closed and in reserve. But the supply of blood, and therefore oxygen, to all these fibres must be increased, as will be readily understood from the statement that a sprinter running 100 yards in fast time requires about 30 times as much oxygen as he would need in normal activity. But while the blood is passing through the capillaries, the organs and tissues of the body are taking in oxygen and nutrition, so that a slow-moving, regular blood-stream is best suited to the interchange of the materials.

On the other hand, the heart is bound to pump blood faster right out to the capillaries of a man indulging in violent action, because the total calibre of the arterial system increases as the capillaries are reached. The blood-flow in the aorta, the great artery, is about 90 ft. per minute when it leaves the heart, but in the capillaries is no more than 2 in. per minute. Further, when the capillaries rejoin to form the lesser veins, the blood-stream is accelerated, because arterial capacity is decreased, and in fact blood returns to the hear through the upper and lower vena cava at half the speed at which it left. The importance of proper training now becomes more apparent than ever, on account of the way in which the intermittent blood flow in the arteries is controlled to provide the regular stream of the capillaries.

Training does and must tend to make the walls of the arteries more elastic, because the smaller vessels and capillaries offer considerable resistance to the blood flow. Wherefore, each heart-beat makes demands upon the elasticity of the walls of the larger arteries, the heart-beats being repeated with just enough rapidity to make the outflow of blood into the capillaries continuous, through the arterial system being distended to the point where the elasticity of the arterial walls will force through the capillaries, between each heart-beat and the next, an amount of blood equal to the amount leaving the heart at each beat. If the walls of the arteries were to become entirely inelastic, the flow of blood in the capillaries would be intermitten, because the heart would pump as much blood as left it into the capillaries and the flow would cease when the heart-beat finished. That is why it is so dangerous for old athletes, whose arteries are becoming hardened, to take part in veterans' races.

Peripheral Resistance is the function which brings into play the elasticity of the larger arteries, the estimate of the force which drives the blood through the tissues and organs of the body is commonly termed blood pressure. This all-important blood pressure depends upon various factors some of which are:

a. the amount of blood forced into the aorta by the heart-beat per minute,

b. the amount of peripheral resistance. The blood output varies according to the heart beats per minute and the strength of each beat, and

c. the greater the peripheral resistance the higher will be the blood pressure.

Human system has means of its own for increasing or decreasing the number of heart-beats per minute, of adjusting the force of the beats and the peripheral resistance to the needs of any particular part or organs of the body at any given time, so that a blood pressure suitable to the needs of the particular circumstances obtaining may be produced. Thus, when a person is reclining the normal heart-beat is about 60, but when that person stands up, the rate rises normally to 75 and in the intermediate sitting position is about 72.

Thus, it can be said that a shorts, sharp sprint will raise the rate of heart-beat per minute by as much as 25 per cent, and so, again we see the need for training, to enable the heart to support the strain. It should be remembered that a hot bath and pleasurable excitement both stimulate the action of the heart. That is one of the reasons why a man limbers-up before a competition to get his body warm, and why a man excited by the hope of winning a contest is likely to do well.

On the other hand, a cold bath or painful emotion decelerate the heart action. That is why the athlete should not stand about stripped out and letting his limbs get cold, and why the man who fears doing badly in the competition for which he is waiting is not likely to win. In this connection, there is a genuine distinction between anxiety and fear. The importance of these matters cannot be over-rated, since it is the alteration in the pulse rate which adapts the heart action to the varying needs of the body, and the higher the pulse rate the greater will be the quantity of blood forced into the arterial system per minute. This energy-output of the heart is under the control of a special system of nerves, which regulate the pace of its beat.

Thus, during muscular exertion, the heart and the circulation make their most important adjustment to meet the immediate needs of the athlete. They do this by increasing many times the output of blood from the heart, both by accelerating the rate of heart-beat and by making more powerful the contraction of the heart at each beat. Now if we thinks back to the fact regarding the relationship between two men with hearts beating at different rates per minute, but doing the same amount of work, and if, moreover, we re-examined the American experiments already referred to, we are bound to arrive at the conclusion that the heart-rate of a trained athlete is lower for a definite blood output than that of an untrained person, when both are performing the same task. It should be remembered that the divergence grows more pronounced as the exertion increases and becomes more prolonged

Proper training produces great contractile power in the heart, so that in the case of the trained athlete, there need be a lesser rise in pulse rate than in the untrained man to secure the same blood output from the heart. Many people are under the delusion that all training consists only of the building up of certain groups of muscles for the acts of performing certain physical skills applicable to perhaps a single type of athletic event. In reality, proper training does far more, since it lays the fundamental basis of all athletic success by building up and developing the heart muscle so that it may meet the demands made upon it to produce blood circulation adequate to the needs of the athlete. Athletic training should build up the heart to full contractile power, because the rate of human heart-beat cannot increase to more than 180 per minute during forced and prolonged exertion. From all of which arises the conclusion that although he may be otherwise physically capable of the feats he wishes to perform, the untrained man works more steadily and regularly at the lower rate acquired by training than at the higher rate which the untrained man must produce for the same effort in competition, with his prepared opponent.

Muscular action increases the heart-rate correspondingly to the violence of the exercise, but, whereas ordinary people have a rate of about 65 to 75 per minute, in the case of an athlete in training, the rate may be as low as 45 when he is at rest, while such rates as 55 are quite common. The point to remember is that these lower rates are normal for the athlete who is trained and in training.

Putting the theory developed in another way, it may be said that a strong heart beating at 45 has a fourfold capacity when its rate rises to 180 under severe exertion, whereas, as in the case of the untrained man perhaps, if the resting rate is doubled, the heart accommodation is halved under maximum strain. After violent effort, the heart-rate decreases gradually to normal, and although the two nerves which govern the heart do not cause it to beat, their action has yet much to do with the deceleration process, because they influence its rate and affect its strength.

The vague nerve, which is an involuntary never and has its starting point in a nerve-centre situated in the under-side of the brain, is concerned with slowing down the action of the heart, whereas the sympathetic nerve-fibres, which have their origin in the upper part of the spinal cord, cause the heart-beat to become stronger and more rapid when they are stimulated. As soon as the athlete begins limbering up, preparatory to competition, the exercise he is taking automatically removes the vagus effect by means of the nervous system, so that his heart begins to beat more rapidly, and almost at once, and equally automatically, the sympathetic nerve becomes active and the heart rate rises still higher.

Before leaving these specific considerations of various questions, in relation to the human heart, here we are taking two final points, which are of vital interest to all athletes and those who are called upon to take charge of them. We do agree that the length of time a man can go on, and the severity of the effort he can make, are contingent upon the amount of oxygen debt he can incur, but the extent to which a man can take oxygen into his lungs depends, inter alia, upon the rate at which his heart can drive the blood around his body. Increase in this pressure imposes an immense amount of work upon the heart, and even well trained athletes cannot take in more than approximately 4 litres of oxygen per minute.

6

Athletic Tests and Measurements of Ability

The modern generation is living in an era of examinations and tests of all kinds, which serve, or should serve, the purpose of assessing, in the first place, general ability as an indication of potentiality, and secondly, specialized suitability. In how far the examination system is better than the methods of our forefathers, one is not prepared to say.

In former times, a man relied upon his judgment of character when dealing with other men, and could pick an athlete or a horse upon their points. The fact, moreover, still holds good that many a boy who never could pass a paper examination has yet turned out to be a brilliant success in life and a great organizer, or leader of men. When we turn to the physical side of life, a rather different state of things obtains, and it is all to the good that the fact is being recognized at last that body and mind are one and inseparable and ergo, realization is slowly, but surely coming that the body is as important in the scheme of education as the brain.

Perhaps, the modern passion for measuring things is more marked in general education than in any other sphere of life, and this measuring os the child's mental capacity is well graded running as it does from the general knowledge paper and essay types of test, to intelligence tests and tests in specialized subjects. With modern recognition of the importance of physical education, the system of examination and testing is spreading to the fields of sport, and again we see the close alliance, which is maintained by the mental and physical sides of our being.

Mentally, there is great variation between one person and another. One boy has a brilliant intellect, another simply cannot learn, no matter how he tries. The same state of things obtains in the physical field. There are many successful and many incapable athletes also. Here the word incapables have been used just in order to deliberately distinction between incapables and incompetents. This distinction is important because there are some athletes whose athletic potentiality had never been tested, and who looked like hopeless cases at first but, who if they did not become champions, showed marked athletic ability when they became athletically educated. By incapables here we mean those youths who simply do not possess the capacity for becoming good in any form of athletic activity. There is a small proportion of genius always, and there are lots of incompetents and incapables, but the research that has been made so far in this subject tends to show that the variation between the genius and moron preserves much the same ratio in both mental and physical ability tests.

According to Prof. McCloy, the general range of athletic ability taken in the mass yields about five or six per cent of very good material of the best university athlete type, 24 or 25 per cent who are just on the border-line of being very good and may, or may not, mature in their second, or third season, 38 to 40 per cent who are merely middle class, and about 25 per cent who are well below the average, but are not yet so bad as the lowest group, who constitute the despair of all physical instructors and athletic coachcs.

Although the eyes of the world are ever fixed upon

genius, it is the lower grades that benefit most from the new systems of measuring athletic potentiality that are gradually coming into vogue. It may be said, with certain reservations, that a good coach can always improve the performances of a genius, how much or how little is a matter of circumstance, provided he is taken in hand sufficiently early.

However, available genius represer ted at the most, probably no more than 5 per cent of the mass. As regards the boys in the lower classifications, who show any signs at all of potential athletic ability, it is fair to say that one can improve them a little by teaching them various physical skills, buy you cannot make a Sievert out of a lad who lacks the essential potentiality in the first place. Nor can you, on general grounds, make, say, a high jumper out of a boy whose athletic tendency is towards long distance running. Early athletic ability measurements give a good indication of the potential coefficient and more or less enable one to say approximately how good a boy may become.

Later one, no doubt, we shall devise a boy is best fitted for of making the boys play certain specified games for which they have little or no natural aptitude and still less liking. In drawing up the various systems of measuring and testing athletic ability which are already in vogue, physical educationalists have had the advantage of knowing what mistakes have been made by those who in the past have been responsible for preparing the tests in the mental syllabus.

Many boys who have done well in class work fail in examinations through sheer nervousness, and the same thing is seen in competitive athletics, wherefore the tests for measuring athletic ability have been devised along lines well calculated to circumvent this particular difficulty. Present-day measuring tests have all been designed for a specific purpose and not as tests of specified abilities.

Capacity represents the natural ability of the subject to perform certain physical skills, the technique of which has not yet been taught to him. It is a test of natural physicals cleverness, therefore, it must be a test of a variety of abilities, all of which must involve fundamental principles of success in athletics. In dealing with this subject, it is pointed out that maturity and size are important factors which have to be considered, and the way in which he arrives at an assessment of their influential values upon the measurement tests is by building up a Classification Indexs.

Other things being equal, the boy who has an advantage of six inches in height usually wins in athletics, although, conversely, the boy who has an advantage of three or four years, again all else being equal, is likely to prove the winner in most types of contest. Having the foregoing points in mind, Prof. McCloy arrived at his Classification Index by using as his factor twenty times the age in years, plus six times the height in inches, plus the weight in pounds. The age, however, becomes a constant factor at 17, boys over that age being reckoned as 17, because that is the age at which research made in America suggests that a boy ceases to mature, although athletically, in his actual standard of performance will rise considerably during subsequent years. There is a lot to be said for the use of this Classification Index, because practical experience has proved that it correlates closely with performances in track and field athletics.

After setting his Classification Index, Prof. McCloy then goes on to measure the amount of horsepower the individual can develop. This is not nearly so difficult as one might be tempted to believe at first sight, if you will think for one moment that all track and field athletics are really a matter of horsepower, that is, relative to the individual's weight. The Standing Shot Put will probably illustrate best how the term horsepower or simply power is arrived at in this connection. A shot-putter has to throw the put over a distance. During that distance the twist of his body, the final thrust of his leg, combined with the drive of his right arm, is accelerating the shot as much as possible. But to gain maximum acceleration, he must employ force over the given distance in which he still maintains control of the shot. Now force employed over a certain distance is work, but to obtain the maximum effect in shot-putting, the work must be done rapidly, wherefore the time factor enters into our calculations and leaving out the question of the angle of departure of the missile, we find that it is the time rate which determines the distance to which the shot can be propelled, and so finally, we reach the conclusion that the time rate of the work is horsepower.

Equally important inferences may be drawn in relation to the jumping events, especially the high jump, in which horizontal velocity is converted into vertical spring at the moment of the take-off foot making its final impact upon the ground, although of course, there are many other factors concerned in the accomplishment of a perfect jump, which is consonant with the athlete's ability plus his natural spring. The force which the high jumper exerts as rapidly as possible in the take-off action of the foot from which his spring is made is exerted, probably, over a distance of not more than 12 inches. He uses that power, in relation to his weight, for acceleration through that 12 inches, and the force exerted and the time taken to exert it over that distance determines the height a man can jump.

Success in athletics depends upon strength and speed, in other words the athlete must have at his command force and velocity, which are synonymous terms for strength and speed, but force-times-velocity is power, and so you see how we arrive at the term horsepower or simply power in relation to track and field athletics. Speed is dependent upon not only the contractile power of the muscles, but also upon how quickly they can be contracted.

According to Prof. McCloy the Sargent Jump provides perhaps the best means of measuring muscle viscosity, and, if he means natural and normal viscosity one is prepared to agree with him, but a bald statement is a little dangerous in this connection, because so much must depend upon the prevailing temperature and the amount of running about, or preliminary exercise, a boy has done jump prior to performing the Sargent jump test. The Sargent jump is simply a leap straight up into the air, the instructor assessing by eye the height to which the jumper's head rises.

However, it is necessary to standardize a method of jumping, so that the boy with some knowledge of style shall not score over the boy who has none, since what these test is for is to measure jumping capacity, in relation to muscular viscosity, not how much the boy knows about jumping. When Prof. McCloy used the Sargent jump in combination with his age-height-weight Classification Index, he found its correlation to the individual's athletic ability to be about .85, while the results of a number of trials taken over a period of days correlated as high as .93. It should be pointed out that in speaking of correlation point so and so, one means simply a measurement of relationship and not a percentage.

Thus, such a high correlation as .9 enables the official carrying out the tests to make a fairly accurate prediction of the boy's future abilities, because the correlationship is working towards plus one, but a low correlation like correlates .2 gives a lesser degree of reliability in prediction. So far we have seen the use of the Classification Index and the use of the Sargent jump for testing muscle viscosity, but there must also be a test for motor educability, that is to say, how well and how quickly the subject can learn new physical skills. For this purpose the Americans use the brace test.

It is important to remember that the brace test does not, and is not intended to, test a boy's potentiality for learning individual skills, but only his ability to learn new skills. It is obvious, therefore, that any test of this kind must combine a number of stunts. The fourth type of test used in America is a test for agility and co-ordination. This was first produced by Mr. R.H. Burpee, teacher of physical education at one of the New York Y.M.C.A. institutions, other instructions have modified it to meet their own requirements. In this test, the subject takes the knees bend position with his hands resting on the floor in front of him. On the order being given, he shoots his feet out behind and immediately comes back in the reverse order to the stand. His movements are stop watch timed and he gets in as many repetitions as he can in 10 secs. The Burpee test of agility and large muscle co-ordination when used by itself correlates about .4 with athletic ability, but when combined with the three other tests, the correlation is as high as .93.

While studying systems of measuring athletic ability, it must always be borne in mind that the mere fact of a subject showing a high correlation does not mean that he will become a good athlete at once, or indeed, that he will ever be a great athlete, simply to instance but two factors of success, because he may lack the patience and perseverance required for training, or he may not have the competition temperament. What the correlation does show quite definitely is his potentiality in relation to his motor ability.

Americans have a test for motor ability, which is known as the Roger's test and they have the ordinary chinning test. Those are the strength tests. Then they have a track and field athletics ability test, which is variable in different schools, but a fair example of such a combination would be a sprint, a potato race indoors, a long or a high jump and a shot put or discus throw. This test is scored in combination with the horsepower developed, and the strength and track and field tests combined correlated about .8 or better, with general motor ability. There is also a method of scoring the athlete according to the amount of the actual capacity which he develops. The use of the battery of four tests, which have been described, when applied to Freshmen, enables the American coach to pick the men who are likely to produce the best results from coaching, and although the others are certainly not neglected, a coach does start at a big advantage when he knows the men he can concentrating upon as being the ones who are likely to make the team.

The athletes, being thus graded, are now ready for individual attention and can be taught the technique of the event they are going to take up. That means that the next tests will be tests of skill, and finally competition itself will be the best acid test of courage, which will show whether a boy has athletic intelligence and the competition temperament. In the athletic achievements tests used at the George Washington High School, the basis of measurement is the examination, the test scores being transmitted into quotients, improvement ratios, percentile and letter ratings, and the diagnosis of a subject's failure often reveals the causes. It is interesting to note that the number of boys, excluding those who were under weight and those with organic disabilities, put through the test in 10 years was 12,622.

Here we have selected seven events alongwith the reason for their selection which are as follows:

a. Rope Climbing—General strength and bodily

agility. Safety in case of accidents.

b. Standing Long Jump—Strength and Leg Sprint.

c. 50-yards Run—Strength and Leg Speed.

d. Press-ups—To develop strength of arms and back muscles.

e. Chinning—To test strength of arms. Reverse grip used and regulation horizontal .bar employed.

f. Number of Goals Shot in 60 Secs.—To encourage the development of skill in handling and dribbling the basketball and accuracy in shooting goals.

g. 25-yards Swim—General strength and speed, and also as a safety measure.

The study of the results of the scores in the various motor events produced two sets of norms, i.e., age norms and combination age-height-weight norms. The former represents an average in any event, and the latter is also an average, with weight considered as a sliding scale performance; standard being the goal of achievement represented by the score reached, or exceeded, by only 15 per cent of those taking part in the test.

When we come to the consideration of physical types for.various events, we shall see that it has been possible to ascertain by measurements and records of 74 individuals what is the ideal built for a sprinter and how the American Society of Directors of Physical Education in College was able to supply for the preparation of Dr. Tait McKenzei's statue, The Athletic charts of student's measurements between the ages of 16 and 25 which had been kept by Dr. Dudley Sargent over a period of forty years, together with Dr. Paul Phillips's dimensions of sprinters and McKenzie's own statistics regarding skaters. The measurement for Dr. Tait McKenzie's glorious statue, which will survive the test of time itself as the epitome and true presentation of the ideal athlete of the twentieth century, were secured by means of a double test, since, of 400 men who had excelled in all forms of sport and had undergone the intercollegiate strength test, the average was taken of the 50 strongest men, as revealed by the strength test during a five-years' period.

The American inter-collegiate strength test is made scientifically by means of a dynamometer. So far as England is concerned, excellent work is now being carried out by the Physical Education Staff of the Board of Education and also throughout the Physical Training Departments of the Fighting Services. A good deal of research work has been done from time to time with a view to drawing up some form of comparative table giving the relative value of performance in various events, since, quite naturally questions have not infrequently arisen as to the merit of, say, 100 yards in 10 secs., as compared with a 12-ft. pole vault or a 6s ft. high jump.

7

Athletic Psychology

Athletic psychology is a big subject, but it is in this department of his craft that the coach does, or does not, establish his claim to greatness. A man may know every single thing there is to know about athletic technique, he may have a perfect genius for imparting his knowledge and yet he may fail to turn out a successful team, simply because he does not understand the temperaments of the various individual athletes committed to his care, or it may be that his own personal anxiety for their success is at the root of the trouble, for when people are working in close association, nothing can be more catching than the communication of fear or anxiety. Nonetheless, there never was an athlete yet, capable of doing a really great performance, who did not suffer from what is popularly termed getting wind up whether he showed his emotion or not.

Here it is important to understand the meaning of getting wind up, for there are two essential factors to the sensation, which varies in the time of occurrence prior to competition in accordance with the temperament of the individual athlete. The right sort of wind up is the sort of sheer excitement that brings a man right up to his toes, ready and eager for the contest, the wrong type is anxiety, which may amount those positive fear and in extreme cases, will cause loss of sleep for one or more nights preceding the day of competition. One has known cases when this type of fear seemed to be inherent and incurable, although, possibly, a psychoanalyst, dealing with complexes, causes and inhibitions, might be able to diagnose and alleviate the trouble. Usually the wrong type of wind up is due to the following reasons:

a. insufficient training;

b. wrong training methods; or

c. over-training, which is tantamount to staleness.

The cure is to establish a complete sense of self-confidence in the mind of the athlete, such as comes from conscientious training of the right kind. And yet, even that will not always suffice, for there was at least one great quarter-miller who knew that he could beat the best men in the world, but always worked himself into such a pitiful state of panic before a race that he frequently lost to men of less perfect physique and ability, but who possessed a far higher nervous potential.

Truly, nervousness is bad, simply because it dissipates energy and is therefore wasteful. The symptoms are readily recognized by undue affability or irritability and a tendency to bodily chilliness. When this condition is apparent, the kindly comradeship of an understanding coach is invaluable. It sometimes helps matters too, if the athlete is given a small piece of hard barley sugar to suck. The coach can do a lot for an athlete in this connection, but the main consideration, when all is said and done, is for the coach to so handle his charges that each one of them will learn to know himself, so that he becomes the master of his own fate. The sensations at the root of the whole matter are emotion and excitement, as witness the phenomenal strength of a madman, for when excitement is at maximum, men can and do, perform extraordinary feats of strength and speed.

However, depression has the reverse effect and makes the performance of physical feats both difficult and tiresome. When a man is excited, or otherwise affected by strong emotions, his heart-rate goes rushing up and the suprarenal glands, deep-seated near the kidneys, release adrenaline into the blood stream with astounding results, for the heart beat is both quickened and strengthened and the man is thereby prepared for the coming struggle. It is, in fact, probable that the presence in the blood stream of this adrenaline is intimately connected with the condition already referred to as wind up, of the right type. The man who first demonstrated the effects of emotion upon human health and human physical activity was the famous physiologist, Prof. Ivan Petrovich Pavlov. It is the researches of Pavlov, Cannon, Carlson and Crile which have made plain the fact, and its converse, that efficient circulation and digestion make for happiness, because pleasant sensations influence the secretion of our digestive juices satisfactorily and also stimulate the rhythmic action of the food-canal.

On the other hand, fear, over-anxiety and, indeed any form of mental disturbance provide a distinct hindrance to proper digestion. In the foregoing connection, it may be pointed out, therefore that freedom from worry has a definite nutritive value, because the well-being of a person is at its highest when his mental and physical harmonies are in tune.

The influence of mind on body is illustrated in the release of adrenaline when strong emotion is felt. The construction of the smaller blood vessels follows, so that blood passes from the peripheral to the deeper parts, the muscles are excited and stimulated and the sugar content of the blood becomes reinforced, an important item. Another surprising thing in connection with what may be termed the psychical side of the athletics is the subtle effect upon the athlete of good news.

Emotion has its physical reactions in tensions and movements throughout the human system and also influences glandular secretion. It is as though there were, and there probably are, repercussions of happiness which are physiological. Beyond that, nothing is more certain that body and mind are one and indivisible. Sometimes the one side is predominant, sometimes the other, but even aesthetic emotion is a mental and physical reaction, wherefore it is essential in the training of athletes to correlate mental health with the physiological ideal of bodily development.

Mind and body, in fact, must work hand in hand, and to that end mental dieting, exercise, rest and play must ever be the natural complements of the similar preparation of the body for athletic competition. It must not be thought, from what has been said, that the mind alone influence the body, for in this respect, it is by giving the athlete interest-driven activities to monopolize his attention that we often succeed in casting our fear, anger, worry and other kindred emotions likely to prove harmful to health if left to flourish unchecked.

Of athletic failure, worrying is a very fruitful source, but, apart from the athlete who is naturally of a nervous disposition, worry is not infrequently caused by the coach who creates a too completely athletic atmosphere in which his charges must dwell. And with worry, we must associate disappointment, for the purpose of the present argument. It is the duty of a coach to get the confidence of his charges, so that they will be only too ready to share their troubles with him, it is also part of his job to inspire them with confidence in their own ability to succeed, but when success does not eventuate, he must be prepared to tide them over their bad periods of disappointment.

Here a difficulty arises. So many coaches, in the hope of getting something rather more than his best out of a boy, will lead him to believe that he can perform feats which are really beyond his compass. He may win, although not so impressively as has been prophesied. If he does win, all will probably be well, for it is easy enough to tell him that he did not produce the anticipated performance because so big an effort was not needed. But if he loses to another, whose own best is far lower than the beaten man was led to believe he could do himself, then his disappointment will led to believe he could do himself, then his disappointment will be proportionately the greater and his faith in the man who is coaching him is bound to be shaken.

It is true to say that sort of encouragement only comes off once in a very long while, and probably only when circumstances have combined to create in and for the athlete that supreme state of excitement which enables him to perform phenomenal feats. Disappointment is not by any means confined to the competitive sphere. Any good coach knows that the laws of training correspond to the rules of exercise and rest, and every coach should make himself conversant with a certain Chart of Expected Rate of Progress for Men in Training, just as he should know the Weight Chart for Men, which is sub-divided into Ligth-Boned, Medium-Boned and Heavy-Boned categories for various ages. If the coach's own knowledge is complete, it should not be difficult for him to convince his charges of the fundamental principles of progress in training.

In the beginning stage, there is almost always great improvement in both skill and ability, such as will inevitably inspire the athlete, who has not been warned what to expected, to look for continued progress at much the same rate. He must be made to understand that, his muscular system coming into a state of activity from one of comparative rest, the muscles will have enough stored-up energy to respond quickly to his will, for the time being while their very looseness will be an asset sin the performance of athletic skills which a more seasoned athlete may still find difficult.

For the man who means to succeed in face of all obstacles and disappointments the first flush of easy achievement will be followed by a period of much slower progress. The muscles will be tired from renewed training efforts, the nerve impulses will, if one may use such a term, be self-conscious of the responsibility of their job in transmitting orders quickly, antagonistic muscles will interfere with the smooth flow and return of effort, but, all the time, the whole system will be readjustment itself to the new life it is being called upon to lead. Presently, when the firsts series of adjustments have been roughly made, there will be further progress for a time and a fairly high level of excellence in performance will be maintained. So far the athlete has had no cause for disappointment, but now comes the time when he steadily goes up, until a peak performance is reached. He is delighted, of course, and unless warned, looks for better and still better things. It is, however, almost certain that one of two things now ensues. If he is a very good athlete and, moreover a person who is neither easily elated nor elated nor depressed, he may maintain the standard he has now achieved. But it is much more likely that, having broken his personal record, there will be such a feeling of enormous satisfaction that he will succumb to the temptation to lie back and rest awhile on his laurels, wondering how in the world he ever did that trick.

In other words, the reaching of a peak is usually followed by a relapse. Yet another possibility is that he will be so tremendously pleased with his latest effort that he will straightaway abandon all pretence at training for style and will go all out to achieve yet another peak. In either of the two last-mentioned contingencies, it is practically certain that the athlete's graph will show a distinct curve downwards after a peak performance. If it has been a really good peak, the readjustment will come with stability at what the coach knows to the boy's proper peak average for that particular season.

The coach who studies the psychology of a player's charges should be constantly on the alert to ward off discouragement. Athletes may do well at first, may then train with admirable conscientiousness and yet seem to be making no progress. But the charting of the progress of athletes by graphs is an absorbing part of the coach's occupation. What frequently happens in the case of pole-vaulters has been explained.

The charting graphically of the progress of a shot-putter does not show the same sudden rises, relapses and recoveries and then the same thing again at higher level, but, rather a series of steps in progression. In the initial stage the upward curve of the graph is great, then come a series of short upward jumps, before the sticking point, which is also the danger point, is reached. From his sticking point the shot-putter will very likely begin to go down in performance and his retrogression may be characterized by some loss of form. He gets depressed and feels like packing the whole thing up, and this is just the point at which the coach must step in with an explanation that the drop is merely temporary and is a perfectly natural phenomenon in the practice of any athletic skill. If he can tide the athlete over this bad period, help him to get his field-events second wind, as it were, the graph will again show a sudden and distinct upward tendency of curve.

Care must be taken, however, not to confuse normal retardation of progress with the symptoms of approaching staleness. It happens sometimes that the athlete who has made an auspicious start slowly ceases to improve and then begins losing ground. Yes, you may say, but that is exactly what you have just been talking about, where is difference. The difference lies in other symptoms. It is one thing if a man appears to go back a little as the natural reaction to doing a bigger performance than he has previously achieved, but if his muscles do not seem at fault, if they fail to respond readily to his will and he feels tired, there you have definite danger signals and a warning to rest him, for if you try to maintain, or to increase, his training his condition will certainly become worse. Other danger signals are loss of weight, sleep and appetite, irritability, restlessness, drawn features and sunken eyes.

The physical evidence is only apparent when staleness has actually set in, the other symptoms should give the experienced coach due warning. The first symptoms to watch for is a desire upon the part of the athlete for more than the normal amount of sleep he is getting. The right safeguard is to give nature a chance of restoring the balance of the man's nerve reserves, the cure, if staleness has set in, is rest, preferably accompanied by change. It is no uncommon thing, both in athletic training and in daily life, to see a person's power dissipated through the wastage of physical power and nervous energy which follows unnecessary fatigue from both mental and physical over-exertion or from a species of over-exertion which comes from unwise attempts to combine the production of big mental and physical efforts at the same period.

The man who is coaching athletes, who are also students, will do well to watch this point, because such men are making a two-fold demand upon their resources, their nerve power and such lads need careful handling and still more careful nursing. Mental and physical fatigue is a natural outcome of exertion, and there is only one true type of exhaustion in this connection, which is the exhaustion of the nervous forces. It may be brought on by failure to appreciate the true value of rest.

However, without approaching near to the danger line, any coach who keeps graphs of the work of his charges will agree with the contention that it is not possible to works both body and mind at maximum pressure at one and the same period. If a boy is studying for an important examination at the same time, that he is training for a competition of equal importance from the athletic view point, it is the curve of the graph of his physical work which will show a downward tendency. If you care to study an freshman, who has gone up to a reputed university, with the real intention of working, you will, if you have the vision a coach ought to have, detect in his features little signs of mental strain after he has attended two or three lectures in a morning, while an air of general lassitude will testify to a form of bodily fatigue. But after his first term, when he has got used to taking noes and knows what points it is important for him to remember, you will see a vast improvement.

But never, during the whole of a man's university career, will you find him capable of giving his maximum effort to training as a Blue at the same time that he is working for the degree that he is not going to find it any too easy to take. An accurate weighing machine should be just as important an adjunct to training quarters as a shower both and the massage table, because the athlete's weight is, of all things, the surest guide to his condition. Moreover, the coach, who does not keep a daily chart of the weight of his charges, either does not know his job or else, he is not doing it. The weight varies with the athlete, and with the type of athlete.

Also with the condition of the athlete, his weight varies, and that is the important point in relation to matters at present under discussion. As a general rule, one finds that a man is a bit over weight when he first goes into training, but in the first week he will sweat off some is his superfluous flesh. In the ensuing weeks, the regularity of life in exercise, rest, sleep and food will probably bring his weight back to about what it was at the beginning of training, but now it will no longer be over-weight for muscle is beginning to take the lace of superfluous fat.

Nonetheless, an athlete of average size, that is to say, a man weighing somewhere about 145 to 150 lbs., is likely to lose anything up to 3 lbs., as his further training progresses, but that is not a matter to worry about. On the other hand, a loss of that amount of weight when a man is approaching the stage of being fully trained should give his coach cause to consider the amount of work that man is doing with a view to the quite possibly necessary revision of his training schedule. If the man continues to lose weight, even though he be but half-way through his training period, there need be no doubt about the necessity for cutting down his training activities. Weight is the best guide to the fitness, or otherwise, of athletes, and a variation of 2 or 3 lbs., may have no special significance, for a man may lose as much as 6 or 7 lbs., in a punishing long-distance race, but whatever the loss, a fit man should regain his weight within four and twenty hours, a decreased of 5 to 6 lbs., which is not made up within the period mentioned, indicates that something is seriously wrong, and the athlete must either have more food or his work be reduced, or possibly, stopped altogether, until he begins to pick up again.

In this connection, rest is valuable restorative. The Americans are very keen on the scheme of charging the weights of men in training, and their food consumption, appetite also being a good guide to condition.

Hillman kept carefully prepared weight charts. If he found that a man was gaining a little or holding his weight at normal, he would work him. If a man lost weight and did not pick it up next day, he would rest him. He is responsible also, for the axiom that a man should not be worked on Monday after a hard contest on Saturday, nor when his weight is low, his appetite poor, or he is sleeping well, otherwise you can easily ruin either an individual or a team in training. Hillman's figures show, further, that four men gained 22 lbs., an average per man of 4 1/3 lbs., four lost 25 lbs., an average of 6¼ lbs. per man, but only one man finished the season weighing the same amount as at the commencement of training. It was also the principle of this authority that the team, to enable them to go successfully through a full season, should have rest period added to the daily routine of training. There were 30 mins. before lunch, and 30 mins. before supper. There were cots provided in the gymnasium, and after the men had worked out and had a shower, they got to their cots and relaxed completely for half an hour, after which they assimilated their food a lot more easily.

For athletes in training, the principle should be the same. After a man has had a gruelling contest, or his coach has asked him to punish himself in training, he has not much fancy or a hearty meal, but if you send him to rest and relax fully for 20 or 30 minutes, he will be ready to tackle his food and to enjoy it.

Sleep is a sure guide to the coach as to the mental well-being of his athletes in training. Sleep, in itself, still provides a baffling problem, and no satisfactory explanation of sleep has yet been furnished by science. The main point upon which physiologists are in agreement is that the blood supply to the brain is checked and that some mysterious diminution of oxygen lowers the vitality of our organs of consciousness. The brain life seems to be entirely suspended at the end of the first hour of slumber, which is therefore the most beneficial part of our night's rest, during which the blood feeds and reconditions tired muscles, and perhaps the protein in the blood we have eaten does its main task of repairing tissue wastage.

Later, there is probably a return of blood to the brain which produces that partial uncontrolled consciousness in which we dream dreams. In some people, automatic response to stimulation occurs, and then they, maybe, walk in their sleep. Athletes who are nervy sometimes talk in their sleep on the eve of a competition. All these symptoms the coach should know and understand.

If a man is restless, or does not sleep well, it is a good thing to give him a warm drink, Ovaltine and Milk is a good thing as anything and something light to eat when he is actually in bed. If the sleep is likely to be disturbed, a thermos flask of something warm to drink may be left on the bedside table, or it may be sufficient to provide a box of jujubes. It often helps to get man to sleep again if he can lay his hand on something to pop into his mouth and suck.

If a coach can divert an athlete's mind from the anxieties of his attempt, he will succeed in achieving better results. In actual training work, sit lessens the strain of learning a particular skill if you break up the routine by giving the boy a complementary allied work. For example, when your long jumper has had his work out on style, but you want him to do some more training for spring, it may pay you to let him see how much distance he can cover in a standing jump, a standing backwards jump or three hops on the take-off leg for spring, or, with a javelin, or discus-throw, how much ground he can make in six throws, three with the right hand and three with the left. All practices of this sort vary the monotony and maintain interest, while still achieving your object in training.

Work for the throwing man, using first one hand and then the other is considered to be very good. Athletes do not seem to worry themselves over-much about the real amount of knowledge possessed by their coach, that he does have the necessary knowledge they no doubt take for granted, and so the thing that really counts is the ability of the coach to inspire confidence in the boys and to get them to confide in him.

8

Nutritional Diet and Facts for Athletes

One should always remember the proverb that One man's food is another man's poison. It is permissible, having regard to the notions about athletic diet which were in vogue in the palmy days of the prize ring and pedestrianism and some of the weird notions which still obtain in our own enlightened age. Right through the first half of the last century, many books were published but three which set forth such astounding theories is that supper is bad for the lungs, potatoes should be eaten only to correct the effect of London made bread. All young meat such as veal and lamb, all white flesh meat, whether game or poultry, are good for nothing. They contain no nourishment.

Soup, fish, pies and puddings were regarded as poisonous to a boxer, and athletes were not allowed vegetables, fish, butter, cheese, eggs. Dry biscuits were always kept handy in training quarter and were given to athletes on awakening, because they are considered excellent for absorption of mucus from the mouth, throat and also the windpipe. The athlete was allowed only the barest necessities of life in the way of liquid. Beer was the main beverage, because water was anathema to the old time trainer, milk was supposed to curdle on the stomach, warm liquids were feared as likely to relax the stomach, which would be weakened by taking broth or soups, since these beverages require but little digestion. Sweating and blood-letting were common practices, and laxatives and emetics in general use.

Here is a nice quotation, if a man's loose meat be perceived shaking on his sides, breasts etc., if it lie about the chops, if is seen he is bladder-headed, and his head must be sweated particularly, dull, heavy eyes with a great disposition to sleep, starting in his sleep, or pricking of the skin, demand that he be blooded, opening the physic should ever follow bleeding. By the time Archibald Maclaren wrote his Training in Theory and Practice, however, the men in training had themselves revolted against such drastic treatment as has been outlined above, and we find this author condemning the use of emetics and puratives and advocating the inclusion of vegetables in the athlete's training diet.

Progress was not being made, hands although meat was still the staple part of the athlete's menu, for the sake of its richness in nitrogen, we find Dr. R. Faries in his book Practical Training for Athletics, Health and Pleasure indicating that bananas may be eaten without ill effects, and suggesting the use of butter, provided it be replaced by oatmeal if not well digestion.

However, the fallacy still obtained was that any form of sugar was bad for the athlete's wind. Some of those old-time prejudices are still extant, and to them we have added some new fads and fancies of our own. The trouble is that new scientific principles, even when their value is fully proven do not easily overcome custom. They may appeal to a man's logic and yet not conquer his deep rooted convictions. The mental lab preserves life, but it does make progress most terribly slow.

The inertia of tradition, however, is not so dangerous as the ill informed theories of some modern faddists. Among the older traditions, which are not yet dead is the purging of an athlete at the beginning of training, the belief that meat is the only strength-giving food, the curtailment of milk and the theory that butter increases weight, and by creating soft-fat decreases the powers of endurance, and that bananas are indigestible and of small food value. Among the newer prejudices are the over-emphasis of an alkaline diet, and the cutting out of meat altogether from the athlete's menu that the newest system of so dividing the athlete's meals that the proteins and the carbohydrates are absorbed at different times.

However, why the shibboleths remain and prejudices persist is that our knowledge of the science of nutrition is yet incomplete, the power of tradition is still stronger than the evidence of scientific experimentation, the faddists defeat the scientists by the plausibility of their advertisements, and men are wary of dropping a system which has suited them reasonably well for another which someone only says will lead to better results.

The competitive life of an athlete is comparatively short, and he does not wish to risk losing a season's form for the sake of experimenting with some new thing which may not prove better for him individually. There is a lot, too, in that last explanation, and planning the dietary of the individual athlete often turns upon the coach having a good knowledge of the likes and dislikes of the particular pupil It is, of course, an accepted principle that the athlete must go into trainings if he wishes to succeed in his particular branch of sport, but one often wonders, so far as diet is concerned, how much need there would be for specialized feeding if the man led a life of moderate training, such as would allow him to accelerate the revivals or building up, of his specialized efficiency when it was required.

African native leads a healthy life and needs no long training to bring him to the highest peak of physical efficiency. He lives in the fresh air and the sunshine, many of them wash from top to toe daily, especially those living on the coast or beside a rivery, they go to sleep at dusk and wake at daybreak, and enjoy the food natural experience has taught them to eat as the best suited to their conditions of life. Palm oil, for example, as Vitamin A, Vitamin B is found in country rice, but if you give them trade rice, from which this vitamin has been taken, they soon deteriorate, the bananas, of which they are fond, contain 20 per cent of glucose.

Vitamin C comes from chicken, dog, bananas, coconuts and limes. The sun gives Vitamin D, while Vitamin E is found in the maize which is roasted as new grain. Since Army diet, and the benefits thereof, have been mentioned, let us see upon what that diet is based. It is in reality the outcome of experiments carried out more than half a century ago with A.S.P.T. instructors submitting themselves as subjects under medical supervision.

In order that the dietary finally decided upon may be the better understood, it should be explained what are our chief sources of nourishment. They consist of proteins, i.e., meat, fish, eggs, cheese, beans, peas, etc., carbohydrates or starchy foods such as bread, cereals, bananas, potatoes and so on, fats, salts and water. The proteins supply energy and replace waste of tissue, they are therefore the actual body builders, and that explains why meat has for so long reminded the staple part of the athlete's diet, for the meat proteins serve his purpose better than do the proteins derived from vegetable sources.

On the other hand, too much stress must not be laid upon the proteins in building up an athlete's dietary, or an undue strain will be placed upon the liver and the kidneys. The carbohydrates neither build tissue nor replace its wastage, they do, however, supply energy, and are especially valuable to the athlete, because they are both easily absorbed and readily assimilated, and so supply him with the greatest amount of energy in the shortest space of time, and glucose sugar, which takes effect almost within a space of minutes. The fats, such as butter, milk and cream are also energizers, but, being slower of absorption and assimilation, are better for storing up a reserve of energy than for supplying it upon quick demand as do the carbohydrates in general and sugar in particular.

In small quantities, vitamins and salts are important. Water is a vital essential, but should not be taken with meals, otherwise there is undue dilution of the gastric juices, nor should it be drunk in large quantities in one or a series of quick draughts. This leads to abdominal distension, and pressure on the thoracic organs deranges the systems of circulation and respiration. Nonetheless, the athlete loses great quantities of liquid through his skin and his lungs when he takes violent exercise, and his organism will become depressed and refuse to function properly if the wastage of fluid is not made goods.

Water has a beneficial effect in flushing the system. As to the quantities actually decided upon as the results of Army experiments, they were as follows, 17 ozs., pure starch sugar, 4 ozs., pure protein, 3½s ozs., pure oil or fat. These amounts, however, applied to pure substances, but most foods contain water, and in addition, one or more of each other in varying quantities, for instance, the 4 ozs. of protein might be ½ lb. butcher's meat, but that would have some fats and similarly the starch food might be some sort of grain, having its own percentage of oil and protein.

Concerning the vitamins, it can be said that a person drinking a pint of fresh milk a day would get all the vitamins that are needed. There are three main requirements which the diet scheme drawn up for the athlete must meet, in that it must contain substances which will:

a. build and repair the tissues;

b. store up and supply energy as muscular and nervous power, and also heat;

c. facilitate certain internal bodily functions.

It is not so much the quantity as the composition of the food that matters. A man may eat any quantity of food in his ignorance, and yet be missing just that minimal amount of some substance which is essential to his physical well-being, as any dietician could tell him in a moment. On the other hand, the diet must be of sufficient calorific value. There are also the minerals of the diet which are present in the form of salts. These help to regulate various important bodily iron, magnesium, phosphorus, potassium and sodium the iron and iodine being present in the protein of the food or the protein of the food or the protein of the body.

Importance of Calcium can be interpreted by the fact that it is contained in the blood at a certain concentration always, and if that concentration became less, the heart rate would be lowered to a dangerous degree, the muscles would become irritable, and the nerves would fail to carry the proper impulses. The calcium level in the blood is controlled by the parathyroid glands, which have no other function. Iron is vastly important, because although we possess but a tenth of an ounce of this element, it is the key constituent of haemoglobin which carries the oxygen from the air in the lungs and distributes it by way of the blood stream to all the tissues of the body.

A man could not possibly do without his one-thousandth of an ounce of iodine, which is concentrated in the thyroid gland. Goitre, for example, is due to deficiency of iodine in a person's composition. Before a coach can prepare a scheme of dietary for athletes in training, he must have knowledge of food values and their suitability for the fare of athletes. For this purpose he must make himself acquainted with the composition of the main food stuffs and their functions in relation to the human organism.

From these view point of composition, the body of the athlete and the food he eats are very similar, since both are compounds in which certain elements combine. The main elements are oxygen, hydrogen, nitrogen, calcium, carbon, sodium, potassium and phosphorus. The constituents of body and its foods are proteins, carbohydrates, fats, mineral matter and water, the three first named being the chief.

Water comprises about 60 per cent of the weight of an average individual, and about one third of the supply to the body is contained in the food absorbed. Approximately 5 per cent of the body weight comprises mineral matter, which produces but little energy, but is of inestimable value to health, especially the potash salts and fruit and vegetable acids which lessen the acidity in the blood. It is in fruits and vegetables that the highest percentage of mineral matter is found. The nitrogenous compounds must remain the most important part of any scheme of dietary, such as the myosin of lean meat, casein in the curd of milk, and albumen in the white of egg.

According to some authorities, proteins, of lesser value to the athlete, are present to a high percentage in cereals, for example, gluten in wheat, and to a lesser degree in leguminous vegetables, for instance, legumin in peas and beans. The albuminoid of inferior body building quality to the proteins, are present in meat, they are however, stimulating and should not be left out of any dietary, if only for their gelatinous value. It may usefully be added that although the old time trainers probably did not know it, the reason their almost sole meat diet for athletes did not entirely break down was because protein can be used as body fuel through the circumstances of chemical changes within the body transforming proteins into fats and carbohydrates. Had they taken the opposite view to the one they adopted, the results would have been disastrous, because, it being impossible for the fats and carbohydrates to take the place of the proteins, there would have been no building up of muscle and no making good of tissue wastage.

Comparative to any other foodstuffs, fats are richer in carbon, their two other constituents being oxygen and hydrogen. They supply about 15 per cent of body weight and constitute the main source of heat. Carbon is more highly concentrated in fat than elsewhere, and fat occurs most lavishly in meat, milk and fish. Such cereals as maize and oats, nuts and such vegetable products as olive oil, have also high fat contents. Carbohydrates are found almost entirely in vegetables, comprise no more than 1 per cent of body weight, and yet are a very real source of energy. They are easily absorbed and in company with fat from the fat foods supply, a valuable reserve store of energy.

The value of the carbohydrates is found in their various contents, the first of which is the sugar in vegetables, fruit juices, and in milk as lactose. Then, the starches from cereals and potatoes and cellulose, or fibre of plants, which aids digestion by stimulating the periostitic action of the stomach and intestines. Carbohydrates occur in the following approximate percentages in some usual foodstuffs:

Milk—4 to 5 per cent;

Oranges—8.7 per cent;

Bananas—22.7 per cent;

Wheat Flour—70.3 per cent.

Vitamin are not produced in the body of animal, but come from the food supplied in the first place by plants, and in many cases plants which have enjoyed a wealth of sunlight. Heat and air are believed to be destructive of vitamin values, and the use of soda in cooking is also destructive to them. Vitamin A is very necessary to the athlete, since its absence from his diet will mean loss of weight. It is not found in lard, but is present in meat fats, in conjunction with Vitamin D, while cod liver oil contains two hundred and fifty times as much of Vitamin A as butter.

For the athlete, Vitamin B is essential, because this is the anti-neurotic vitamin and since it is of vital importance that the athlete should not be subject to nervous disorders, it is necessary to give him the things that contain Vitamin B, for example, wholemeal flour, yeast, liver and kidneys, while a manufactured yeast product, marmite, is also excellent. Then there is Vitamin C. This anti-scorbutic vitamin is found mainly in fresh fruit and vegetables, while Vitamin D, rather like Vitamin A, but anti-rachitic, occurs in milk, yolk of egg, green leaves which live in sunlight, and in fish liver oil.

Vitamin E and Vitamin F are found together, and come from the germ of cereals, the green leaves of plants and vegetable oils. These two vitamins have an important effect upon certain functional processes of the body. The most easily absorbed of all the foodstuffs are the carbohydrates, sugar being assimilated to the last particle, and giving satisfactorily quick reactions from the athletic point of view.

Fat is very completely absorbed in comparison with the proteins. An average adult requires for daily consumption about 100 grammes proteins, 75 gm. of fat, and 450 gm. carbohydrates, reckoning the gramme at 15.7 grains. The athlete in training requires a rather higher proportion, especially of the muscle-building and tissue-renovating proteins. Food, when consumed and oxidized in the body, furnishes energy and heat for the execution of mental and physical work, the energy produced by nutrients of food can be assessed on calorific value, the measurement being a calorie, or the amount of heat required to raise one kilogramme through one degree centigrade, or, as mechanical power, the heat required to raise one ton through 1.54 ft. To ascertain the fuel value of a food, it is necessary to know the proportion of nutrients it contains, especially the amount of fat that is present. The percentage of protein and also carbohydrate must then be multiplied by 4.1 and the fat content by 9.3 to ascertain the number of calories contained in 100 parts of the particular foodstuff in question.

Sauces, condiments and other forms of spices and seasonings supply neither body building material nor heat and energy, so far as we are concerned, but in certain circumstances, they serve a useful purpose on the training table, since they sometimes render palatable a food for which the athlete does not particularly care, and thus aid digestion. Athletes vary considerably both in their likes and dislikes, and in the quantity of food which suits them best.

These all the matters for grave consideration of the coach in drawing up a diet table for men in training. A mixed diet is not only best, it is necessary because of the following reasons:

first, because it will kept the athletes more contented,

secondly, because no one kind of food contains all the things that are needed in the proper proportions, and

thirdly, it is by designing a mixed diet, with plenty of fresh fruit and vegetables included, that we ensure a proper supply of the vital vitamins to the individual.

It is very necessary to give men a diet they like. Not only does this plan keep them contented, but the mere anticipation of pleasant food predisposes the digestion to activity, or else why does a dog's mouth water at the sight of meaty bone and the glutton smash his lips with satisfaction when he smells good cooking. The cost of feeding athletes satisfactorily is often brought into question and here a fallacy frequently entraps the ignorant.

It is a fact that certain shopkeepers should be better known as psychologists than as honest men, for they have a practice of charging one price to one customer and one to another. One person wants the best at the lowest cost and gets it, other person does not believe that he is getting the best unless he pays through the nose for it, and the shopkeeper charges him accordingly.

There you have the fallacy that a foodstuff must be good because it is expensive. It is the nutritive value of food in relation to its cost which must be studied. For instance, cheese is about half the price of English beef, cheese contains 33 per cent protein and beef about 20 per cent, but no coach in his right senses would think of feeding his charges entirely on cheese, or again a high class cheeses is far more expensive than American cheese, but contains no more nourishment.

For an athlete, in comparison to vegetable proteins, animal proteins are betters, because they are more readily digested, wherefore it is true economy to pay more for the former than less for the like food value of the latter, where athletes are concerned. The coach should also take into account the actual food values in the production of energy of protein rich foods.

Vegetables and cereals contain a higher percentage of proteins in their raw state. In the process of cooking, they increase in bulk by absorbing water. The main sources of carbon are the fats and the carbohydrates, and here the coach must be careful, for the latter, although cheaper, are more bulky, but the former, although more expensive, are highly essential to the athlete's well-being.

Climative conditions must be taken into consideration. The coach to a team in Northern Europe would naturally rely mainly upon fatty foods in planning a training dietary, whereas a coach in Japan, India, or even, possibly South America would realize the value of rice, which is rice in starch, but deficient in fat. Even in England and America, there should, in this respect, always be a difference made in the summer and winter training diet of the athlete. Fish makes a welcome change in the diet of the athlete, but is of lower food value in comparison with the same weight of butcher's meat, is less stimulating and less satisfying, but it is more readily digested, on account of the fibres of fish being generally shorter finer, and more easily separated than the fibres of meat.

White-flashed fish is not so good a muscle-builder as lean meat, because it provides less tissue-forming protein. Fat-fish has a higher protein value, but still not so high as that of lean meat. As an energizer, however, fat-fish has much the same food value as meat, but the proportion of fat in fish varies from less than two per cent in whiting to twelve per cent in salmon.

Than mutton, beef is less digestible, because the fibres are coarser and the connective tissues more closely packed. Veal is both nourishing and readily digested. Mutton has this disadvantage, that the large percentage of the fat stearin makes that part of it less digestible than beef. Lamb is more digestible than veal, but is less nourishing than mutton.

Pork is a food always regarded with suspicion by athletic coaches, perhaps through tradition, or perhaps because they know that the fats between the fibres makes pork indigestible, and, the pig being an unclean feeder, the meat may harbour parasites if the beast has been carelessly reared or its flesh is not well cooked.

Bacon, however, is an essential item in the breakfast menu of most athletes. Recooked meat or fish should be utterly barred. Both have already lost some of their nutritive value in cooking, and the rehash not only deprives them of natural flavour, but also makes them difficult of digestion by reason of the toughening of the fibres and the hardening of the proteins. Chicken and turkey, as training treats, or to titivate the appetite of an athlete a bit off his feed, are excellent because they are readily digested owing to the fibres being short and the fat being beneath the skin and round the intestines instead of interlining the flesh.

Better modern understanding of the high value of vegetables is bringing about the greater introduction of both raw and cooked vegetable dishes in training menus. They should certainly be served as adjuncts to meat dishes, and also as vegetable interments, while others, when young and tender, should be eaten raw, as radishes, or as salads to accompany cold meat.

Vegetables, however, should always be absolutely fresh, since green vegetables, in particular, ferment quickly. It is only pulse, such as peas, beans and lentils, which aid in muscle-building, through their rich protein content. Other vegetables are of low protein value, but are rich in mineral matter, and principally potash salts. They contain carbohydrates, in the shape of starch, cellulose in their fibrous framework, the starch content being high in potatoes and much less in green vegetables.

Sugar, the great, quick energizer, is most plentiful in beetroot, carrots and parsnips, while the carrot is also particularly rich in mineral salts and vitamins. It is the mineral salts and vitamins in fresh vegetables which comprise their value as a part of the daily diet, since the mineral salts purify the blood by lowering its acidity. The cellulose in old vegetables is not easily digested, but has a periostitic value. Too much old vegetables should not be given to athletes, as it is likely to cause fat flounce.

Green vegetables, whether cooked or raw, are of major importance to the bodily well-being of the athlete, and must form a part of his daily diet. Fruit, like vegetables, is coming into ever greater favour with first class coaches who really take the trouble to make themselves masters in every branch of their profession. The athletes, too, have contributed their quota to the sum total of our present knowledge.

Fruit should undoubtedly figure prominently in the diet of the athlete, who, since he is all the time striving to build muscle and replace tissue-wastage, must be regarded in much the same way as one regards a growing child, to whose health fresh fruit daily is essential.

The mains value of fruits lie in their fruit acids, sugar, vitamins and mineral matter. Fruits contain a high percentage of water, a reasonable proportion of carbohydrates, and a certain amount of starch and cellulose. The proportion of fat and protein which occurs in some fruit is almost negligible. It is best to eat fruit raw, because cooking lessens the high vitamin value. Fruit sugar is readily absorbed and assimilated and is easily digested.

The most nutritive fruits, those containing the highest sugar content, are bananas, apples and grapes, among fresh fruits, and in the dried variety, figs, dates. All fresh fruit must be ripe, or the acids and cellulose will be present in too great quantities. The water content has been mentioned, and while this is very high, it serves a particularly useful purpose where athletes are concerned, since they often suffer from thirst, and the water contained in fruit is a convenient means of assisting the replacement of body fluid wastage.

The water content in the general composition of fresh

fruit is 85 to 90 per cent, then there is protein 0.5 per cent, fat 0.5 per cent, carbohydrates 5½ to 10½ per cent, cellulose 2½ per cent, and mineral matter 0.5 per cent. Constituents vary as much as in the case of the strawberry, 90.3s per cent, one per cent protein, 0.6 per cent mineral matter, carbohydrates 5.3 per cent.

In order to understand anything about what the athlete should or should not, eat in the way of bread, pastry and cake, it is necessary to get down to the fundamental foundation of all three, which is flour Otherwise we cannot determine the food value or the suitability for the diet of the athlete. If a grain of wheat is examined under a low-power microscope, the germ will be seen at the base of the grain. This is the young plant, very rich in gluten, the flesh-forming protein, and fat. The centra part of the grain is the endosperm, which contains a high percentage of starch. Then there is the outer casing of bran which comprises cellulose and a preponderance of mineral water.

In different wheats, the proportions of gluten and starch vary and different grades of flour are obtained by breaking the whole grain up in the process of milling, and then by mechanical sifting, blending in various proportions to produce different grades of flour. The two chief classes are the ordinary house holds and the patents, or pastry whites.

The pastry flours are poor in gluten, but rich in starch, whereas the household flour contains more gluten and so is more nourishing. Wholemeal flour and bread have a considerably higher food value, and may be considered, therefore, the best for athletic dietary. It is a moot point whether butter or dripping should be used in any pastry that may be made for athletes.

On the whole, perhaps, good, wells-clarified dripping is to be preferred to butter, as being the more readily digestible in this particular connection. The average composition of cow's milk is 3.5 per cent protein, 4 per cent fat, 4.75 per cent lactose, mineral matter, 0.75 per cent and water 87.25 per cent. Nonetheless, the fact that milk is the natural diet of all young mammals, when they are growing most rapidly proves the food value of milk. Its suitability is found in its lime salts and certain vitamins.

A rich supply of lactose takes the place of starch. Milk has casein for its protein, and contains fat in the form of a fine emulsion floating on the surface as cream. The fat constitutes the degree of the milk's fat value, and is the only one of its constituents which varies to any marked degree. When milk is drunk, it virtually ceases to be a liquid, because the rennin, or ferment, of the gastric juices causes the casein of the milk to clot. That is why the athletes should not be allowed to gulp down a glass of milk quickly. If too large a clot is formed, digestion becomes difficult.

The older time trainers missed their mark when they held that milk curdled on the stomach. Clotting and curdling are two entirely different things, because it is the gastric juices acting upon the casein which causes the clot, whereas the curdling of milk is due to the presence in the air of some souring bacteria, which acts upon the milk sugar and produces lactic acid, the casein held in solution by the lime salts, being precipitated. Skim milk, despite its loss of fat, has a high nutritive value, because the casein, lactose and mineral matter still remain. Provided that milk puddings, on account of the farinaceous ingredients, are well cooked, they are both nourishing and digestible, but must contain sugar, some starchy food and preferably eggs as well.

For the coach, eggs are of greatest service. They are rich in protein and provide a meat substitute in concentrated form, which is invaluable for such purposes as giving a man a light meal a couple of hours prior to competition. At other times, however, eggs, on account of their deficiency in starch, should be combined with a farinaceous food, to supply bulk. Eggs have the same constituents as meat, in a more concentrated form, and although not quite so rich in protein are richer in fat. This fat is found in the yolk in a high state of emulsification, making it easily digestible, and the yolk has further good characteristics in its content of calcium salts, iron, phosphorus and Vitamin D.

The white of an egg comprises principally water and egg albumen in solution. Athletes should be given only new laid eggs, because these are the most nourishing and the most readily digested. Giving the athlete a couple of raw eggs whipped up, either alone or with milk. Raw eggs are the most easily digested of all, otherwise the degree of digestibility depends upon the cooking.

Hard-boiled eggs should not be given to athletes. And in planning a dietary, the coach should remember that eggs, on account of their lime-salts content, have the opposite effect to say, brown bread and fruit, which have a mildly laxative effect. An excellent drink for athletes in training is the juice of a couple of fresh lemons squeezed into a tumbler of water and then saturated with a tablespoonful, or more, of glucose sugar. It is a great thirst-quencher, and has also a quick energizing effect.

When athletes are concerned, such beverages as tea, coffee, and cocoa present a somewhat difficult problem. Tea contains theine, tannin and volatile oil, coffee comprises caffeine, tannin, and again, volatile oil, while cocoa is made up of theo-bromide, an astringent not unlike tannin, fat and starch. Tea and coffee are both mild stimulants, by reason of the alkaloids represented by the theine and the caffeine. These constituents tend to lessen the acid-absorbing power of foods, cocoa, on the other hand, increases this power.

Tannin is an astringent less powerful in coffee than

in tea, but if tea is allowed to stand too long the tannin becomes tannic acid, which interferes with digestion and irritates the mucous lining of the stomach, it tends also to harden the coagulated albumen of meat. For that reason, coaches should never allow athletes to indulge in high tea. Tea and coffee in moderation serve a useful purpose. Taken in excess, they are harmful to the athlete.

Thus, it is concluded that from more than half a century of personal experience and experiments, combined with the views of dieticians and first class athletic coaches who have made a close study of the subject, is that athletes in training should primarily be given the food they like, provided their choice of menu makes it possible to furnish the proper nourishment to fulfil the three main requirements of dietary, and that the diet therefore be corrected in composition and sufficient in quantity.

Athlete should be fed with special care upon the day preceding the contest, he should have his normal breakfast on the actual morning, and two hours before competing, if this suits him, two lightly boiled eggs and a cup of weak tea, or the lemon and glucose drink. In any case, give him a good quantity of glucose, with or without orange-juice, according to his taste, just before going out to limber up, say twenty minutes to half an hour before his competition.

Point to be kept in mind is that a man cannot do himself full justice physically if his physical effort is called for soon after he has eaten a substantial meat. Muscular exertion makes big demands upon the heart and the circulatory system, since during exercise the muscles need much more blood flowing through their arteries than when at rest. The extra blood supply can only be obtained by restricting the flow through other tissues and organs, especially in the stomach, intestines, liver and spleen. Now the abdominal region is rich in blood vessels and may at any time contain fully one third of the total blood content of the body. This big blood reservoir is known as the splanchnic pool and the vaso-constrictor nerves, control the splanchnic area.

When the muscles need more blood for violent effort, they draw it from this area and the splanchnic vessels become strongly constricted. If at that time the digestive process is strongly active, owing to a heavy meal having been eaten just recently, it follows that the need of the muscles for blood to help them perform their task, and the need of the digestive organs for blood to help them perform their duties, become strongly at variance, and consequently maximum effort is well high impossible, and at the same time digestion is deranged. This brings us to a subject often debated, not without acrimony, in athletic circles, for officials do love a good banquet after a big event.

One admits, quite frankly, that the athletes, too, like to dine together and thoroughly enjoy the celebration at the time. An end of the season dinner would no doubt be an excellent thing but the sort of banquets we are discussing are those that follow an international match or a championship meeting and so occur normally right in the middle of the season of competition. Apart from the considerations that athletes attending these banquets drink wines to which they are not accustomed and are kept out of bed long after the hour the training regimen requires for their retirement, there is the vital question of in how far it is advisable for an athlete to eat a big meal upon the evening of the day during which he has imposed the heavy strain of competition upon his organism.

It is a normal thing for the athlete to feel especially hungry after taking part in a contest. Demands have been made upon his mental and physical abilities. Nature warns him that there is wastage to be made good, and also he has enjoyed only an abnormally light lunch.

Logically, therefore, it would seem wise for him to partake of a large meal. This is not so. We have only enough blood to look after one of two systems at a time, regarding in this connection the muscular system and the digestive apparatus as separate entities. When muscles are working at full pressure, there is but little blood in the intestinal tract, and vice versa, the blood is in the intestinal tract and out of the muscles when the stomach is full of food and the athlete is properly rested.

In human body, it is the vasomotor centre in the brain which controls the blood distribution, but the blood is not redistributed from the muscles to the digestive apparatus with the speed of magic, and a man quitting the stadium after a strenuous competition has still most of the blood in the muscular system and very little in the intestinal tract. If he then sits down to a heavy meal, he is likely to feel anything but well upon the following morning.

After a big competition, a light evening meal is undoubtedly beneficial to the athlete, and if he still feels tired the next morning, his diet should be light on that day as well. The moment, however, he begins to feel fit and refreshed, he should be allowed to eat his ordinary training meals, with, perhaps some table luxury thrown in as a reward.

9

Mathematical Evaluation in Athletics

The fact that many runners have succeeded in eclipsing that hitherto mythical mile time of 4 mins. 8s secs., or the relative time for 1500 metres, reopens the age-old question as to what is the absolute limit of human record breaking capacity. For many long years, there have been those among us, good judges too, who have maintained the possibility of a man averaging the almost incredible time of 62 secs per quarter mile for a distance of one mile. That has been done, and now we are asking each other if an average of even 60 secs. per 440-yards lap is beyond the compass of a human being.

A mile will be run in the level 4 mins. within the experience of the present generation. Athletic science is still in a stage of adolescence, and it is probable that the acquisition of greater scientific knowledge rather than the athlete himself, will allow distance runners to return faster and yet faster times. Take the four fastest 440-yards laps in one mile record-breaking history and you will get a four mins. two secs. mile, made up as follows:

Taber's first quarter in 58 secs., when he returned 4 12.6, Lovelock's second quarter in 62.2, when he showed 4 07.6, Cunningham's third quarter in 61.8, when he did 4 06.8, and Jonse's fourth quarter in 58.2, when he did 4 14.4.

Above figures, however, represents the efforts of four

individuals, but the machine runner will eventuate. Meanwhile, just as Nurmi, with his constant speed theory added something new to distance running, so Cunningham also has contributed rather more than a world's record to the history of the mile, for he has proved the possibility of running the first half-mile as fast as the second, with a fast third lap and an even faster fourth quarter. He has, in fact, laid the foundation of the theory of constant acceleration and has proved the feasibility of conquering the previously apparently inevitable let up the third lap. This he has done by returning for the third lap 63 secs., when he made his record of 4 09.8 and 61.8 secs., when he returned 4 06.8.

The nearest approach for a third lap time was by Jules Ladoumegue, when he got wonderfully close to constant speed running by returning for his four laps 60.8, 63.4, 63.8 and 61.2 secs. The claim that Cunningham has, by running, the second half of a mile faster than the first half, added something entirely new to the theory of one mile, running is not, however, admissible. When the first real international match took place between the New York A.C. and London A.C. at Manshattan Field, Tommys Conneff, U.S.A., running against his countryman, Geo, Orton, and the Englishman W.E. Lutyens, who won the mile for Cambridge against Oxfords for four years in succession, now only made a world's record of 4 mins. 18 secs., but produced both the most constant speed lap running and the fastest second half mile on record, the latter being in proportion to the total time taken. His lap times were 65, 65, 64, 64 secs. and he covered the first half mile in two mins. ten secs., and the second half mile in two mins. eight secs.

The early pioneers of scientific athletic instruction concerned themselves with effect and dimly apprehended cause, but they missed the third great factor, which is the proof by quantitative measurement of the connection between any two or more actions. Paavo Nurmi of Finland held practically every distance record, from one mile in four mins. 10 2/5 secs., to 11 miles 1648 yards in one hours. He was well named the Phantom Finn for behind the whole sheaf of his amazing records lay hundreds of miles run in silence and solicitude upon frozen, pine fringed Finnish roads, with a battered old stop watch for his only friend and mentor.

Credit to revolutionized the distance running goes to Nurmi, when he set himself the task of maintaining an even pace throughout his races. Why or how, he hit upon this principle one does not know. He has coached many Finns to go after his laurels and hoped that Viljo Heino, whom he had trained to break some of his records, would win the 10,000 metres and perhaps the Marathon. For generation, it had been the custom for millers to run a fast first lap, hold as much pace as possible in the second, and ease off in the third to store up energy for a shattering final 440-yards burst.

Nurmi, it has been said, did not possess a finishing spirit. The truth of the matter is that he did not need one, for he set and maintained such a pace in all his races that no opponent of his was ever left with the ability to sprint even the last fifty yards. The Nurmi's running system was the right one can be proved scientifically and Prof. Kennelly of Boston, U.S.A., has suggested that more than one long distance running record might easily be broken by the aid of a mechanical pace maker, on the principle of the electric hare used in greyhound racing, travelling at a constant speed and so adjusted that the runner, by keeping up with it at his known best speed, would just break the existing record. In this manner, runners would be trained to produce constantly increasing even pace until the personal best speech of each man trained in this way would be discovered.

The man who can run a mile in 5 mins. should cover 352 yards in one minute, while a mile in 4 mins. 8 secs., which approximates to the three best world's records, would mean a constant speed of just over 425 yards per minute. Speed, however, must be adjusted to the distance to be run, just as the motorist has to change his gears to suit the gradients over which he is driving his car.

Two points present themselves to the student of the physiology of running. Apart from psychology as a factor of success, the three essentials for breaking distance records are, obviously, style, speed and stamina, combined with pace judgment. The first point, therefore, involves the consideration of whether one standard, uniform style can be stabilized for the use of short, medium and long-striding distance runners, while the second point deals with the question of the degree of marked and material differences in the mode of progression of good and bad runners.

These matters have been the subject of exhaustive experimentation at the Physiology Institute of the University of Breslau. By the making of slow motion films, it was possible to dissect and analyse the running action of three of the world's greatest middle distance runners, Erling Wide, Sweden, and the Finns, Ville Ritola and Paavo Nurmi. The method of making the cinematograph films, of both good and bad runners, produced a record of the graphic curves described by certain parts of the body in the function of progression by running. The parts of the body selected for recording graphically in their path were the head, the pelvis, the knees, the feet and the toes.

However, very little variation in physiological movement was discoverable in the action of athletes with differing stride lengths. This was especially pronounced in the initial strides of progression from a stationary start. Such variation as there was bore direct relationship to speed and stride length rather than to style. The divergence between the action of educated and athletically uneducated runners was, however, very pronounced.

Incidental to the main motive of the experiment were certain discoveries concerning the much debated question as to whether or no first class runners do, in fact, first make contact with the track by placing down the heel at the termination of each stride.

In this case, the theory is really based upon race-walking, the contention being that the placing down of the heel at the end of a stride produces greater stride length and firmer poise. The film's made at Breslau showed, clearly that Nurmi and Ritola both placed the heel down in the way described. Wide, on the other hand, quite obviously first made contact with the track with the sole of his foot. Between Wide, Nurmi and Ritola at their best, there was but little to choose, and the point must remain debatable as to whether Wide would have been supreme had he used the heel contact style favoured by the two which are as individual as their own handwriting and to have attempted to convert a Wide to the style of a Nurmi would have been a highly hazardous experiment.

First class runners do not alter the carriage of the body above the hips in running. There exists a close relationship between the carriage of the head and thc pelvis, while the pelvic curve portrays a flexibility of hip action, which is the very poetry of running. The Breslau experiments proved equally clearly that the untrained athlete invariably runs badly. Running of this type is bound to prove exhausting to the runner.

If one compare the fine regularity of the geometrical curves produced with the faulty irregularity of the curves produced by a bad runner and the other by a good runner, there seems a lot of difference. The difference may be actually assessed by quantitative measurement of the two sets of curves, when the value of regularity in forward

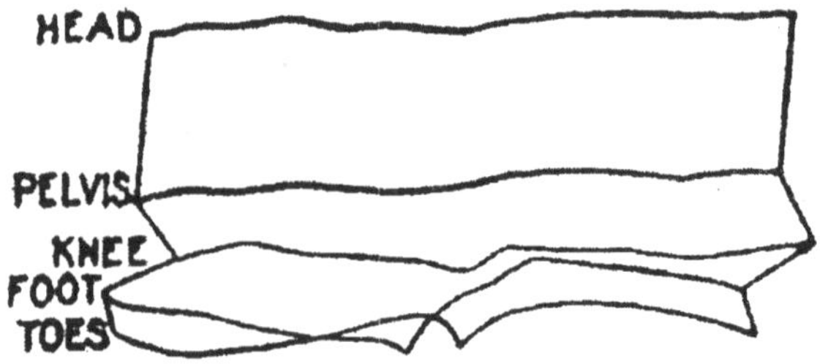

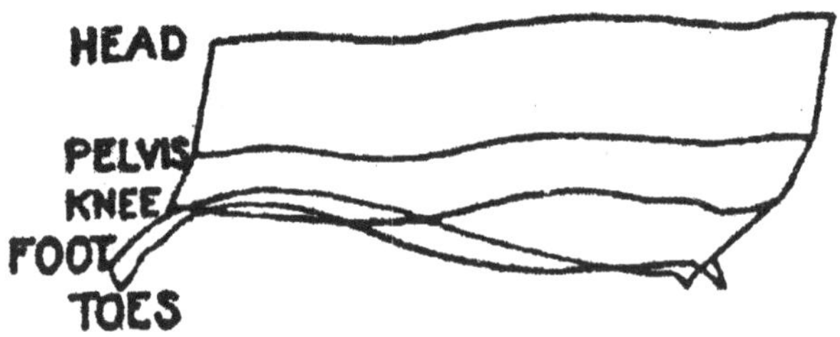

movement as a factor in record breaking will be readily appreciated.

The study of both this curves show that the bad runner wastes much of the velocity of his body carriage through lack of rhythm and balance, and by his jerky action expends a disproportionately great amount of energy in keeping himself on the run, whereas the good runner, properly poised and constantly striving to catch up the weight of his forward momentum, sails smoothly along with little or no break in the rhythm of his action. The latter is a mode of progression designed, and well-calculated, to delay the intervention of physical exhaustion as long as possible. To summarize, it is a highly debatable point as to whether man, as man, has improved sufficiently in physique and nerve force during the last half-century to account for the fact that many men have improved by well over ten secs. upon the world's record made by T.P. Conneff, or to take Haegg's record of 4 mins., 1.04 secs., as representative of the mean of record breaking, there is clear evidence that the record smashing miller, travelling a bit faster than 7 yards per second, could give the world's record holder of forty years ago just about 70 yards start in a mile and yet beat him by more than two-fifths of a second.

Altogether, we cannot account for the improvement of some ten seconds that has taken place by quoting Nurmi's discovery of the fundamental principle of running to level time schedule, since Conneff showed 65, 65, 64, 64 secs. for his 440-yards laps when he made his record of four mins., 18 secs., and also shows the best schedule, in that respect.

Thus, we are bound to assume that a better style of running, as revealed by the experiments carried out at Physiological Institute of the University of Breslau, has been evolved in the affluxion of time. Taken in conjunction with other circumstances, germane to the general issue, such as time schedule running for the discovery of optimum speeds for individual athletes, better running methods must be regarded as the main factor accountable for the ten seconds' superiority of the present generation of middle-distance runners over their predecessors.

One should kept in his mind that there is a lot of difference between the optimum and best speed. To have an optimum in relation to energy expenditure some form of resistance outside the body must be overcome, as occurs in throwing and shot putting, and in part, in pole-vaulting. In track racing, there can be no optimum, because there is only wind resistance, and the movement of the limbs of the athlete. Where movement against resistance is concerned, certain experiments can be carried out and a graph drawn to show what is the optimum which will represent the best speed of movement in the particular connection.

At speeds higher than the optimum, we get more speed and less work, and on the other side, we have less speed, less work; therefore, it will be readily understood that, in the case of certain events, the finding of the optimum is most important. In the foregoing connection, too, we have to consider the question of the load. If the load is so great that rapid muscular movement is impossible, or even if it is too much retarded, the result is unsatisfactory. That is why shot putting became, and remained, unpopular at school levels, so long as the use of the 16 lbs. instead of 12 lbs. shot, as now used, was in vogue.

An immature schoolboy could not move the load, represented by a 16 lbs. shot, quick enough and there was waste of energy through the muscles being maintained in a state of activity too long. On the other hand, to give a strong lad of 17 or 18 years of age, the shot used in women's competition to put with would be almost as wasteful, because he would be able to make his muscle movements so rapidly that he would really do but little work at each movement.

There are no competitions in field events in which the handicapping is done by adjusting the weight of the missile, instead of allotting start by feet and inches, otherwise some interesting results would materialize through men finding the optimum weight of a missile suited to their own physique. Things being as they are, all a man can do is, first, to build up his strength in proportion to the weight of the missile he would be asked to propel, and secondly, to find the best speed in the turn, glide or approach run which will allow him to apply his optimum delivery speed in overcoming the resistance, outside his body, of that missile.

All of these may sound rather complicated, but it is surprising how quickly, through the trial and error of experiment, one does, in training, discover these optima and best speeds. In using the term best speed, it is necessary to understand clearly what we are aiming at in each particular connection. That is to say, is the best to be in the saving of time, or the saving of energy.

The sprinter, obviously, wants to save time, whereas the object of the distance runner should be the conservation of his energy. The difference between sprinting and distance running is really a difference in gear ratio, and that gear ratio, for each individual runner, represents the speed at which it suits him best to move his legs for the attainment of his particular object.

Thus it can be concluded that in actual fact, a best speed at which a runner must progress if he wishes to cover a given distance in a given time with the least waste of energy. The amount of energy that is expended in a speed burst during a race is not compensated for by running more slowly at other stages of the contest, and to run at varying speeds is far more exhausting than to run at a constant speed.

If a man is paced in such a way that the speed is bound to remain constant, he cannot waste energy by running too fast at some stages of the distance and too slow at others. In theory, it is not a difficult matter to ascertain how to run a certain distance in the required time, provided that distance is to be run at a constant speed. If you know the distance and the time to be taken, it is simple enough to find the speed in feet per second at which one must run, and in practice, i.e., without the aids of a mechanical pace maker, a man must first train himself to stride with absolute regularity and at the same time must so educate himself in pace judgement that he can tell within the margin of a fraction of a second the speed at which he is covering each 440-yards lap.

Pace judgement and the regulation of pace come rather under the heading of the physiological factor in training than under the mathematics of athletics, but, important scientific principles are involved, since it was through the researches he made in oxygen consumption during violent exercise that Prof. Hill was able to confirm Nurmi's theory that the preservation of even speed throughout a race is the method least productive of fatigue.

Constant speed is the most economical. The man who cannot tell the speed at which he is travelling is likely to run himself clean out very quickly, when the competition is such that another runner has a pace-maker to break up the opposition. On the other hand, the man who knows his own best speed and can judge the pace at which the race is being run can generally afford to let the field go until he knows that the time has come for him to strike.

Pace judgement may be acquired in a number of ways. The Sport Clock will be invaluable, meantime, in training, the stop watch carried in the hand, at any rate for distances of a mile and over, is still the best mentor. Many a man has lost the race he should have won through his inability to judge the pace at which he was travelling. But it is equally true to say that although constant speed running is the most economical, and perhaps the surest way of breaking records, it does postulate a tremendous strain on the nerves, despite the possession of an iron will, to stick to the schedule and await the orders of your stop watch, when the whole field may be going right away from you. And yet it is only the old story of the hare and the tortoise put into modern dress.

All the same, there are times when temperament and tactics enter into a race to such an extent that any thought of uniformity of pace a distance of less than a mile would seem like athletic suicide. The discovery that bamboo poles are light to carry, allow a man to run at greater speed, and yet are strong enough to bear his weight when vaulting to height, together with the introduction of slide way, which affords a fulcrum to the pole point, are factors which account largely for the circumstance that the record has improved nearly 4 ½s ft.; but science has contributed to the dynamics of the event by teaching the athlete how a delayed swing, a strong pull and a quick push up, following a very fast approach run, may enable him to propel his body over a lath set as much as 18 ins. above the height at which his hands grip the pole wherewith he makes his vault.

In order to value the effect of approach speed upon the height the athlete is able to clear, or should be capable of clearing, it is first necessary to find the height to which a body will rise against gravity, when its horizontal velocity is converted into vertical velocity. We will assume, therefore, that the athlete approaches his take off at a race of 25 ft. per second, i.e., 100 yards in 12 sec. The symbols to be employed in our calculation are v=velocity, h=height obtained, g=acceleration due to gravity, and t=the time taken for a body with velocity v to reach a given height. Then

$$v = gts, \text{ or}$$

$$t = \frac{25}{32} \text{ secs.}$$

Now,

$$h = \tfrac{1}{2} gt^2$$

$$\text{so, } h = \tfrac{1}{2} \times 32 \times \frac{25^2}{32^2} = \frac{25^2}{64} \text{ ft.}$$

$$= 9.76 \text{ ft. or } 9 \text{ ft. } 9 \text{ ins.}$$

But this height obtained applies to the centre of gravity of the body in question. Assuming the centre of gravity of a man when running is at the mid-point of a line drawn between the upper ends of his femur, it would be approximately 3 ft. from the ground and the line of his take off, and should be raised by merit of his speed of 25 ft. per second to a height of 9 ft. 9 ins. + 3 ft. = 12 ft. 9 ins.

However, if the athlete is capable of running 100 yards in 11 secs. i.e., his approach run is made at a speed of 27.3 ft. per sec., then the height is found to be 11.7ft., so that he should be able to raise his centre of gravity to and propel his body over a cross-bar raised 14 ft. 7 ins. above the ground. The foregoing figures relate purely and simply to the merit of the speed of the run-up, and such factors as friction of the pole point in the slide-way and air-resistance have not been allowed for, although the latter is a very large factor indeed, which must have an adverse effect upon the height obtained.

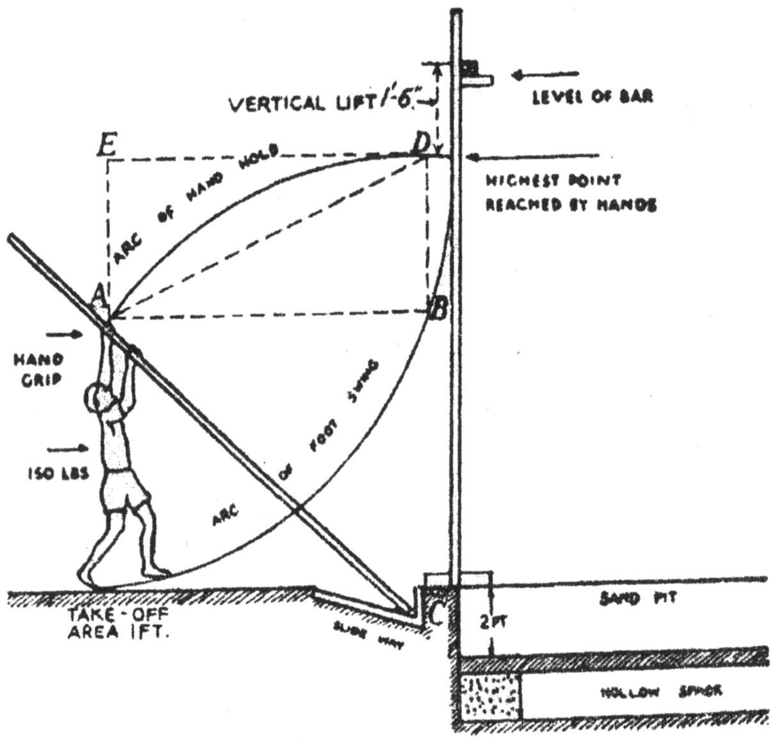

While, on the other hand, no favourable allowance has been made for the vertical life whereby the vaulter raises his body a considerably way above the height of his hand hold upon the pole, when it has reached a vertical position. Nonetheless, in the Pole Vault, the conversion of a strong and rapid pull into the action of a quick and forceful push up should be worth at least 18 ins., especially if maximum foot elevation has been obtained.

Even so, the whole case is open to considerable argument, but one point the figures do bring out is the enormous importance of speed in the run up, since the height attained in the swing-up is proportional to the square of the velocity when running, so that an increase of speed equivalent to even one-fifth of a second less in 100 yards provides an addition of over 4 ins. to the height reached in the upward swing.

We assume for our calculation that the athlete shown in the above figure weighs 150 lbs. He has finished his run, planted his pole, the point of which is just about to strike the end of the slide way at point C, and, as the pole point strikes, his right hand will complete its shift on the pole, and the two hands, touching, will consolidate their grip. Then he is in the process of converting his forward momentum into upward momentum by means of sprint.

Here two forces operate simultaneously, one due to his weight and the momentum of his run, the other due to the force of his spring in taking off. The resultant of these forces gives the magnitude and direction of the force existent as the instant of take off. Of the two forces at work simultaneously, the one along the line AB represents an energy of 937 foot-lb., due to his weight and the velocity of his approach run, while the other along the line AE is equal to 600 foot-lb., due to the energy of his spring. If the two lines referred to are joined to make the parallelogram, ABDE, we get a resultant along the line AD representing a kinetic energy of 1,120 foot lb., and its direction, which is the force existent at the instant of take off, along the arc AD. Again, the diagram serves to emphasize the importance to the vaulter of building up maximum approach speed commensurate with strong spring and a well balanced take off, for it will be readily followed that the longer the lines AB and AE, the greater will be the resultant AD, and consequently the greater will be its value on scale, and the more easily will the vault be made.

If it is postulated that a man weighing about 11 stone raises his body 2 ft. by the pull and another 1 ft. by the push, then the work he does has been calculated approximately as follows:

On pulling—raising body say 2s ft. = 300 foot-lb.

On pushing—raising body say 1 ft = 150 foot-lb.

Total comes out to be 3 ft. = 450 foot-lb., or a force equal to about three times the weight of his own body.

This type of calculating is of the greatest particular value. A coach, using a stop watch, can time the approach run of the athlete, he is teaching from the start of the run to the instant of take off, and from that time obtained, he may deduce how high the pupil should be able to vault. He knows, also, from the kind of calculation given above, what should be the contribution of pull and what the contribution of the push, but how is he to assess the contribution of these two integral parts of the vault. He should stand on a pair of steps to the side of the jump, so that his eyes are on a level with the bar. If the feet shoot up, then the coach may be sure that the vaulter has put in the maximum amount of pull in exactly the right part of the vault.

Whereas, if the seat rises over easily at a low height, the coach may know that full advantage is being taken of the athlete's ability to push his body up. Or, if vaulting is at maximum heights, then the form is not right, for he has managed a full arm extension in the push up, despite the fact that his action is unbalanced. If, on the other hand, the coach, perhaps up on his pair of steps, see the sort of flat lay out, then he will know the athlete has swung round the pole, and consequently has got off balance.

So far as the high jump is concerned, some geometrical considerations in relation to the take off and landing. It has been stated as a fundamental principle, moreover, that half the secret of successful high jumping is to be found in the ability of the athlete to get all the heavy parts of his body down to the level of his centre of gravity in effecting bar clearance. Before the athlete arrives at that stage, however, he must learn how to raise his centre of gravity to bar level and just how high he needs to raise it for each particular height he is attempting. This information can be obtained by what may be termed stop watch calculation, but for timing a high jumper, it will be best to use a watch split to hundredths of a second.

Prof. Hill, when making tests of this kind, discovered that a man clearing 5 ft. is off the ground for 4/5th sec., between take off and landing, and deduces that virtually half of the time is spent going up and the other half coming down, with an infinitesimal fraction of a second spent in wriggling over the bar. Perhaps, however, the subject of the experiment was not particularly expert as a high jumper, for the real masters of the arm seems to get a distinct pause period in the execution of their turn cumuli out over the bar. The time occupied in the jump, however, supplies the basis for the calculation of how high the centre of gravity actually rises.

To revert to the analogy of our pole vaulter, by assuming that the man's centre of gravity is at the middle point of a line passing through the upper ends of his femurs, we can say that in the case of the high jumper also it would be approximately 3s ft. above the ground at the instant of take off, but if the jump occupies 4 to 5 seconds, then the centre of gravity is raised 2½ ft., i.e., 6 ins. higher than the height of the cross-bar. But this is unnecessary, if a man jumps in correct style, using either the Western Roll or the Easterns Cut-off, since both these styles bring the legs up and trunk down, to the centre of gravity.

Further useful and interesting mathematical calculations can be made in relation to other events. The long jumper, for example, can calculate what should be his maximum elevation in jumping if he is to reach certain given distances and can assess also the force and the energy he will be employing.

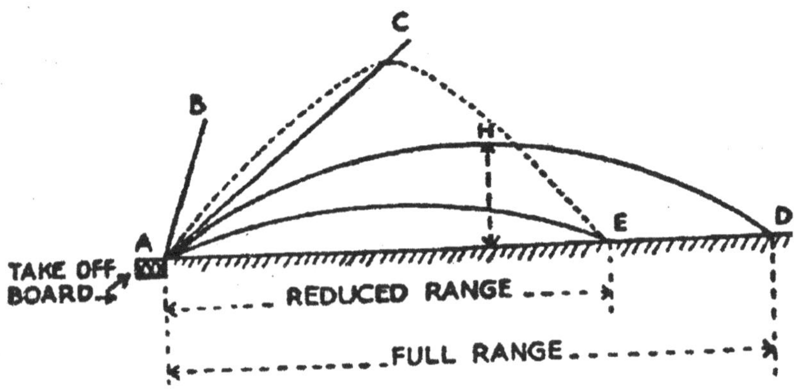

In the above figure, the point A represents the ordinary take off board sunk flush with the ground. AB denotes the correct sprinting angle of 75 degrees which the jumper holds during his approach run and at which his body should be pitched when he is taking off. Let it be noted that the line of the body's forward inclination AB and the ground line AD form the angle BAD, which is an angle of 75 degrees. The line AC indicates the true direction of take off, and with the ground line AD, forms the angle CAD of 45 degrees. This, in sits turn, produces the true parabola of flight AHD, which is the path of the jumper's centre of gravity. If the jump is made at an angle greater or less than 45 degrees, the range will be reduced as shown at E. H is the maximum vertical height when the jump is made at the true departure angle of 45 degrees. This height can be calculated for any jump. A proper body inclination at the take-off brings the jumper's centre of gravity beyond the board and ensures that his high point will be reached at two thirds of the parabola of flight, and not half-way, which would cut down the clearance distance.

While dealing with the pole vault, the relationship of speed in the approach run to success in jumping, but, before going on to that again, it should be made quite clear what one means by the statement that the true angle of jumping is one of 45 degrees.

As first sight, this may well suggest that one is going to jump too high. In point of fact, 45 degrees is only the angle at the instant when the body immediately enters upon the path of its parabolic flight curve, and is steadily acted upon by the force of gravity, which rapidly destroys the energy existing at the start and becomes nil at the highest point of the trajectory.

If the earth did not attract a body to itself, the jumper would go on in a straight line for ever, but it is this attraction which causes the body's flight to follow a curved line. During the first half or two-thirds of the curve, the attraction of the earth is a retardation, but during the latter portion it acts as an accelerating force. The distance a man can clear depends also upon the velocity of projection, governed by the amount of impulse generated. To make this matter clear, let us assume that the jumper weighs 140 lbs., that he jumps 22 ft., and approaches the take off three times at varying speeds of 40 yards in 5 secs., 40 yards in 6 sec., and 40 yards in 7 secs. These speeds represent velocity of 24, 20 and 17.14

feet per second respectively, and, an initial velocity of 26.5 ft. per sec.

Therefore, it will be seen that this gives an increase of 2.5 ft. per sec., on the first speed, 6.5 ft. per sec. on the second speed and 9.34 ft. per sec., on the third speed.

Impulse generated can be found by the following formula:

P = m (u-v)

where, m is the mass, viz. 140 lbs., u and v are the first and second velocities respectively.

While working this out, it will be found that the impulse of the force required is:

for 24 ft. per sec., 350 units of impulse;

for 20 ft. per sec., 910 units of impulse;

for 20 ft., per sec., 1320s units of impulse.

This shows clearly that the greater the speed acquired in the approach run, the less units of impulse will be needed for the jump. In other words, the greater the speed a man can command in the run-up, the more units of the impulse he will have at his disposal to put into the jump.

Let us now look at the question from the point of view of the jump itself, and to eliminate all complications of speed velocity and increased acceleration, we will take the case of a man weighing, let us say, 168 lbs., who intends to jump a distance of 10 ft. from a stationary position. He will, swing his arms, lean forward, and crouch to generate the impulse for his spring, but at the actual instant of take-off, his body will be fully extended before his toes leave the board. The velocity with which he leaves the board will be one of 17.8 ft. per second, and his initial horizontal and vertical velocities will be 12.6 ft. per second, the compressed force exerted being

93.45 lb., and the kinetic energy 831.6 foot-lb.

If the jumper jumps at the correct angle of 45 degrees, according to all laws of dynamics, the highest point in his parabola of flight will be reached at 2 ft. 6 ins. midway between take off and landing. As in the above figure, during the first part of the jump from A to H the jumper will be fighting to combat the resistance due to the attraction of gravity, but after he has possessed H gravity will assist him to increase the length of his jump, provided his own centre of gravity continues to follow the true path of the parabola. This brings us to another point which is that it is the problem of preventing the heavy upper parts of the body from coming forward as momentum is lost, and by disposing the weight forward, forcing the heels to the sand pit earlier than they need reach it.

It should be kept in mind that at the point H in the curve AD in the figure, the force of the initial impulse is facing defeat, and from the point H to the point of landing at E or D, the force of gravity is overcoming the athlete's powers of resistance.

In this connection, it should be remembered that the hurdler cultivates a forward body dip, forcing his trunk down over the thigh of his leading leg, for the sole purpose of driving his foot down to ground on the far side of the hurdle as speedily as possible. Also, the bringing down of the heavy parts of the body to the centre of gravity does not help the long jumper, because he uses no sideways twist and no turn for the sake of raising his hips over a bar, as does the high jumper. What he does want to do is to prevent the forward weight of his body from driving his legs down, and so he uses some combination and arm and leg actions, now to create an additional explosive force to add a purely mythical fresh velocity to his body in flight, but rather to so dispose his balance that his centre of gravity may continue to follow the true path of its parabolic curve.

Throwing perhaps provides a wider field for scientific research than any other department of track and field athletics, because, in throwing, sheer skill will always beat mere brute forces, even when a really large disparity in strength and size exists between any two competitors. Even with the high gearing ratio with which the throwers work, no human muscles are capable, in a simple movement of producing a velocity, comparable with that with which a cricket ball is projected.

A cricket ball has been thrown more than 1¾ times as far as a javelin and nearly 2 ¾ times, as far as a discus but a cricket ball comes readily to the hand, weighs approximately 5 ½ ozs., and must always travel with an even centre of gravity, since it has all points of its circumference equidistant from its centre. On the other hand, a javelin weighs 1 lbs., 12 ¼ ozs., and is 8 ft. 6 ins. in length, while a full sized discus weighs 4 2/5 lbs., and has a circular dimension of 8 5/8 ins., with a thickness through the exact centre of not less than 1 ¾ ins. These missiles, therefore, are subject to forces reacting through their shape to make them unstable in flight.

However, when a cricket ball, having all the advantages, just enumerated, is thrown to a distance of 150 yards, the energy of its projection is about 75 ft.-lbs. that is to say, there is a velocity of projection of 120 ft. per second, or 80 miles per hour. If you compare the cricket ball throwing record of about 450 ft., with the javelin record of 251 ft. 6 ins. and the discus record of approximately 172s ft., you will see the tremendous forces the athletes concerned must have employed, in comparison with the cricket ball thrower.

Now let us consider the contributory factors leading up to the production of maximum performance in throwing. We will ignore such questions as training, co-ordination of muscular effort and the crucial angles of delivery. Speed in the actions leading up to the projection of a missile is, however, a factor of major importance.

In the case of the Shot Put, the initial impulse is generated by the swing of the left leg, the falling forward of the body, and the powerful drive from the right leg, when the body is just crossing its forward point of balance. The more powerful the forward drive can be made, commensurate with proper balance in the putting stance, the greater will be the speed acquired, and therefore less units of impulse will be needed for a put of a given distance, or, conversely, the greater the speed of the glide, the more units of impulse a man will have available for his use in the delivery of the projectile. Where hammer and discus throwers are concerned, it is the turning movement within the throwing circle which generates the initial velocity of body movement, which will subsequently be converted into the propulsive force of the throwing action.

However, neither in running, gliding nor turning can a man generate the force for a velocity of projection of 120 ft. per second, there must be other contributory factors. Perhaps the analogy of a huntsman cracking his whip will best illustrate the point, for when he does so no very great momentum is generated by the swinging of the crop, but when the loosely swinging lash is arrested with a sudden jerk, a wave of impulse flows along it and there is a loud report as the energy reaches the silk cord at the end. This proves that the energy released has travelled along the lash as fast as found travels. Now translate that analogy into terms of any athletic throwing feat and you will see that the hand of the thrower must be moving at the velocity with which the missile is projected at the moment of delivery, but there is one condition precedent involved here, and that is that the arm should be kept absolutely loose until the jerk intervenes.

Even so, the missile must be released at exactly the right instant and in exactly the right position, that is to say, the jerk or explosion must be concentrated at the right point in the throwing action. These things, however, cannot be done at will, and a perfect throw is the outcome of long and very careful training. There is another important matter yet to be examined, and that is the question of range.

Hammer and discus-throwers are able to hurl their missiles to phenomenal distances, because the circumstances of throwing allow them to take advantage of the fullest range of swing that the arm or arms can compass. The javelin-thrower does not fall quite within the same category, while the shot-putter is more restricted in this respect than any type of field events exponent.

While considering the throwing events, we get, perhaps the most striking and interesting examples of how the theory of dynamics enters into the scientific study of athletics. Hammer-throwing, for instance, is probably the most strenuous event that an athlete can adopt. The questions of initial impulse and progressive acceleration, however, are all important, for whereas all the momentum has to be generated within the restricted area of a 7-ft. circle, two turns are insufficient to build up maximum rotary velocity for conversion into the propulsion of delivery, five turns are practically impossible, and although four turns seem to be mathematically the right number, most men find difficulty in mastering three with the ability to remain in the circle after the hammer has been released. The strain imposed upon the human body by the feat of hammer-throwing is very great.

Assuming that a man, using four turns and thereby generating the necessary cumulative velocity, throws a 16 lbs. hammer 150 ft., the centrifugal force exerted, which represents the actual pull upon his arms will be 366 lbs., the velocity of the hammer at the instant of release is 69 ft. per second, the greatest vertical height attained in the parabola of flight is 37 ft. 6 ins. and the time of flight will be just over 3 seconds.

The range of hammer-thrower's arm effort is approximately the same as that of the discus-thrower, but he is able to exert a greater pull, because he uses both arms, and, moreover, the hammer-head at the end of the shaft, which provides a prolongation of the arms, gives the head of the projectile itself a far wider range of swing than is the case with the discus, the outer rim of which lies directly under the thrower's fingers. It may be said, therefore, that the 4 feet, representing the all over measurement of the hammer, gives the thrower that much advantage over the discus-thrower in range of swing, and explains why a 16 lbs. hammer has been thrown 189 ft. 6½ ins. as against a throw of 171 ft. 11½ ins. with a discus weighing only 4 2/5 lbs.

The fact that many records have been refused on the grounds that the athlete was assisted by a following wind proves clearly how little was known to many judges concerning the exact science of the events of which they took charge at competition. A strong following wind is undoubtedly of assistance to the short-distance sprinter, who runs the whole of his course with a breeze behind him. It is for less certain that similar benefit is derived by the hurdler, high jumper and pole vaulters, while the effect of a following wind upon certain missiles propelled through the air is definitely detrimental.

A following wind was considered to constitute a favourable circumstance, and officials, passing on records, were in the habit of assessing the strength of a prevailing wind by the deflection of a handkerchief, quite irrespective of such considerations as whether the handkerchief held up was of light silk and dry, or of heavy linen and damp. As a safeguard against this sort of unfair treatment of possible record-breakers, has invented an automatic anemometer. No event, presents such possibilities for research where wind effects are involved as does discus-throwing, but it should be understood that from the moment the index finger of the thrower's hand imparts to the missile, the last ounce of the energy in projection, right through until it comes to earth, there are two main movements, which affect its flight. These are an even balance of the missile itself and a perfect parabola of flight.

To make this matter clear, let us imagine the discus as an ordinary fly-wheel, uniform in weight and shape, and having a true centre, round which centre the discus revolves at the greatest speed which can be generated by the final spin imparted by the fingers, as the final phase of a cumulative effort, at the instant of projection.

The effect of wind resistance in relation to the angle of throw has been recognized for a long time as providing two of the most important problems awaiting solution, and many authorities, actuated by the knowledge that an aeroplane takes off best against the wind, have long doubted the soundness of the contention that a following wind was of assistance to the discus-thrower.

It was realized also that only experiments carried out in a wind tunnel would solve the problem of the effect of a wind against the flight of a discus and the effect of a wind following the flight of a discus. In order to ascertain the effect of a given wind against a discus at various angles of inclination, and to determine the most advantageous angle of throw, a discus was suspended in a wind tunnel by means of attached to delicate measuring and recording instruments. By these means, it was possible to chart the drag, or tendency of the discus to the pushed backwards, and the lift or elevating tendency, due to wind resistance against the under-surface of the discus, with contingent partial vacuum behind and on top of the discus, at various angles of inclination of the missile, varying from the horizontal to the vertical and back again.

In addition, slow motion pictures were taken to determine whether the discus changed its angle of inclination during flight and what ratio of revolutions were involved. It is concluded from the various pictures that initial path angle and the angle of inclination to the ground were identical and consistent from the point of delivery, although the angle of the missile to the resultant wind was continually changing. This, it is suggested, may be due to the spin of the discus on its own axis having a gyroscopically stabilizing effect, which helps to prevent any large alteration in the initial angle of inclination.

Other pictures established the theories for it was found that the discus in flight made from 18 to 21 complete revolutions, or enough to steady the flight, although not enough in aerodynamic effect to otherwise increase the distance thrown. Further the experiments produced a component of three forces beside gravity, which is constant. These forces were drag, lift and momentum.

In this connection, it must be remembered that whether the discus is moving forward against still air, or in air in motion, the character of the force is the same, although the strength of the force varies. Moreover, an object moving forward tends to create a vacuum and the shape of the discus is such that a partial vacuum is created behind and on top of the missile, when it is thrown at an angle upward from the horizontal and less than the vertical, and consequently the discus is being constantly pushed up into its partial vacuum by the pressure resulting from its own motion and from whatever wind may be blowing against its flight.

This is the lift which helps the discus to overcome the force of gravity and causes it to progress with what is know, in athletic parlance, as a true scale. The best scale is seen when the discus is flying through still air, or against the wind. The first inference would appear to be, therefore, that the stronger the head-wind the higher the discus will mount and the further it will fly, but this is only true in part, for there is bound to come a point at which the strength of the head wind will kill the momentum of the missile. When this point is reached, the discus will certainly mount higher, but it will fall more steeply and distance will be lost in consequence.

It reminded to discover the optimum point at which the lift would be greatest as compared with the drag, and the experiments carried out in the wind tunnel proved finally that the elevating effect of a head wind up to between seven and eight miles an hour was increasingly helpful to the discus-thrower, there being, after that, a steady decrease in the benefit up to 14.5 m.p.h., while beyond that point, a head wind became definitely detrimental. The results of the experiments made with a tail-wind were startling and upset all the pet theories of the alleged experts, who had refused to pass records made, with the aid of a following wind.

The argument that, logically, any force which propels an object must increase its speed of flight was not contested by the scientists carrying out the experiments, but it does not follow, necessarily, that the distance of flight will be prolonged commensurately with the additional speed. What the experiments carried out in America did prove was this, that a following wind, or even a quartering wind, creates a very marked decrease in the partial vacuum formed behind and on top of the discus, which is further deprived of all essential lift through lack of air-resistance to its under-surface when it flies with the wind behind it.

In other words, the discus is not only deprived of the lift, which should be pushing it up constantly into a partial vacuum, but is actually forced downwards by the pressure of a following wind striking at an angle against its tilted upper surface. Consequently, a discus-thrower, with a following wind gets less lift, less drag and less height at the top of the path of the parabola, so that the missile is maintained in flight for a proportionately shorter period of time than when it is thrown against a head wind of not more than 14.5 m.p.h.

The conclusion one arrives at, therefore, is that the stronger the tail-wind blowing behind the discus, the less distance will the athlete be able to throw the implement. Another thing proved by the experiments, was that the initial path angle and the angle of inclination to the ground were identical and consistent from the instant of projection and further that the correct angle of projection when the best conditions obtain is one of 35 degrees. The inferences to be drawn from the experiments made in America appear to be that the discus-thrower should make full use of all head on winds up to 14 to 15 m.p.h. and should throw with an angle of inclination of 35 degrees and an identical initial path when the adverse wind eos not exceed 8 m.p.h.

Secondly, when throwing against a wind of over 8 m.p.h., he should decrease the angle of inclination to decrease the drag by lessening the surface offered for wind resistance. At the same time, he should rely upon his cumulative momentum and the velocity of projection generated in the explosive jerk, as the main contributory factors for getting distance in the throw.

Thirdly, it must be remembered that the athlete has a 90 degree sector into which to throw his discus, and when the head wind is over 14 m.p.h. he should throw in such a direction as will enable him to use a quartering wind, but in that case, he must give the discus a flatter angle of inclination.

Fourthly, if the existing circumstances compel him to throw with a following wind, he should make his discus high, so that the wind pressure from behind may bear against an almost vertical face, thus partly neutralizing the loss of vacuum, while taking advantage of the propulsive force of the following wind.

Proper angle of projection for the javelin, shot and hammer is one of approximately 45 degrees, and that of the discus 35 degrees in ideal conditions. Most athletes know that these are the correct angles of delivery, and yet how seldom one sees the discus- and javelin-throwers getting their implements away along the proper parabola of flight. When a discus is throw properly, it rises from the thrower's hand with its whole face inclined to the ground at an angle of 35 degrees for some few feet and then tips slightly inclined inward to the left until it flattens out at the topmost point of its parabola of flight. Then gravity exerts its power and the fall of the discus earthwards is accelerated.

If a perfect throw has been made, the discus will follow the rest of its downward patch inclined inwards to the right. That is to say, the high point of the rims inclines inwards to the left as the discus mounts upwards, it then flies gyroscopically flat for an instant, and, filling, has the high point of the rim inclined slightly inwards to the right. If the head is dropped back the thrower will sweep his arm up, rather than across, and so make the delivery angle too steep and the arm sweep too short. If the wrist is bent back on the arm and discus may still depart at the true angle of 35 degrees, but will be unstable in flight, because the final pull of the fingers, which impart the spin to the missile, will be uneven and the last flick of the wrist itself will be lacking. If the discus shoots along the ground upon landing, that is sure sign that it has not been thrown high enough.

A discus that has expended the full force of its propulsion in the air pancakes, or bounces, when it hits the ground. When a javelin is properly thrown it enters upon its path at a true angle of 45 degrees, but here we have conditions to consider which do not affect the shot-putters and hammer- and discus-throwers. The weapon itself weighs but 1 lb. 12¼ ozs., but the fact that weight is distributed through a length of 8s ft. 6 ins. of steel head and more or less pliant, tapered wood-shaft makes it an awkward implement for the novice to handle and control.

In throwing the javelin, the whole result, from a dynamical point of view, hinges upon two main circumstances, i.e., the speed and strength of the thrower in combination, and perfect balance. In the examination of errors that arise, the factors of strength and speed need not, for the moments, concern us, as we will assume that the thrower is physically equipped for the feat he wishes to perform. The only way strength need be considered is in relation to the fact that the stronger a man is and the more his strength is applied to an incorrect balance, the greater will be the resulting error.

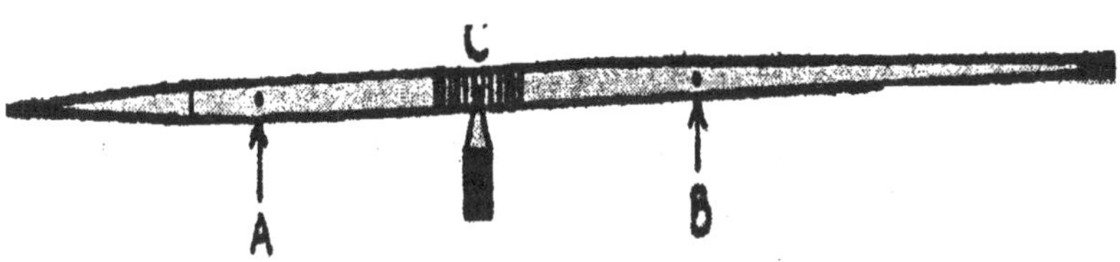

If this truism is borne in mind, its force will become more apparent as the question of balance is dealt with. We will deal with this point in some detail, since it is most important one, and the one which governs the perfect throw. By balance, one means, of course, centre of gravity. A body will be in stable equilibrium, when it is so suspended that a slight swing to either side will cause it to oscillate gently until it comes to rest again with its centre of gravity vertically under the point of suspension.

The figure above represents a javelin, drawn somewhat out of proportion. Let C be the centre of the gravity of the whole javelin, if it be suspended or balanced at this point, it will remain in equilibrium. This now divides it into two parts, each of which, again, has a centre of gravity at A and B respectively, and it is these two centres of gravity which keep the whole weapon in equilibrium when held in the thrower's hand. Now the force applied in throwing the javelin must pass through its centre of gravity, i.e., at C which is the centre of the weight of the whole body. But supposing the javelin be thrown with the hand grasping it at B, then, as just stated, the whole weight to be moved lies in C, and therefore, any force applied behind this point must be push.

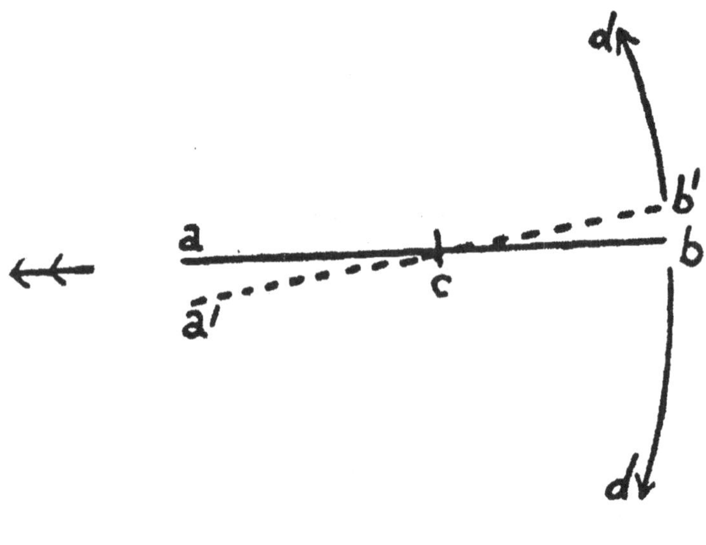

Again, supposing the weapon be held at A and thrown, and then as this point is in front of C, it naturally follows that the force applied must be pull. Pull in throwing is far less likely to produce error than push. Let AB represents a javelin travelling in the direction of the arrows heads and C its common centre of gravity.

Now assume again that the weapon is grasped at B and thrown. It would naturally be very hard to hold the javelin in this position and maintain the true direction of flight, i.e., along AB; therefore, assuming the error is a' b', a force applied at B and with a direction parallel to AB would produce an upward tendency to rotate round C, as shown by the arrow, and it will be seen easily that the nearer the javelin is held to the centre, the less likely is the error to occur. Or should the weapon be held at a point near A, the tendency will be to drop it in the direction D.

Despite the fact that the power must be transmitted longitudinally to the shaft, it seems to me that when the javelin is in flight, the parabola of that flight must pass continuously through the actual centre of gravity of the weapon, for if the flight of the javelin merely follows the tip of the steel head, the weapon will pitch too steeply and much distance will be lost.

It is true that the angle of projection is one of 45 degrees, but it is equally true that the best and the longest throws show the javelin in flight travelling almost parallel to the ground. In point of fact, in very long throws, the javelin, having encompassed half its flight, seems suddenly to mount to a higher plane, upon which it sails on for a while before pitching earthwards as its impressed forces dwindle. A characteristic of a good throw is that the weapon descends on a gradual slant, entering the earth with the shaft almost parallel to the ground and the point only just breaking the turf.

Therefore, to maintain the javelin in the line of its true direction of flight it is essential that it be thrown with the hand hold established at its exact centre of gravity.

There is the question of direction, for the rule governing the contest ordains that all throws shall be measured perpendicularly to the scratch line or the scratch line produced.

In this connection, the keeping of the javelin above the line of direction during its alteration from the carry to the throwing position, while the four final strides are being made, is important, but the whole secret of making a straight throw lies in the ability of the thrower to square his chest to the front, by a quick twist of the shoulders, before his arm strikes. There is one more point. In order that the centre of gravity of the weapon may furnish the path of its parabola of flight, it is necessary that the javelin should be lifted off the palm and be released when the hand is directly above the shoulder. If the release comes later, the javelin will be dragged down, and may also fly to one side or the other of the true line of direction, which is perpendicular to the scratch line from behind which throwing takes place.

10

Track Events

Track Events, as the name implies, is not any single event, but group of various events. For this, it can be said that many events jointly constitutes the track events. Basically it can be said that all those events for which particular and proper track is prepared, are included in the track events.

To explain this in more simple term it can be said that it is a part of Athletic. As we know that Athletic event includes both track as well as field events, and in this chapter we will discuss about these track events and in the succeeding chapter about field events. Thus, we can say that in order to understand and learn the event of Athletics properly, we have divided all the events included in it under two separate headings, namely the Track Events and Field Events.

Track Events are important part of Athletic Event, as without which Athletic cannot get the proper shape and existence. Today, these events have become very popular throughout the world and has become an income event in Olympics also.

Now the question arises that which events are included in track events, so to clear this point we can say that following events are called the Field Events:

a. Hurdling,

b. Sprinting,

c. Running,

d. Steeplechase,

e. Walking, and

f. Cross-Country.

In this way we see that above mentioned events are the ingredients of Track Events. In this chapter we will discuss all these events one by one in detail. Before going to the skills and rules of all the events, we have mentioned prior introduction relating to these events, so that no beginner have to face any difficulty in understanding these events. By this manner, any one can take advantage from the chapter and discussion of the present study.

HURDLING

Hurdle races are another face of sprint races. In such races, sprint techniques are used for clearing the various obstacles, for which speed is required. Combining this with an optimum stride length as well as an economical clearance of hurdles perfectly is important. To become a successful hurdler, one should possess the physical ability to keep himself ready for the full distance.

Some 130 years back this game is believed to take birth. In the beginning, this event comprises of running and jumping requiring the competitors to stop to turn sideways on to perform a scissor jump across the barriers. Sheep hurdles were used as barriers and they were attached to the ground. They were designed so that any runner unfortunate enough to fail to clear the obstacle could sustain quite an injury. Than after, hurdles were made just to stand on ground rather attached. The original hurdles were quite literally sheep fences, being very sturdy affairs fixed into the ground.

In initial years of its beginning, hurdling technique was not so complicated as it is today. Athlete used to tend to leap over the barrier with bent lead leg across the front of the body.

In 1886, for the first time straight lead leg were used. The person using such kind of barrier was an Englishman, named Arthur Croome. The man who developed this technique in international athletics was the winner of 1900 Olympic Gold Medal who was Alvin Kraenzlein of the USA.

Alvin Kraenzlein is considered the father of modern hurdling. In 1896, for the first time, hurdling event was included or taken up in the Olympic Games, however, it was only a hurdle race over 100 m. After 4 years, this distance increased to 110 m but remained this for a long time.

400m hurdle was included in the Olympic Games as an individual event for the first time in 1900. That time, hurdles of 3 feet was used. In 1904 they were only 2 feet 6 inches high, but they reverted to 3 feet in 1908 at which height they have remained.

Hurdling of women's took quite a great time in becoming fully civilised or developed. In 1926 it was decided that the distance for women will be 80m, however for the first time this event for the women was included in Olympic in the year 1932. After 1968 games, the distance was changed to 100m with the hurdles at 2 feet 9 inches. In 1969, the first official world record in this event was established. In 1971, the 400m hurdles for women was introduced, which became full international event in the year 1975, however, it was till the year 1984 that it had to wait to be included in the Olympic Games.

Earlier, this event was developed with an aim of measuring the sprinting and jumping capabilities of athletes. Over the time, the technique has developed and improved.

In the 100/110-metre hurdles, elite athletes aim for three strides between each hurdle. They also attempt to spend as much time as possible on the ground sprinting and, conversely, as little time as possible in the air over each hurdle. To do this, athlete should possess the knowledge of hurdling technique, for which a concentrated program of sprinting, hurdling and related flexibility exercises is needed.

Height of hurdle can be changed according to the age and gender of the athlete. For younger athletes, the height is decreased and vice versa. Thus, young athletes run shorter distances using fewer hurdles, not only this, their height from the earth is decreased according to their physical abilities. In the same way, the height of hurdle is more for male athletes than for the females. Divisions of the athletes is generally done on the basis of age factor.

Over 110m and 400m for men and 100m and 400m for women are the hurdling events which are being organised or included in the Olympic Games. Hurdler should be tall and should possess the full and thorough This is particularly the case in the men's 110-metre hurdles, where the hurdles are 3 feet 6 inches tall.

Today, Hurdling has gained worldwide popularity and people of both sexes are playing it in various countries of the world. Now, it has become an integral part of Olympic Games.

Skills and Techniques

As mentioned previously that Hurdling is quite same as sprinting, thus it should be learned or taught in the same manner as sprinting. Coach should keep in his mind that he should taught the athletes to clear the hurdle as a run over action and not as a jumping event. For clearing the hurdles properly, height of the athlete makes a lot of contribution.

To become a good hurdler, one should have a good height, speed, flexibility and a kind of coordination between his physical and mental capacities.

Thus it can be said that to become a good and successful hurdler, one should possess the following qualities:

-sprinting;

-strength and mobility;

-general fitness;

-technique.

Without possession all of these qualities, one cannot become a good hurdler. It is clear that a person who is a good sprinter can become a good hurdler. So, it can be said that without becoming a sprinter, none can become a good hurdler.

Of all the Track events, hurdling is considered the most attractive event, both to take part in and to watch; there is a special thrill for competition and spectator alike in the perfectly timed, rhythmic rush, and the rise and fall of the racing bodies as they clear the hurdles, apparently without effort, and by the closest margin of inches for safety.

Any person can learn to run, but for this event, he should also have mental capabilities. One who is impatient cannot become a good hurdler. There are many hurdlers in the world, but not a lot of great hurdlers. This is because of the reason that a man requires many other qualities for this event.

To become hurdler, a man must be tall, strong, well split-up, quick on his feet, a good jumper and very fast on the flat. On the flat a man may attain no small degree of distinction by his speed or staying power alone.

It is not too much to say, indeed, that a fast sprinter with a good spring will almost always be beaten by an infinitely slower man who has mastered the hurdler's art.

While selecting the students for coaching, coach should thoroughly check that the he should possess all these qualities which have been mentioned above. If he can stand upright and flick up his leg so as to bring the muscles of the thigh just above the knee hard against the shoulder; and if he can sit on the ground with body held upright and the leg, which throws first over the hurdle, stretched out straight in front of him, with the whole underside of the limb flat to the earth, while the thigh of the other leg is at right angles to the hip, with knee and inside ankle bone flat to the ground and heel touching back of the thigh, without doubt he will do.

Position of Hurdler while Performing Crouching Start

In the beginning, hurdler should keep his fingers on Scratch Line. His hands should be separated from each other so that back leg can come freely through the front. We assume here that he advances his left foot, the place for that foot is just about six inches behind the scratch line. This simply mean that the hurdler's left knee should be only just behind the Scratch line in the On Your Marks Position. While in this position, the knee of his right leg should be level with ankle bone of the left foot.

It is the duty of the coach to check the athlete's position. If athlete finds himself comfortable then should dig small holes for the forepart of his feet, taking care that the holes are strong enough and the back wall of each firm enough to allow him to get a good push off when the starter fires the pistol. They should be arranged in such a manner that each foot of the athlete is directly behind the knee to which it belongs.

Once the starter has given the caution by order On Your Marks, athlete is advised to follow it with Get Set. The whole secret of successfully Getting Set is to let the weight of the body go forward on to the front foot and the fingers before the back knee should raised from the ground; at the same time sufficient weight must be kept upon the back foot to prevent the body falling forward; otherwise, it will be impossible to make the spring into action from both feet, as player should do when the pistol bangs.

Another most important thing to remember is that one must concentrate the whole of one's mental energies upon the matter in hand, holding both body and mind in perfect control between the starter's warning "Get Set" and the report of the pistol which flings the body forward in a state of eager activity. Above all, learn to keep deep steady on the mark.

The man who swings backwards and forwards upon his fingers and toes may anticipate the gun by a fraction now and again; but generally, he is the one who is caught napping. To the hurdler, even more than to the sprinter upon the flat, it is of the first importance not to wobble in the first few strides. A man who does so is bound to be unbalanced as he approaches the first hurdle, and will, most likely, have to ease up and buck over it, instead of taking the obstacle easily and gracefully in his stride.

The first few strides from the pistol should be accomplished as quickly and smoothly as possible, with the body gradually rising through an inclined plane to the right angle at which it will be carried throughout the running part of the race. Once the race is on, the hurdler has got to remember that the shortest path between any two given points is always be straightest. From this axiom he may learn two lessons:

First, to run straight on the flat, and to fly low over fences. The higher the body rises over the top rail of each hurdle so much the longer will it take for the athlete to get his lending foot to the ground again coming down from the fence. The player should be taught, if possible, to start the race with that foot advanced, which it is his custom to throw first over the hurdle; the starting practice will then serve to build up the muscles of the back leg which help so much to lift the body forward over the flights of hurdles.

The first flight of hurdles is set up 15 yards from the scratch line, that the athlete should reach his take-off for the first flight in seven or eight strides, and that the take-off should be about two yards in front of the hurdle. It is almost as important for the hurdler to make sure, by practice, of always getting accurately up to the take-off for the first hurdle, as it is for the long jumper to learn always to hit the take-off board squarely with the ball of the foot. Most men find that their stride over the hurdle from take-off to landing is just about 12 feet, but they should not lose sight of the fact that the whole object is to get the foot to ground as quickly as possible upon the far side of the hurdle, for which reason they should aim at coming down as near as possible to the obstacle. It is, the player's duty to see that the training is done in no haphazard manner; and one of the first principles is that when men go out to work the first hurdle must be set up fifteen yards from the starting point.

When the coach has taught his players to take the hurdle properly, he has still got to teach him to get his stride right between hurdles, so that he can cover the distance in three strides.

The first trouble will be to get the player to open out his legs sufficiently while retaining proper control over his body, the three strides in such a manner that he will have sufficient momentum to carry him over the next hurdle. These, however, are difficulties which will be overcome by practice, proper body carriage, and the physical fitness and strength engendered by training.

Beginning Position

The beginning position at the hurdle is as follows:—

The leg he would naturally throw over first should rest on the top rail, and the body is doubled down on to it. At this stage, coach should watch him to see what he does with his arms. The chances are about a thousand to one that he will arrange them in absolutely the best way to suit his own balance. This he will do instinctively, and the instructor needs to take note of it for future reference, for once the tyro starts running over the fences his arms are apt to fly in all the ways at once. It will be best to keep him to his first instinctive arm carriage if it seems likely to distribute his weight in the right way.

After the player has got himself properly arranged, with the left leg resting upon the top rail of the hurdle, he should place both hands forward on the top rail while the coach should draw his left leg forward, while the player at the same time should raise his weight on his hands. This is the stage at which the coach should note what means the player adopts of drawing up and carrying over his back leg; for it must be remembered that the fork between his legs will only just clear the bar as it will do when he his running in is fences properly later on. Consequently, it is worth while finding out if he has a natural inclination to manage his back leg in proper manner, or if he shows evil tendencies, which must be checked at once and as quickly as possible eradicated.

The next thing that the coach should teach the athlete is that if his right arm has gone forward over the hurdle with his left leg his shoulders will have remained square to the tap and he will have alighted on the ball of the left foot. He will also keep his chin in front of his leading leg all the time. Now the athlete should balance himself with the knee of the right leg on the top rail of the hurdle behind him as the right foot rests upon the ground; stand in front of him and draw his right hand a little forward towards himself. This gives his body the forward pose.

Then, coach should tell him to let his right leg swing through to the front, and, as he takes the step, make him swing his left arm through to the front and slightly across the body, at the same time pointing out to him how greatly the arm-swing helps the forward movement of the right leg, and also how it tends to keep the shoulders square to the tape. When these elementary principles are firmly fixed in his mind, coach may teach the player to take one hurdle, insisting that he should alight upon the ball of the foot and sprint forward a few strides upon landing from his fence. Coach cannot impress upon him too strongly the vital necessity of being nippy.

He must be off like a flash of lightning the moment his leading foot touches the ground. If he can master this he will learn instinctively to work his arms to aid his body, and to snap that rear leg through to the front for the next stride forward just as fast as ever he knows how.

Teach the player that he must never, under any circumstances, land upon his heel. To impress this upon the player, make him go over his tracks every time he runs, to see that he has not been guilty of this unforgivable error. At this stage of the proceedings beginning players should do plenty of walking practice over hurdles, because it is the best method to make him fast over fences, which has nothing at all to do with being fast on the flat between flights. At first the coach will almost always find the player regarding him with a sceptical eye when he tells the player that he should have no difficulty in covering the ten yards between flights in five fair·heel-and-toe walking strides, flicking over the fence like a flash of lightning at the end of the first step, and bringing the rear leg past the one on which he has landed in equally quick time.

It is quite often that one finds a man who is excellent in almost every respect. He is smart and stylish over timber and travels well on the flat, but he has the fatal fault of letting down his heel spikes as he lands from each fence. This is where patient perseverance, becomes necessary. A man showing such a fault has only one hope of salvation. He has got to strengthen his ankles, and the quickest way for him to do that is by tramping the track stiff-legged and on the tips of his toes. He will in this way acquire such a cramp as will make him curse the day he met his trainer, but that disability will soon be got rid of by having the sore places well massaged. If the coach himself is lissom and a hurdler of any note he can teach the tyro many tips and practically all the essential positions in the dressing room, by posing himself and the pupil, and letting a high table take the place of a hurdle as a leg rest to the foot of the leading leg.

As a variation of the five step and over walk method of instruction or exercise, one usually finds that the Americans before a race travel the whole 120 yards hurdle course with five slow, short running strides between fences, and a lightning-like passage over them. In training, they usually walk the whole length of the ten flights just outside the hurdles. A man who hurdles right leg first would be to the right of the flights, and a man hurdling left leg first to the left of them. The hurdler takes five walking steps to the hurdle, kicks up his leading leg beside it, so that the foot goes to the height it would reach if he was actually on the fly; then as the leading foot comes to ground and the body goes forward, the back leg is flicked up and over the hurdle with heel tucked back.

It will be noticed that in this exercise one foot is always on the ground but the leading foot goes above the height of the hurdle while the foot of the rear leg is still on the ground. This is as it should be in actual practice. It will also be noticed that the knee and ankle of the rear leg are raised over the top rail of the hurdle itself, while the foot of the leading leg is on the ground. It will be obvious to anyone of average intelligence that the man who can get his rear leg to that height while the other foot is on the ground, and can, moreover, walk through at the side of ten flights of 3ft. 6in. hurdles and repeat the performance ten times, has no need to waste time and energy in jumping high over the hurdles in competition.

The trainer has to guard against two things in the country. One is the risk that his charges, who not infrequently do their preparation in raw cold weather at the beginning of the year, may take cold. For this reason, they should be encouraged to wear sweaters with high necks, and long pants beneath their running shorts. The second caution applies all the year round. Every beginning player will knock his legs about terrify if he is not properly looked after, but any trouble of this sort is avoided if the trainer sees that his charges are fitted out with padded knee and ankle guards for practice purposes. To avoid falls, it is as well to get hold of half a dozen of Foster's Patent Hurdles. This hurdle consists of a frame 2ft. 6in. high, with a swinging, wooden gate 2ft. high; the swinging joint being six inches from the one side and eighteen inches from the other, so that the height of the hurdle can be set at 2 ft. 6in. or 3ft. 6in.

It is invaluable for practice purposes, since it can be changed from one height to the other at a moment's notice, by means of a clamp lever which allows the wooden gate to swing free if the hurdler should touch it in practice, or binds it firmly in position when it is desired to use the hurdles for purposes of competition. These hurdles, like so many patents, are, unfortunately, rather expensive. It therefore behoves the club or institution which cannot afford luxuries to build up some type of hurdle which has a top rail that can be fixed at will at 3ft. 6in., and a lower rail which remains fixed at 2ft. 6in. or 3ft. Player should bear in his mind the he should never train his charges over more than two or three hurdles at first, and that the real object coach in view is to make the players hurdle mechanically and run correctly between flights without ever giving a thought to the matter. After that it is up to him, or to the man who trains himself, to get busy and build up that determination and nervous energy which will enable the athlete to speed up the movements he has learned to make with mathematical precision in such a manner that when he comes to the competition for which he is training he will both fence and run faster ever he has done before, and without losing the perfect style which his trainer has been at such pains to inculcate.

Start

Starting in this event and Sprinting is not same as there exists a difference. This difference is that hurdler must come up to the running position sooner. Generally seven to eight steps are taken by a high hurdler to the first hurdle, twenty one or twenty two by a intermediate hurdler. The hurdler who takes an odd number of steps to the first hurdle will have the same leg forward in the blocks as leads over the hurdle. With an even number of

steps, the lead leg over the hurdle is the back leg in the blocks. By attempting to hurdle with each leg, hurdler will determine the lead leg.

The Approach to the First Hurdle

As has been described above, twenty one or twenty two strides to the first hurdle will be employed by an intermediate athlete. They should employ last five strides to the first hurdle being in the same rhythm as that to be used between hurdles. This is more applicable to the hurdlers attempting thirteen strides to use twenty strides for the first hurdle, while for those athletes who are taking fifteen strides should take twenty two strides.

Guidelines

i. In the first stride, hurdler should concentrate on a short fast movement;

ii. Till third stride, hurdler should not look at the hurdle. He should resist the temptation to throw the head back and stand up out of the blocks;

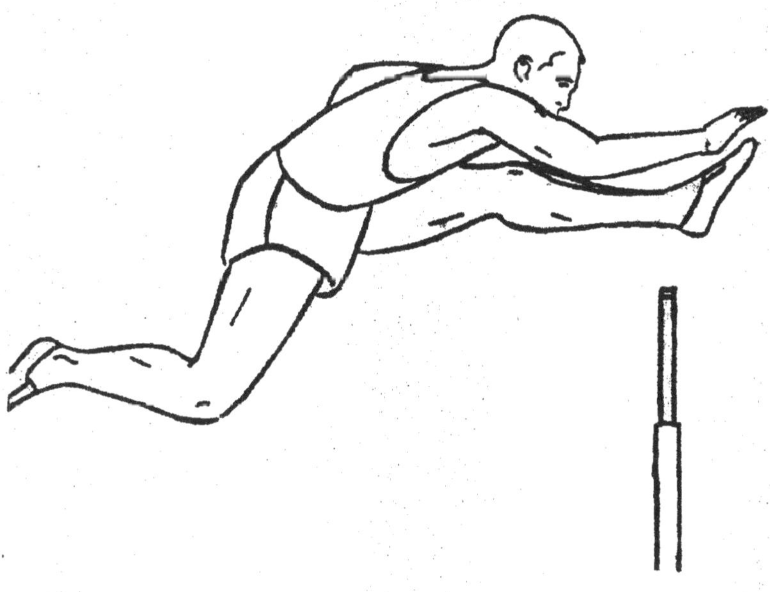

iii. Final stride should be shortened;

iv. Quickly, he should get back down to the ground;

v. Then, he should get to the first hurdle first.

Running Between the Hurdles

As has been said earlier, that to become a good hurdler, one should be a good sprinter, so, it can be said that hurdler must be primarily a sprinter. Many beginners not require any kind of changes of sprinting action between the barriers because the distance between the hurdles presents no problem at all for them. The problem with youngsters more likely is that the hurdles feel too far apart. Whereas, senior sprint hurdlers have the opposite problem; in most cases the hurdles are too close together.

Athlete should modify his sprinting technique to make it fit the gaps. A fast leg cadence is needed and a shorter stride length. This can be achieved by training over hurdles that are slightly closer together than normal. The athlete may have to use a lower knee lift than in normal sprinting. The emphasis should be on leg speed.

In the highs, a hurdler must take 3 steps and in the intermediates 13, 15 or 17 steps. The intermediate hurdler can use a 14-stride pattern if the lead leg is alternated. The hurdler must concentrate on good sprint action between the hurdles, running up on the balls of the feet, with knees high and arms driving hard with relaxation. Good sprint rhythm between the hurdles is important. The hurdler should never gallop or overstride which often is caused by not getting a good step off the hurdle with the trail leg.

Guidelines

i. The first stride should be shorter, which should not be kept deliberately short but must be the optimum between length and speed. If too long, it should be slow and other strides should be shorter. This usually results in the athlete being too close to the next hurdle. If too short, the athlete may be too far from the next hurdle;

ii. The second stride should be longest. The athlete should train to run off the hurdle;

iii. Third stride should be shorter as it is considered to be the preparation for take-off.

CLEARANCE

In this event, the flight path of athlete is determined by manner of movements which he makes while leading up to the take-off. Once athlete has broken contact with the ground, his flight path cannot be changed. A hurdler's flight path and his efficiency depends to a great instance to approach strides and take off action.

In the athlete's line of running, leading leg must be snapped up. It is very difficult to correct the fault of a hurdler whose leading leg swings at the hurdle across the line of running. There are few athletes who swing the leg outward and other inwards. Both produce a corkscrew action over the hurdle with an off-balance landing on the other side. To correct this, it is not an easy task. Athlete should give full attention in training on lifting the thigh in line of running and also on shooting the heel across the hurdle.

While talking to the athlete, coach should care a lot of care. He should make use of words which are straight, clear, and have only single meaning.

Between the obstacles, the hurdler should take at least three strides. The principle of shortening the stride before take-off holds good for each obstacle. Hurdler should run between obstacles fastly and smoothly. The important factor to fast-moving legs frequently lies in the speed of the arm action. All the times, arms should be worked vigorously, and especially between the hurdles. Athlete should keep his head straight.

Important words while describing hurdle crossing technique are knees and the attack. Knees as it is the knees that lead the leg action and attack because the hurdler must attack the hurdle aggressively. Basically, the hurdle crossing action is a modification of the normal sprinting technique. The action of legs should be exaggerated which allows the hurdle to pass under the body.

Movement of Legs

The last stride of the approach to the hurdle should be shortened to allow the take-off leg to move rapidly under the hips, which ensures the sprinter that a fast effective drive can be made across the hurdle. At the hurdle, he should drive the knee of his lead leg. Lower leg should be left low and extended once the knee reaches the height of the barrier. The knee should be picked up just parallel with the vertical centre line of the body. There should be no tendency for the knee to be pulled across the body or for the lower leg to go out and round. As the heel of the lead leg passes the barrier, it must be pulled down and back to land under the body. Player is not required to keep his legs straight over the top hurdle. He should straighten them as it descents towards the ground.

Trailing Leg: As soon as the lead leg rises, trailing leg of the sprinter should drive the body. If drive is to be completed, he should begin to recover the trail leg from behind the body. The sprinter should feel the trailing knee sweeping wide and flat over the hurdle. This should be a rising leg with the high point of the knee being ahead of the hurdle as the lead leg lands. As the leg crosses the hurdle, foot of the athlete should cocked at the ankle to avoid hitting of barrier. After crossing the barrier, he should raise his knees and come round in front of the body. If athlete drop the trail leg off to the side after crossing the barrier, first stride will result very short and pull the athlete off the balance. The trail leg should be pulled high and fast, so that the first stride is fast.

Thus, various parts of the body of sprinter will remain at following positions while crossing the hurdle:

Leading Leg: The leg which goes over the hurdle first comes up in a normal sprint with a high knee lift. As the thigh is coming through, almost touching the chest, the lower leg straightens and the heel is thrown at the top of the hurdle. Leading leg and foot are brought down quickly, snapped down, ready to drive in the first stride towards the next hurdle.

Trailing Leg: This leg provides the motive power for driving over the hurdle. If it drives full, it will trail and there will have been a split of the thighs. Now, as if to catch up, the trailing leg crosses the hurdle in a bent position with the inside of the leg almost brushing the top of the hurdle and the knee and ankle at right angles. It is important that the thigh eventually comes through near to the chest. If this happens, sprinter will get a good first stride after landing.

Movement of Arms

The arms should act to balance the body and counter the rotations produced by the legs. The arm opposite to the lead leg should lead the action into the hurdle. Sprinter should keep his arms in the following positions while crossing the hurdle:

a. Hurdler should push his opposite arm forward as soon as lead leg rises while in normal sprinting action he should take back his other arm. As the trail leg comes round, he should swing his leading arm in backward direction while keep the other arm in normal position. In sprinting phases of hurdling, sprinter should keep his arm in normal state. The hips and shoulders should be kept square to the front throughout the drill. Athlete should keep his hips as high as possible. There should be no sinking either at take-off or on landing.

b. With knee driven at the hurdle, sprinter should fully flex his lead leg and should drive the opposite arm forward. He should keep his hips at maximum height and rear leg drive almost completed.

c. Sprinter should open out his leading leg and recover the rear leg. There is a good range of movement as the lead foot approaches the top of barrier and the trailing foot is only just off the ground. This position is termed as split position which is proved to be very effective and valuable at this stage. At this moment, he should raise his leading arm slightly.

d. Sprinter should continuously open out his leading leg across the hurdle half-way, it is anatomically straight, while not the locked. He should not raise his shoulders and keep his eyes on the next hurdle. Around the side, he should recover the rear leg with foot travelling inward towards the body.

e. Then, the sprinter should bend his lead leg and take the shortest route down to the ground. At the moment, he should concentrate on pulling the heel back under his body. With foot lower than the knee, he should recover his trailing leg. Throughout the drill, sprinter should now raise his knee more than trailing foot, then, to counter the rotation of the trailing leg, he should bring his leading arm round to the side.

f. This is the final stage where sprinter has to land. Now, to land, he has to straighten his leg and touch the ground. Over his this foot, he should pivot his body while keeping the knees straight. In front of his body, he should recover his trailing. Throughout the performance, he should keep his hips high. At this time, the athlete should concentrate on sprinting away from the hurdle.

Finish

The distance between the last hurdle and finishing line is definite and in set number of strides one can clear it. Athlete can determine whether it is worthwhile to practice a dip or lunge at the line, he can observe the footballs made by him. It is a good plan to dip on the stride if the foot comes down six or seven feet around 180 to 215 cm short of the line. After landing off the hurdle, this will be the sixth stride.

TEACHING THE HURDLING

While coaching, coach should treat all his hurdles separately, however, sometimes it cannot be possible for coach to do this, then he can make use of the squad system. Squad system of coaching should be used by the coach when he thinks that his players need to be motivated.

Coach of this event should develop a coaching eye, which is a time consuming thing. This quality emerges in a coach with his experience. As an athlete knowledge of the event from the coach, so coach should have thorough knowledge of each and every aspect of the event. Not only this, he should be capable of using his knowledge properly in giving the athletes instructions. He should be capable if analyse the action of his athletes. He should pinpoint each and every fault of athletes, irrespective of the extent of it.

Coach should understand that merely noticing the faults of athletes is not his duty, but to provide them with proper instruction is his duty. To increase the field of vision, coach should stand well back from the athlete. Once he has decided that beginner is taking advantage from his instructions, next, he should take him to hurdle so that he can learn balance and position. In the beginning, he should give the athlete some help by assisting him, however, with passage of time, he should let the athlete perform this independently.

A high hurdler's starting position should be suck that can help in producing the greatest acceleration and also bring him to the take off point which is required for slick first hurdle clearance.

While teaching the hurdling skills, a coach should keep all the following important points in his mind or it can be said that following should strategy he should follow or use:

Presenting the event

Organisation of a classroom presentation is the first thing done while presenting the hurdles to a beginner. With this, it becomes easy and effective to acquaint the new athlete with the event. In such kind of classroom presentation, coach should firstly make use of the loop films. Through this medium, players gain the feel for event and these help in arising the interest of athletes in the event.

Coach should tell the athletes that they have to run over the barriers and not to jump over. Stress the lay out action over the hurdle and keep on representating that through a race, a number of hurdle's head remain at the same level. Tell them how important are rhythm, balance and smoothness while performing. Coach should tell them that in the first and in between hurdles, they have to take a definite and particular number of steps.

The Start

Concerning the technique of teaching, there exists not a vary vast difference between coaching the sprinting event and this event. Methods to teach the techniques are quite same in both these events. However, there exists some difference which is that in high hurdles, the boys and girls should come up into full sprinting stride less gradually than a sprinter would. In high hurdles, the distance of first hurdle is 15 yards, however, this distance is less for the girl's athletes.

Atleast two strides before the take-off, the hurdler should be in full sprinting stride with which it get proper drive into the take off. Still, a high or girl hurdler should come out of the low blocks, like sprinter, however, he should come up comparatively quicker but less gradually. This problem does not arise in the intermediate hurdles.

To the first hurdle, most hurdles run eight steps. Related to this, a question arises that should the lead leg be changed or should the block placement should be changed so that the hurdler uses the most natural foot placement in blocks . There arises no problem if the athlete leads as well as start with the same leg. But, this is not the reality. If athlete face with this decision, you should leave the lead leg and just change your block position. It has been seen that to change the back and forward feet in block is not so disruptive as over the hurdle, changing the lead leg.

On this factor, the number of steps athlete will take to the first hurdle depends. An even number of steps to the first hurdle is best if athlete leads over the hurdle with his left leg as well as start with his this leg back in the blocks. On the contrary, athlete should take odd number of steps to the first hurdle, if he leads with his left leg, but prefers the right leg back in the blocks.

The takeoff position to the hurdle

There is not any particular position relating to take off position because from athlete to athlete it changes. However, a standard position can be mentioned in which from the hurdle, athlete set around seven feet. However, for some athletes, the ideal spot can be a little in either direction, but this range should not be more than six to eight feet. Coach should emphasize the bent knee lead leg drive and should aim the lead heel at a point around six inches in front of hurdle and about four inches over it. From this point, also stress the downward action of lead leg. In doing so, if a beginner afraid, it becomes the duty of the coach should raise his morale and put confidence in him. For a beginner, it is advised too high over a hurdle inspite of continuously hitting it. With progress, coach can bring him down. From banging into the barrier, coach should not discourage him.

The main problem a coach faces in this event is to teach the beginners the location of take off point. Seven and six feet are more for a beginner. It is found that beginners desires to take off nearer to the hurdle, which becomes an important factor when coach begins to teach steps in between hurdles. Beginners take off from incorrect point because it is just a kind of psychological problem found in athletes, the duty of finishing and overcoming from them lies with coach. For this, coach should possess such qualities by which he can do this work easily.

Arm action

For an athlete, movement of arm is very important. Coach should keep a hurdler's arm as near as possible. You should not let the athletes to exaggerate the extension of opposite arm to the lead leg. To get the trail knee higher than the crossbar, extension of opposite arm should be sufficient. Inside the chest line, extend it slight and bring the elbow slightly to the outside as soon as it bring to the rear. Beginners should not be allowed to swing their arms laterally, as it can prove dangerous for them. Coach should know and keep in his mind that to keep the body straight and in a balancing position is the necessity of hurdling technique.

Bar Clearance and Lead Leg Action

While coaching the hurdling techniques, coach should use the low hurdles in the beginning, and with the progress of athlete's performances, can switch to high hurdles. Initially, let the beginners walk over the hurdle, stress a bent lead leg. They should keep their thigh, knee and foot straight and note that they use the knee first and then the foot while bringing the lead leg above the hurdle.

While teaching the hurdle clearance position, you should allow the athletes to possess the same position as they did while doing exercises, and then insure that in three right angles, they are positioned, in such a manner:

-the angle formed by the inside of the thighs of the lead and trail legs,

-the angle of the thigh and calf of the trail leg, and

-the ankle— foot angle of the trail leg. Many youngsters lack the flexibility to get into this position and stay there in good balance.

While sitting on the ground, if the athletes are unable to possess this position, it is certain that they will not do it swiftly in midair while clearing the hurdle. For this reason it is always said that to become a good hurdler, one should have flexibility in his body.

Body Angle and Trail Leg Action

If you are assure that now the hurdles have perfectly

understand the lead leg action and proper position over hurdle while bringing the trail leg, switch them to stand over the hurdle while keeping their lead leg on the ground. With the trail leg in the just-described right angles, have them bring it through, emphasizing driving the knee up as close to the chest as possible and out to the front. Once they have drilled on the trail leg action, let them walk over the hurdle. While this, you should keep a keen watch on their lead and trail leg movements and tell them to keep the shoulders square, eyes in upward direction, left arm fully extend in forward direction if their right leg is leading.

Now let the athletes to jog over the hurdle. While doing this, they should continuously increase their speed with their experience. A device called "gimmick" is used with the trail leg action which tell them to imagine that they have two eyes on the inside of the knee of the trail leg and those eyes should be looking at the inside of the other leg as they pull it through. You should start to emphasize the forward lean of the body as soon as they start to run over the hurdle. On the height of the hurdle and leg split of the athlete, amount of lean depends.

Timing and landing

As has been said earlier, with progress, coach should come down or get down over the hurdle. Lead foot of the athlete should land on the toes at a distance of about four feet beyond the hurdle. It should be slightly to the right of an imaginary line which is down the centre of the lane.

Athlete should get down faster after the lead leg begins its downward action. Not only this, he should bring his trail leg very quickly. While landing, the position of a hurdler should be same as a sprinter. While landing, the centre of gravity should be over the lead leg while keeping the trail knee at the chest.

Perfecting Hurdling Skills

The process of perfecting the technique of hurdling is a long, painstaking job for the athlete and the coach. The basic means for this is hurdling exercise. Their multiple repetition is essential for every training session. The variety of exercises creates a great variation in their application.

Walk Overs

This drill corresponds very closely to the walking sprint drill. The method is very much the same. The athlete performs the full hurdling skill at a waling pace over low hurdles set at 1m to 1.5m spacings. Walk over drills can be used as the preliminary exercise in teaching hurdling or as the first exercise in a hurdles skill session.

Trail Leg Isolation Drill

This particular drill is designed to work only the trailing leg. Hurdles should be placed from 3 to 4m apart and initially should be lower than normal race height. The athlete should first perform the exercise by walking down the side of the flight of hurdles taking the trailing leg over the hurdle. The lead leg must go past the line of the hurdle before the trail leg is used. Once the drill has been mastered at a walking pace, the speed should be increased. The drill can be done using three strides or one stride between close spaced hurdles or by using five strides between normally spaced hurdles.

Isolation Drill

These drills are so termed because they are in isolation with certain parts of the hurdling drill. They can be used for improving hurdling technique and for teaching hurdling to small groups of beginners.

Lead Leg Isolation Drill

This drill should be performed alongside the hurdle. It is difficult to do at a walking pace. The athlete should attack the hurdle in the normal way but only take the lead leg across it. The trailing leg should trail alongside the hurdle. There should be a good range of arm movement, with the opposite arm leading the action.

Athlete is required to keep his hips high and eyes ahead at the next hurdle throughout the drill. As before this can be done by using three strides or one stride between closed spaced hurdles or five strides between normally spaced hurdles.

Drills for Improvement

Active Exercises

Active mobility exercises are those exercises in which the athlete is in total control of the movement. These can be done either through the full range of movement or in the end position. Active exercises through the full range should be done slowly and gently so as not to build up momentum and risk injury. Fast exercises through the full range will also bring in the stretch reflex and have little mobilising effect.

In the end position there are two further methods of doing active exercises. The first or static method is to hold the end position for approximately six to ten seconds. The second or kinetic method is to utilise very small gentle movements in the end position. The athlete should not bounce nor attempt to force the range of movement.

Passive Exercises

Passive mobility exercises are those in which some factor external to the athletes is in control. Passive exercises should always be done with care and only under the coach's supervision. The external factor can be pressure applied by another athlete or the coach.

Ballistic exercises can be loosely classified as being passive in the sense, that when great speed is built up the athlete is no longer in complete control. Passive exercises should only be done in the end position under the guidance and direct supervision of an experienced coach. The athlete being mobilised must first get himself to the end position before the coach begins to apply pressure.

In this end position, the coach can then apply steadily increasing pressures for six to ten seconds. The athlete must still remain in normal control and when he feels that the joint has been taken to its limit, he must tell the coach, who must stop immediately. A joint must never be forced beyond the point that the athlete feels is possible. Pressure must never be appointed quickly or sharply. Passive exercises must never be done through the full range of movement.

Progression

In general terms, active exercises maintain mobility range whilst passive exercises increase them. It is apparent, therefore, that passive exercises are only required when the athlete's mobility is insufficient for the event. During warm-up, only active exercises and some ballistic exercises are necessary. Occasionally, it may be necessary for one or two passive exercises to be included, usually for psychological reasons.

Ballistic exercises which, when done with care, are

active in nature and can very quickly become passive. They should never be done cold. If the minor injuries which are often incurred in warm-up are to be avoided the following progression should be used.

Hurdle Sitting Position

i. Athlete has to make three right angles, one between front foot and ground, one between body and ground and other between his legs;

ii. Heel of trailing leg should be tucked into the body.

Hamstring and Lower Back Stretch

Athlete should begin from hurdle sitting position then should leave over the lead leg, which he should keep straight. This mobilises the hamstrings, lower back and adductors. This drill should be used by the athlete in stages two or four.

Adductor Stretch

From hurdling sitting the athlete should attempt to place his hands on the ground beyond the trailing knee. This position can be attained by using a gentle sweeping movement from the Hamstring and Lower Back Stretch drill. This mobilises the adductors and lower back sideways. Athlete should use this drill in stages two and four.

Back-Lying

From hurdle sitting position, athlete should place his body flat to the ground. This mobilises the quads and some adduction. This drill should be done by the athlete in the second stage.

Astride Sitting

To perform this drill, athlete should keep his legs straight and chest on the ground. This mobilises the lower back, hamstrings and adductors. Athlete should use this, in second and fourth stage.

Seated Adductor Stretch

Athlete should place the soles of his feet flat together and heels pulled into the body. He should attempt to push the knees down till the outsides of the legs are on the ground. This mobilises the adductors. This drill should be used in first, second and fourth stages.

Reverse Adductor Stretch

Athlete should keep his lead leg straight and trailing leg at right angles to the body, which faces the front throughout the drill. The athlete should attempt to rotate the trailing leg till the outside of the leg is flat on the ground. This mobilises the adductors. Use in stages one, two and four. This drill should be used in first, second and fourth stage.

Sprinter's Splits

In the beginning, athlete should keep his front shin and body vertical while both feet pointing forward. He should attempt to straighten the rear leg from the starting position without raising the hips and also push back with the rear heel. This mobilises the quads, hamstrings and Achilles tending region. Athlete should use this drill in the second stage.

Hurdler's Adductor Stretch

Athlete should keep his body upright, while knee and toe of the trailing leg on the hurdle. Many athletes will have to work quite hard to achieve this position. Athlete should begin with a lower hurdle and increase the height as mobility improves. This mobilises the adductors.

Adductor and Hamstring Stretch

Athlete should begin in such a manner that his left hand grasp the left ankle and the body twists to bring the chin to the trailing knee. This can also be done by bending the body sideways instead of twisting. This increases adductor stretch and brings in a small amount of hamstring stretch of the support leg. This drill should be used in the second stage.

Hamstring and Adductor

Athlete should keep his support leg straight and attempt to bring the chin to the knee of the support leg. This mobilises the hamstring of the support leg while maintaining some adductor stretch. Athlete should use this drill in second and fourth stage.

Hamstring Stretch

The starting position of this drill is quite difficult. Athlete should begin with a lower hurdle and gradually increase its height. The heel and not the Achilles tendon of the lead leg should be on the hurdle. Both legs should be straight and the body upright. From this starting position, the athlete should attempt to put the chin down onto the knee while keep both his legs straight. This mobilises the hamstrings. This drill should be used by the athlete in second and fourth stage.

Variation on Hamstring Stretch

Athlete should perform this drill just after completing the Hamstring Stretch drill. Thus, beginning position of this drill should be end position of hamstring stretch drill. Gradually, athlete should bend his support leg while maintaining basic position. This increases the hamstring stretch of the lead leg whilst stretching the quads of the other leg and bringing in a little strength work on the support leg. This drill should not be performed by beginners. Athletes should perform this at second stage.

Passive Hamstring Stretch

The athlete should reach the active end position before going to begin the passive work. The toe should be cocked, i.e., pulled back towards the head and not pointed. The mobiliser should place his shoulder at the back of the athlete's ankle and his hands around the knee. The leg should be kept straight and pressure should gradually exerted to take the foot further down over the his head. This stretches the hamstrings. Athlete should use this drill at fourth stage.

Athlete should keep in his mind that a far greater range can be achieved by using passive mobilising, but great care should be used when doing any passive exercise.

Forward Leg Swinging

Athlete should swing his leg forward and backward. The extension behind the body should be greater. He should keep his body upright and leg straight throughout the drill. Athlete should perform this drill on adductors and on hamstring in third stage only.

Leg Press

i. For any hurdler, this exercise is preferred to any form of squatting as it places no loading on the back;

ii. Athlete should begin by keeping his feet flat on the plate at an angle of around 90° while hands firmly grasping handles;

iii. He should finish the drill with seats still in contact with the chair, legs straight and toes pointed to bring in calf muscles.

Leg Extension

i. In the beginning, athlete should keep his body upright;

ii. He should keep his legs fully extended;

iii. Little or no body rock-back;

Athlete is advised to perform this drill fast up and

controlled down.

Chinnies

i. From back-lying, the athlete should perform a sit-up and at the same time rapidly bring the knee near the chest. The body should also twist slightly towards that knee;

ii. his knee should make contact with the chest.

Leg Biceps Curl

i. This drill is considered the reverse of Leg Extension Drill. In this drill, athlete face down on the bench with the heels under the top bar;

ii. From this position of full extension, he should bent his legs at the knee to attempt to bring the heels to the buttocks;

iii. Athlete should not raise his hips off the bench;

iv. Then, he should perform the fast flexion and slow extension.

Sit-Ups

i. Sit-ups are a simpler version of chinnies and can be done in several ways:

—with feet free and hands behind head; and

—with feet free and knees bent to 90°;

—with feet anchored and hands behind head;

—with feet anchored and arms folded on chest;

—on an incline with weight held behind the head.

—on an incline with feet anchored; and

ii. athlete should use his waist while performing the sit-ups.

Bench Press

i. Athlete should perform this drill while keeping his

head and shoulders on the bench;

ii. He should keep his feet apart and place them firmly on the floor;

iii. While attaining the standing position, he should bent his arms below 90°. If free weights were used, the bar should touch his chest;

iv. Till arms lock, he should press the bar straight up.

LOW HURDLES

Hurdle races of beyond 120 yards are termed as Low Hurdles. This kind of event became popular in few countries of the world some of which were America, Sweden and France. It was in 1900 in which for the first time that the event of such distance was included in the Olympics. At that time, three races of distance of 110, 200 and 400 metres were used. Again, in 1904, this was a part of various events included in the Olympic. In 1908, this event was included, but distance changed to 110 and 400 metre. In 1912, its measurement was 110 metres only and again in 1920, its height was 110 and 400 metres.

English Amateur Field Events Association promoted a 220 yards hurdles in 1911, and 1912 however in 1913, a 440-yards hurdle was introduced. Later in 1914, A.A.A. included this event in their own championships. In 1919, this event was not taken in the event, however again in 1920, it was included in the championship.

Ten flights of 3 ft. hurdles are included in 220s yards. In this at a distance of 20 yards from the scratch line, first flight is set up, between the flights, twenty yards exists, and there exists a gap of 20 yards between winning post and the last flight.

Hurdles should be train for both the hurdles, i.e., 120 yards high and 220 yards low hurdles. The technique while working on this barrier and the high hurdle is quite the same, however, the only difference lies in clearing the bar. Amount of endurance is required more in the longer races. Athlete should know how to take the low hurdles in the stride.

Coach should keep his eye on the performance of hurdler and while training check two important points which are:

-The building up of sufficient strength and staying power to carry the athlete through; and

-Teaching him the trick of covering enough distance in crossing the hurdle and in taking the correct number of strides between each flight. Over the hurdles, athlete should show perfection of form. In the beginning, player should try to limit his work to run over three hurdles and should attempts to attain a seven stride method between flights and over an obstacle, to contrive a thirteen ft. stride.

It can be said that athlete has got to work up to cover 47ft. in seven strides and a 13ft. stride on the rise and fall over hurdles. Nine strides between flights are permissible at first, but the athlete must always have in mind his main object of ultimately working up to the seven-stride method, because a good seven-strider will always beat a good nine-strider.

While coaching for both 120 and 220 yards hurdles, firstly coach should master the style over high hurdles, work low hurdles practice into the schedule, and increasing the distance in his track work. To hold the form and keep to the seven stride method over the last three fences of a hard run race, he must possess the stamina.

In case of quarter-mile hurdle race, ten 3ft. hurdles should be set up at a distance of 50 yards from the scratch mark, 40 yards apart the flight and 30 yard should be the distance between the last hurdle to the winning post.

The aim of the coach should be to cover the distance between flights in 13 strides, but may at first, particularly if he is short in the leg, take fifteen strides for the intermediate runs. Moreover, this training must be designed with an object of building up the greatest possible faculty of endurance, and he should tell the athletes to perform with accuracy.

In both the longer races over low hurdles, it is the fight for the lead, over the last three hurdles which weed out the unfit and although the hurdles, are low, falls are far more frequent in the longer races. With increase in the distance between flight, athlete has to increase his speed of running.

400M HURDLES

Start

A modified medium start is being used for the 400m hurdle. To the first hurdle, top class male hurdlers take 20 to 21 strides, whereas female hurdlers take 24 strides. The lead leg should be placed in front block if an odd number of stride is taken, on the contrary, if an even number of strides is used the take-off leg is placed in the front block.

In all forms of bend running, the athlete should stay far from inside of the lane. To ensure a good fit of the stride pattern to the first hurdle, he can make alterations in his position. Athlete should begin with the other foot forward in the blocks if the wind conditions are not favourable.

Similarity in Technique

There is not a lot of difference between sprint hurdler and the 400 m hurdler's technique. Body will be more upright because the hurdles are low. For success in this event, hurdler should distribute his effort equally, for which athlete should keep himself always relaxed. Down over the hurdles, he cannot afford to use up energy snapping.

Stride Patterns

Spatial Awareness is necessary for performing successfully in 400m hurdling. Athlete should be able to know relating to a hurdle while he is still some distance away from it. By this, his stride will become proper.

It is found that speed of hurdlers often decreases while approaching to the hurdle, which is because of the reason that while doing this, last few strides get chopped. If athlete's speed has decreased, he should regain it before crossing the hurdle. Hurdler should keep himself working speedily. Chopping for a hurdler is not desirable as it causes decrease in his speed as well as well loss in his physical energy. Thus, it can be said that while performing this event, hurdler's run should be smooth and without any obstructions.

Rules

Standard distances are:—

For Men and Boys: 110m, 400m

For Women and Girls: 100m, 400m

There shall be ten flights of hurdles in each lane, set out in accordance with the following.

Women and Girls

For races of 100m distance

Distance from start line to first hurdle 13m

Distance between Hurdles 8.5m

Distance from last Hurdle to finish line 10.5 m

For races of 400m distance

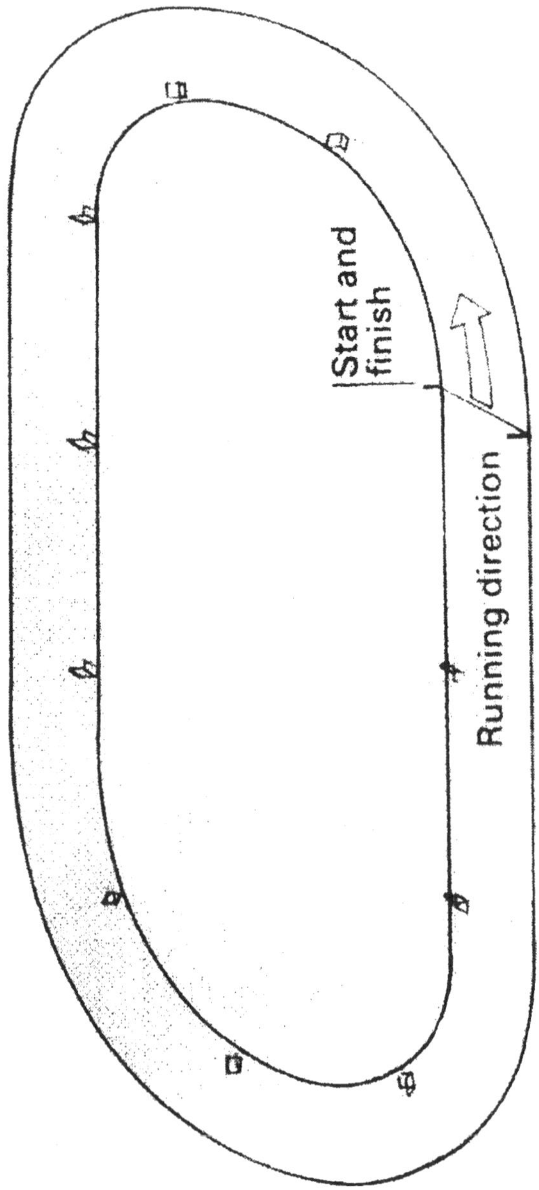
Start and finish
Running direction

a. Distance from start line to first Hurdle 45m

b. Distance between Hurdles 35m

c. Distance from last Hurdle to finish line 40m

For Men and Boys

For races of 110m distance

Distance from start line to between first Hurdle Hurdles 13.72m

1 Distance last Hurdle to finish line. = 9.14m

Distance from = 14.02m

For races of 400m distance

Distance from start line to between first Hurdle Hurdles 45m

Distance last Hurdle to finish line 35m

Distance from 40m

On the track hurdles should be placed in such a way that the feet of the competitor should be on the side of the approach and the edge of bar nearest to the approaching hurdler should coincides with track marking nearest the athlete.

Constructing the Hurdle

There is not any particular metal which is used to construct the hurdle or in other words any metal or any material can be used to construct the hurdle and top bar of it can be of wood or any other suitable material. To support rectangular frame there should be 2 feet and 2 uprights reinforced by one or more cross bars which should be fixed at end of each base, and it should be design in such a manner that to overturn it weight of at least 3.6kg has to be applied to the centre of the top edge.

APPROVE HURDLE (110m H.)

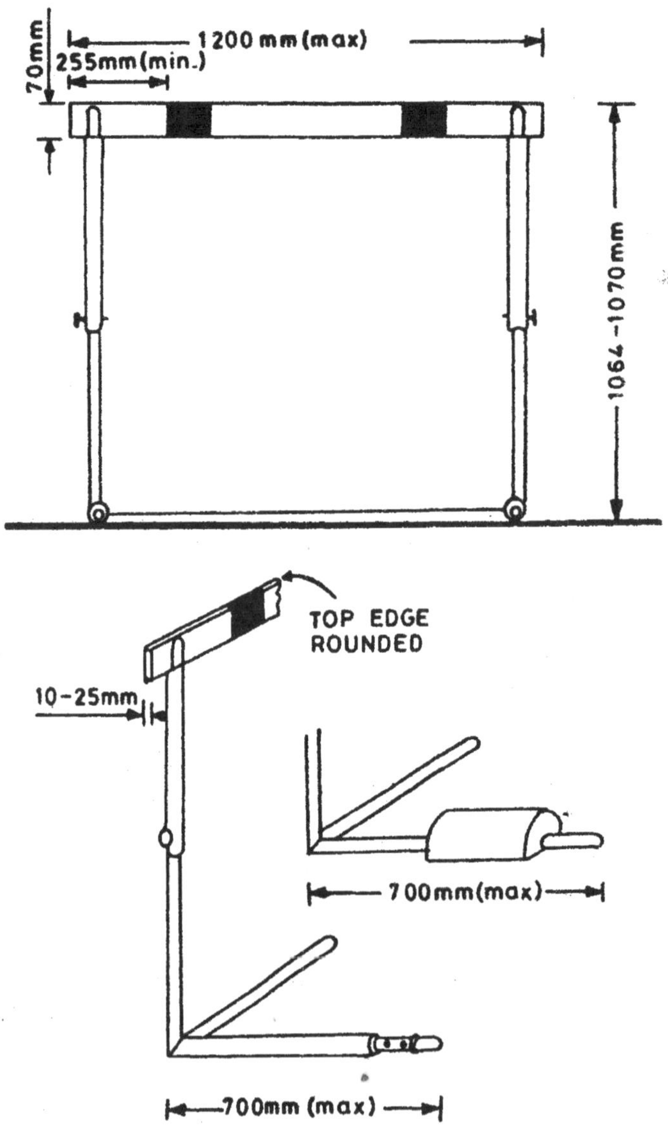

The hurdle and the counterweights should be adjustable so that at each height at least a weight of 3.6kg but not more than 4kg can be use to overturn it. Hurdle can be 1.18m to 1.20m wide and 70cm in length, but its weight should not be less than 10kg. However, there may be some change upto 3mm above or below the standard height because of manufacturing reasons.

-White and black stripes should be used to paint top bars or any distinctive contrasting colours can be used.

-Top bar should be 7cm wide. The thickness of this bar should be between 1cm and 2.5cm, and the top edges should be rounded.

-In all races a competitor has to keep his own lane throughout the event.

-A competitor may be disqualified if he trails his foot or leg below the horizontal plane of the top of any hurdle at the instant of clearance, or jumps any hurdle not in his own lane, or in the opinion of the Referee deliberately knocks down any hurdle by hand or foot.

The hurdles shall be made of metal or some other suitable material with the top bar of wood or other suitable material. They shall consist of two feet and two uprights supporting a rectangular frame, reinforced by one or more cross bars, the uprights to be fixed at the extreme end of each base. The hurdle shall be of such a design that a force at least equal to the weight of 3.6kg applied to the centre of the top edge of the top bar is required to overturn it. The hurdle may be adjustable in height for each event. The counterweights shall be adjustable so that at each height a force at least equal to the weight of 3.6kg and not more than 4kg is required to overturn it.

The width of the hurdles shall be from 1.18m to 1.20m. The maximum length of the base shall be 70cm The total weight of the hurdles shall be not less than 10kg.

In each case there shall be a tolerance allowance of 3mm, above and below the standard heights, to allow for variation in the manufacture.

Important Terminology

Start

For all races run wholly or partly in lanes the start shall be so staggered that the distance from start to finish shall be the same for each competitor, and for all races which are not run in lanes the starting line shall be curved so that wherever it occurs on the track all the runners can cover the same distance in the race.

In 400m race the starter in his own language gives the command, "on your marks" and "set", and in all longer races "on your marks" command. When the competitors are all steady in position the pistol is fired.

Distances

From the edge of the starting line farthest from the finish to the edge of the finish line nearest the start the distance for race is measured.

Heats

Heats or rounds are held when there are too many competitors for a satisfactory single round competition. Except in some circumstances any competitor cannot participate in a heat in which his names does not appear in the program.

Starting Blocks

In races up to and including 400m the starting blocks may be used. They must be constructed entirely of rigid materials. They must be adjustable but should be without springs or any other device whereby the athlete might obtain artificial assistance. Athletes in the "set" position must have both hands in contact with the track.

Lanes

Races shorter than 800m are run completely in lanes. Also run in lanes are the first bend of the 800m and the first three turns of the 4×400m relay.

Lanes are decided by lot. Any competitor who leaves his land shall be disqualified from the game. However, this rule does not apply to the following mentioned cases:

If in these cases competitor does not gain advantage or obstruct another competitor:

a. if a competitor runs out of his land in a straight;

b. if a competitor is forced out of his lane; or

c. if a competitor runs outside the outer line.

Shoes

Shoes having maximum of eleven spikes in the sole are worn.

Pistol

In order to start a race a pistol or similar apparatus is fired upward into the air.

Assistance

No person except an official timekeeper shall indicate intermediate times to a competitor. Coaching may be given to the competitors from the spectating area but no any other assistance is allowed.

Obstruction

Referee may disqualify the competitor who jostles, runs across, or obstructs another competitor on track. After this a referee may order the race to be re-run or permit any affected competitor to compete in next round.

Timing

Times are taken from the flash of the pistol to the moment where the competitor's torso reaches the finish. Fully automatic timekeeping equipment is used for the Olympic Games and most other major meetings, otherwise timing is by timekeepers using stopwatches is used.

Longer races are timed to 1/5 sec, but recorded as multiples of 2/10 sec. Fully automatic electric times shall be regarded as the official time and are timed to 1/100 sec.

The Finish

Competitors are placed in the order in which any part of their torso reaches the vertical plane of the edge of the finish line nearest to the start.

Ties

In case of tie for first place in a finale race the referee if think practicable may decide to re-start the game. If a tie in a heat affects qualification for the next round, the tying competitors run again, if it is impracticable for both to qualify. All other tied results stand.

False Start

A start becomes a false start if a competitor:

i. start before the pistol is fired;

ii. fails after a reasonable time to comply with the command "set"; or

Competitors are recalled by a pistol shot after a false start. The competitors responsible must be warned. In case of decathlon competitors are disqualified after causing two false starts and in heptathlon after three false starts.

SPRINTING

The competitive play of every civilization has an important place for racing short distances. This is a fact which is revealed by the literature of every people. Evidence shows that in ancient Greek Olympics, this kind of event possess much important place. It was till the fourteenth officially recorded Olympiad that the *stade* race covered one length of the stadium, which varied in distance from 192 to 210 metres. On the programme, it was the only running event. In modern times, the threat of physical punishment is not known.

To an accurate degree, the style of ancient sprinters are portrayed on Greek vases, according to which, the runners were well upon their toes, used to keep their body erect and knees raised.

During the entire 19th century, professional racing became very popular in England which gave birth to sprint races.

Professionals were the source of all the methods of management during the early years of American Amateur Athletic Sport. Because of lack of open competitions, running was limited, while the distance was about one yards or ten miles. In these match races, as there were but two starters, the method of getting away were more primitive than at present and had been cunningly devised by veteran professionals to give the expert an advantage over the novice.

Different kinds of styles were used, one of which was Break Start. In this method, judge used to stand on the starting line, the men went back fifteen or twenty paces, stood side by side, joined fingers lightly and trotted up to the judge. As they passed on either side of him, his body broke the touch of their fingers and they dashed away at full speed. If according to judge, the start is right, he did not say anything, but if he thought that any athlete has done incorrectly, he recalled him in order to avoid any kind of unfair advantage. The cunning of professional runners had devised methods of outwitting inexperienced opponents. Some steps away from the judge the expert would slacken his trot and the other almost invariably would do the same. Expert would quick as soon as he reached the judge. Because it required some fraction of a second for the other to follow this example, the men would pass the judge almost exactly abreast, the expert more than likely a few inches in the rear, but he would be running, while the other was only trotting. Thus, the benefit of two or three yards in first twenty five yards of the race is being provided.

Another method or style used in that time was Mutual Consent. In this method, a line was drawn across the track about fifteen or twenty feet starting scratch. Between these lines, athletes were placed. While standing there, athletes had to begin by their mutual consent. Whenever two men touched the ground in front of starting scratch at the same time with any part of their persons, they were considered to have begun. This was an amusing kind of event. Between the lines, men stood facing each other, up to the starting mark sideways, pranced, and man standing ahead used to put his foot down over the mark. Other man had to follow his action. If the second man started, they were considered to have been started with first man a foot or two in front, however, if he is not followed by the second man, orders were given to the first man to go back for a fresh trial.

Over an hour, starts of this kind were lasted. However, possibilities of this increases if one of runners was not anxious for a race. Thus, this system was very time consuming because of which everybody felt need to bring some changes in this method. For which, this system was modified by inserting in the articles of agreement, a clause substantially as follows Start by mutual consent, if not off inside an hour, then to start by pistol.

These professional used to travel and prowl in pairs, one going first to a town , where he used to secure some kind of job, exhibiting his proficiency as a runner to a select few, and at last made a match with and beating the local champion. Then everybody would came to know about the teacher or coach through winner. Negotiations would be opened with the stranger and a match arranged.

Persons winning in the first race desired to double their gains, this interest of people arose in this event. Partners used to go from one place to another with different names and identities. If, after beating the local champions in races under ordinary conditions, any money still remained in sight, the professionals tried to secure it by offering contests on novel terms, and with such conditions as seemed to the uninitiated, foolhardy and sure to lose.

Many methods to start were used, one of which was Lying Down. In this method, player used to stand in his usual position whereas on his back, professional lie flat while keeping his head at the scratch and his feet pointing away from the finish. With the pistol shot, race used to begin. However, this method proved not very successful, because as soon as the pistol was fired, professional turned on his face, rose to his hands and feet and found himself in attitude which is now being adopted by present day sprinters. This preliminary movement cost the professional about half a second, or five yards, and as this was about half the handicap, he could beat the novice in 100 yards. He usually caught his man near the seventy-fifth yard mark.

It seems rather evident how such experiments in starting would naturally lead to the trial of a crouch start. However it was not until 1887 that this method of beginning became much popular.

Earlier, the stand up starters used the Dab. In this method, on their forward foot, they kept their body weight in a well balancing manner. They used to bring their same arm forward. With the forward foot, a very short and fast dab was taken simultaneously while the in the forward direction, opposite arm was swung.

To achieve greater acceleration, quicker movement of the front foot was used. However, in later years, it was found that this policy or such doing was wrong. From then, the initial push in stand-up starting came from the back leg, and a normal arm swing was used.

In modern track history, technique of correct body, leg and arm position while making the crouch start developed very soon. It was in 1920 that an athlete placed his front foot about 17 to 19 inches back from starting line and his back foot around 10 to 12 inches behind the front line. However, this method did not gain much popularity because critics said that it led to the sprinter at a distance from the starting line. However on the basis of various experiments, this technique was declared to be the most fastest way of clearing the starting blocks. Orthodox start with the back knee at some point between the toe and the arch of the opposite foot is considered to be the best.

No evidence or sequence of development forms of sprinting is available, because sprinting is a natural and simple activity that can be present without any specialized coaching. In the same way, there is not any particular pathway of development of technique of finishing. Charley Paddock, who is considered to be the world's fastest human during the period of 1920s, used a full jump at the finish. There are many other techniques used while finish, one of which was the Lunge Finish. In this method, sprinter used to throw his body in forward direction and chest out and arms forward and backward.

Another method was originated which was named the Shrug, in which sprinter had to throw the side.of his body into the string with one hand held high, and the other keeping back behind the body.

Introduction

All the races in which an athlete has to run with his full speed over the whole distance, are generally categorised as Sprint Races. The maximum distance of run in such event is 300 yards. Usually the 100-yard and 220-yard dashes are included in the outdoor meets, while on the indoor programs, the distance of 40, 50, 60, 70 and 80 yards are organised. Indoor distance is greatly affected by the space available.

100 metre and 200 metre races are the two important sprint races included in the Olympic Games. Today, there is no dearth of students for the sprint events, the reasons of this can be the simplicity and of the event or it can be the universality of running.

The universality of running and the apparent simplicity of sprinting requirements are no doubt responsible for the fact that there is usually no dearth of candidates for the sprint events. One might think that a person who can run faster can become a good sprinter, but this event involves so much complicated techniques which makes this quitc difficult and valuable.

Many evidence have shown that in the early contests, 220-yard dash is now run more than three seconds faster. As a race category, this involves all distances upto 400m, while race of 400 m is considered the long sprint. Races having more distance than 400m are not included in this event, as they becomes the part of other event called the middle distance running.

The technique of sprinting is required in all the races, with an exception of marathon. Thus, any person who want to become any kind of runner should possess the knowledge of this event first. In case of short sprints, the source of sprinters's energy is what he has stored in himself. With increase in the distance, demand on the athlete's anaerobic capacity also increases.

To become good sprinter, one should possess the qualities of fast reacting, good acceleration and running in an effective manner. Sprinter is required to develop maximum speed and maintain it for a longer time. This is the reason that a sprinter's training sessions generally begins with drills which help in generation in himself the power and technique.

When competitive season seems close, sprinter should switch to quality high speed sprinting and reduce the power and sprint endurance training. Now in this session, athlete should sprint with maximum speed without any trouble and with utmost ease. The sprinter who has not much time to prepare should perform such drills which help in improving the basic sprinting techniques in him and make him sprint speedily.

Essential for Sprinters

We cannot classify any kind of particular criterion for sprinters, but on the basis of top class sprinters, we can give some idea of physical and mental capabilities of the sprinter. Top flight sprinters are seldom found who weigh less than 130 pounds or more than 170 pounds. Their normal height ranges from 5'7" to 6'3". Drive power is very important for fast sprinting, thus it really does not matter whether the sprinter has short muscle length or long muscle length.

PHYSICAL QUALIFICATION

As has been explained earlier that all the athletes cannot become successful sprinters by merely possessing the quality of running fast. To become successful sprinters, one should possess some extra qualities which are as follows:

-short reflex time,

-short reaction time,

-pure dominance,

-strong power of inhibition, and

-motor mindedness.

-Reilex Time

It is believed that fast start is conducive to a fast race, thus in this way, the sprinter having a short reflex time is always at an advantage. This implies that an athlete having a short reflex time is always benefited before his slower opponent is off his marks. It is found by many measurements that sprinters should have a short reflex time, as it helps them in performing successfully.

-Reaction Time

Because many of the adjustment required of a sprinter are voluntary in nature, the athlete who can make them quickly and efficiently is at a distinct advantage. Sprinting ability and reaction time are highly correlated with each other.

Dominance

Preference to the one side of the body is given while manual acts are performed. Dominance is an inherited character. Right dominant is the name given to those persons who give lead performance to the right side of their body, on the same way left dominant are those who show preference to their left side. There are some person who do not fall in both these categories, i.e., who do not show any kind of preference to their body are called lack dominance.

The difference which exists between these kind of athletes is that the left dominant individual places their left foot back while right dominant athlete places their right foot back while leaving the marks. However, both these kinds of individuals perform the same sequence of movements.

Reversing the feet at the beginning of a race causes an interference in coordination while getting into the first stride. It is believed that the loss in time in getting into stride is overbalanced by the benefit which is the result of changing the number of strides.

Motor Mindedness

If with experience athlete is able to perform the various skills of the event quickly and with comparatively ease, it should be considered that athlete's level is improving and in this way, a progress is seen in his performance. This thing is the evidence of his becoming master in the techniques of event.

While starting off, sprinter should not only emphasize on starting, but also on the sound of gun shot. If the sprinter starts of any other sound than shot of gun, it will be concluded that he is not giving attention to the gun shot but only in starting. Thus, he should be able to keep in his mind that he has to start only with the shot of gun and not with any other sound.

Inhibition

The concentration of the athlete should be on the his

task in the event. In this context it can said that a good sprinter, while performing should continuously concentrate on performing well. He should not give any kind of importance or not to take in his consideration any sound or any comments which are generally given by the audience. By giving attention to such comments, his performance affect to a great extent.

Skills and Techniques

This event has an important characteristic which attract the most of the people towards it. Mere a sheer blinding speed makes top class sprinters. No important is given to the quality of the performance, but the speed of the athlete. This is the main reason which have made the event popular throughout the world.

It is believed that the qualities needed for sprinters are present in a human body right from his birth. These qualities cannot be generated, but are god gifted. To some extent this statement is true. In a sprinter's career, natural abilities play a vital role, however there are various examples of exceptions of this also.

In reality, there is not any particular formula for success. Top class sprinters use the same equipment as others use. The only positive or effective factor which they possess is the hard work they do. The continuous practice of skills and techniques of the event give so much good results that make an athlete top class or world class.

START

It is believed that start is the basis on which the performance of an athlete depends. If start of an athlete is good, it is believed that his whole performance will be excellent. For a long time a lot of work was done to find the ways for decreasing the starting time of the sprinter. Some fifty years ago, it was found that this objective can be achieved by adopting the crouch.

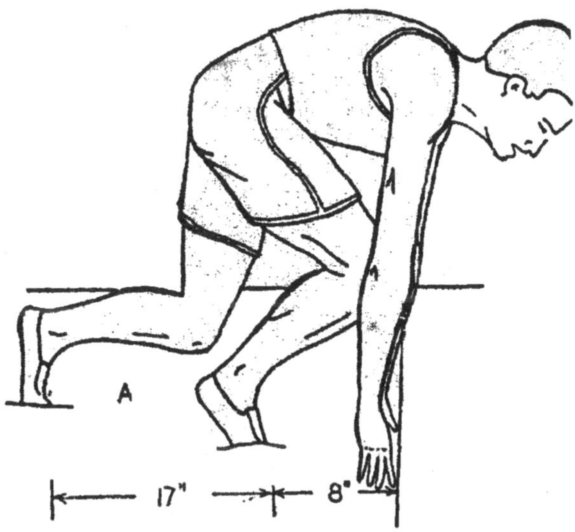

Without any doubt, start is the most practised part of a sprinter's training schedule. It started as soon as the athlete receives the first command of his coach. The first command or order athlete will receive from his coach will be to remove all his outer garments and take the tracksuit. The next order he will receive from the coach will be to stand 3 m behind the line. Before receiving the command of On Your Marks, athlete can make any kind of adjustment in his socks, dress, or can prepare himself in all the ways.

On receiving the command On Your Marks, all the athletes should walk forward and together should go down. This is the condition where gamesmanship in the athletes rise because only one athlete is allowed to stand up while all the others have to remain down. One should not make himself upset, because by doing this, you are putting off not any other, but only yourself.

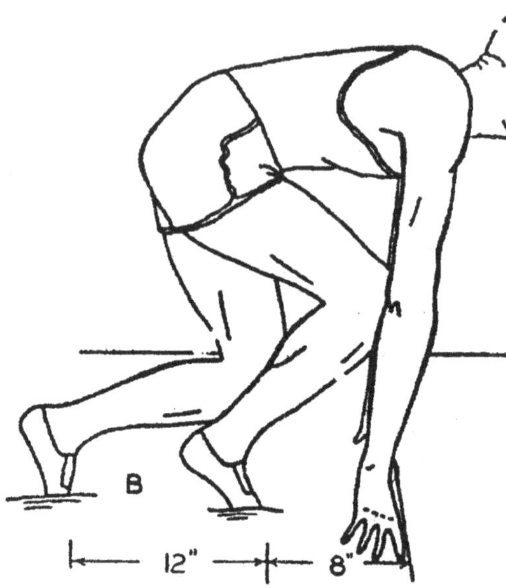

Acceleration of body mass with maximum efficiency is the main oojective of sprint starting, and the athlete receive this power to accelerate the body mass, from his legs. Athlete is not allowed to dissipate this generated power.

To accelerate the body, athlete should operate his legs in such a manner that it work behind the mass of body. Athlete should tilted his body in forward direction. He should take such a starting position that with the sound of gun, his legs give the force to whole body to drive down the track.

On receiving the command of On Your Marks, athlete should walk forward from behind the assembly line to a point which situates ahead of the block. Immediately, he should put his hands on the track and then back against the block faces. He is advised to make adjustment in his first foot prior to rear. He should make confirm that spikes have fitted into cut away sections of the block. Behind the line, hands should be kept. While doing this, all his fingers should remain together and should be turning in outward direction. Fingers should make a high bridge with the thumbs which should be turned inwards just behind the line. He should keep both his arms straight and parallel to each other. His shoulders should remain as high as possible over the hands. With the trunk, head should be in natural alignment. His eyes should be fixed on the track.

Thus, it can be said that while receiving the very first command, athlete's position should be like this:

-from the line, his front foot should be between 16 to 24 inches;

-behind the front foot, back foot should be around 16 inches;

-over the hands, shoulders should be vertical;

-The fingers which are 'up to but not touching' the line form a high bridge.

-with the body, head should be in natural alignment. About one metre down the track, eyes should be focused. Athlete should not look at the finishing line;

-hands should be slightly more than shoulder width apart;

-by the fingers, high bridge formed;

-to right of the front foot, rear knee is about at a distance of three inches.

In this way, athlete is positioned in such a way that his body weight is shift to the thumb and fingers. However, this is not the particular and only way a sprinter can start. There are some sprinters who transfer their weight only on their thumb and on second joint of the finger, while some others throw their weight on thumb and knuckles. Thus, it can be said that the important and only factor is the comfort. Athlete will take only that position in which he feels comfortable.

Any position an athlete can take, but he should kept in his mind that his hands should not be in front of the scratch line.

While receiving the command of On The Marks, athlete's arms should be extended to the full extent but should not be flexed at the elbow. They should be far enough apart to insure free knee action in getting "set". Sprinter is advised to take such a position in which he feels comfortable. His should be in a well balanced state.

To inform the athlete to move up into a steady position is the objective of Set command. Starters should be placed in such a manner that they can easily keep a check on every athlete and see if every athlete is rock steadily while gun is being fired.

It is advisable for the sprinters to move into their Set Position and try to hold this position for some time. This is very important drill or exercise because a poor or bad set position can ruin their whole performance.

While receiving the command of Set, athlete is advised to raise his seat in a controlled movement in order to open his legs to angle of about 90 degree at front knee and 120 degree at rear knee. Very slightly, he should move his trunk, however, not like lower shoulder. Fingers and thumbs will bear more strain, although he should put his legs in such a manner that more power can be generated.

In case of normal medium spaced start, opening the legs out to the above mentioned angles will need a position of the seat which is a fraction higher than the shoulders. However, there is an disadvantage of this position. At the time of firing of the gun, shoulders of the athlete should be lifted into line of drive.

It is not very difficult to obtain a position in which

seat and shoulders are in equal line, but it will bring the legs near to each other and the angle between them will decrease. Athlete can move the feet further back and keep the angles at the knees, but in this position, when the gun fires and the hands are removed from the track, the result is usually disastrous. To avoid this, feet of the athlete should remain in a medium spacing and should be placed sensibly. This allows the seat to be just a shade higher and over the shoulders.

After athlete has obtain the correct angle of front knee and in relation to trunk has properly positioned it, automatically his rear leg will make an angle of about 120 degree while spacing of 15-16 inch 38-41 cms is used. There are some athletes who think that they cannot in this position apply pressure against the back block and slight adjustments must be made so that they can feel the pressure of the foot against the block. On this back foot, there should be no supporting weight, however against the block face, there must be a definite pressure.

As it is not easy to drive effectively with an already straight knee and there would be a time lag after the gun had fired in order to flex it, thus athlete should not keep his rear leg straight.

In the Set position, athlete should keep a natural alignment with his torso, and there should be not any kind of tension in his neck muscles. On this command, it is essential for the athlete to inhale deeply. This action helps make him steady and he can concentrate on the action of start. Start action should be a power explosion action with forward drive against both block faces.

To start effectively, athlete is advised to focus his attention on his action rather than on the sound of the gun. Athlete's sudden reaction to gun's sound shows itself a short backward action in heel of the rear foot. This is considered the first movement made by the sprinter before clearing the hands and rear foot from the track and is caused by the release of the inhibiting muscles.

Position of the Head and Eyes

Sprinter should look downward the track while receiving the command of Set. If sprinter begins from a state in which his trunk is parallel with track, without cramping the track, he will found some distance. The distance of vision will be decreased if he employ the high hip position.

To guide the direction of the body, sprinter should raise his head high so that he can see far enough. Once he has started the run, he should fix his eyes on the direction in which he has to run. If he focus his attention on the people or activities going around himself, he can lose his balance. With the help of peripheral vision and sound, sprinter should be provided with important and required information.

The Position of Hips

Kind of foot spacing employed by the athlete is the main factor on which the height to which he elevates the hips in relation to shoulders depends. It is believed that in shorter longitudinal spacing, hips elevated increases.

In case of Bunch Start, hips remain about 25° above the shoulders. For medium start and elongated position, this angle decreases. Higher hip position is recommenced by experts.

Position of the Trunk

While the sprinter is waiting for the command of Get Set, he can change his body position. Now, he can obtain that position in which centre of weight is well in front of it, rather than in behind. Kind of foot spacing employed and forward tilt of the trunk are two important factors on which this position depends.

Basically, to which height the hips should be raised to the set position, depends on the comfort and efficiency of the sprinter. If the trunk is tilted to its backward limit, there is but little weight on the arms, and, when the command Get set is given, the sprinter must move his trunk forward and upward. Sprinter is conscious of strain on his arms and hands if his body position is too far forward.

Than the longer foot spacing, a short foot spacing is more conducive to extreme forward trunk. Degree of trunk tilt is very much affected by the amount of leg bend and hip elevation. The back leg is likely to be straight, if the forward lean is very extreme.

An On the Marks position which permits the sprinter to get Set merely by raising the hips is most desirable.

Thus in relation to Set Position of the sprinter, following are the important guidelines:

-At the front knee, angle should be about 90°;

-an angle of about 120° should be made at the rear knee;

-above the shoulders, hips should be positioned;

-slightly ahead of the hands, shoulder should be;

-with the body, head should be in natural alignment;

-one metre down the track, eyes of the sprinter should be focused.

The Response to the Gun

We cannot expect from a beginner to properly respond to the sound of the gun. This is with experience that he learn how to respond the shot of run properly. Sprinter capable of responding the gun without any thinking is said be motor minded, whereas athlete who first think after receiving the sound of gun is called Sensory Minded. Such kind of persons just waste their precious time in doing this.

After attaining the set position, sprinter should be always ready to go any instant. The interval which the athlete is held in set position is in hands of the official.

A sprinter who is mentally as well as physically poised can be likened to powder in shell which is going to be fired. As soon as spark come in contact with the powder, it explodes with great force and with the shot of gun, energy of sprinter automatically explode and with a vicious drive, he springs in forward direction.

While receiving the command of Go, sprinter should be in such a position:

-The arm drives backwards

-Head remains steady

-The leg drives, and the first stride should come through low and fast. The action should resemble an aeroplane taking off.

While leaving his marks, sprinter should be able to execute a vicious drive with his legs. On spacing of the feet, amount of force exerted and distributed of this force depends. Greatest drive is executed but the front foot when the feet are nearer to each other.

Equal force is exerted by the legs when the foot spacing increases. Legs exerted the equal force in case of Medium Start. As the foot spacing is increased still further, the force exerted by the back leg exceeds that applied by the front. Force applied by front leg is not effected by foot spacing in any way. With increase in space between the feet, force exerted by back leg also increases.

An average sprinter exerts a force of 195 pounds with his front foot. With the back foot he exerts a pressure of about 150 pounds, when the feet are near or closer to each other. Pressure exerted by back foot increases with increase in foot spacing.

On-the dominance, the sequence of movement which a sprinter follows while leaving his marks depends. Right dominant athlete places his right foot back. In leaving the marks, the movement pattern employed is reflex.

Left hand, right foot and left foot is the order of movement of a right dominant athlete, whereas right hand, left hand, left foot and right foot is the sequence for a left dominant sprinter. After the gun is fired, a fully trained sprinter requires about 0.3 to 0.4 second to leave his marks.

Sprinter should keep in his mind the following important points while receiving this command:

-Vigorous use of the arms through a great range.

-Fast and vigorous forward and upward drive of the right leg.

- Full extension of the left leg.

-There is virtually a straight line from the head through the body to the driving foot.

-Body is kept low.

-The head is still in natural alignment with the body. There should be no tendency to throw the head back nor to tuck the chin onto the chest.

Movement of a Sprinter

In the full sprinting action, a full range of movement should be used.

Arm Action

Behind the body, crucial part of the arm action takes place. With his arm, sprinter should try to attain a powerful drive in backward direction which should aim for high elbow. At the front of the body, hands should be lowered than the shoulders. No sprinter can get full range of leg movement without full range of arm movement.

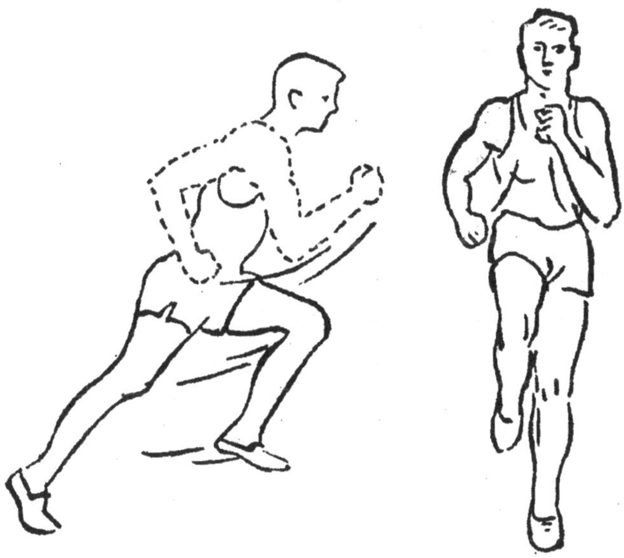

High knee lift is very important and useful for good sprinting which is being provided by rear action of the elbow. At the front position, arm will be open out slightly at the elbow as it moves backwards. As hand passes the hip, greater angle will be make, but then this angle will reduce upto 90 degree. Arms not only help to cancel out undesirable rotations resulted by the leg action but also assist the legs to do their work. The body of the athlete rotate backwards with help of vigorous forward and upward movement, which is nullified by the high rear elbow drive.

As the action of the legs is not central to the line of the spine, the sprinter's body has a tendency to rotate about its vertical axis. Much of this tendency is counter by the arm action. This can be shown by trying to run faster with hands held firmly down to sides or in the pockets. While sprinting, young athletes are found to have tension in their neck and shoulders. However, in experience athletes also this tension is found, while ending the race.

There is a concept of typing up which is the result of upper body tightness. With relaxed muscles, sprinter should learn to run. While running, athlete should keep his shoulders down instead of lifting them. In keeping upper body relaxed, a much important role is being played by the hands. They should be in the relaxed position.

To the lower arms, hands in this event should be merely appendages. Tension in hands will cause tension in the whole body the athlete. Tightness can create problem in breathing and by this much of the athlete's energy will be wasted which is important for him to run.

Leg Action

Following factors are important in relation to good sprinting action:

-completion of the drive, and

-high knee lift.

In sprinting, athlete drives his body in forward direction. Behind the body's vertical line, drive should take place. Ahead of the body, foot will land and then in forward direction should drive, when the speed of the body will have taken it over the foot before the drive can begin.

At no any other time sprinter should attempt to reach out with his foot and claw the body in forward direction. While driving, driving leg of the athlete should be fully extended behind the body. Many athletes fail to complete the drive, snatching the foot away in an attempt to get extra leg speed. While running, athlete should keep his hips high, because it helps in drive completion as it is difficult to snatch the leg off the ground too early when the hips are kept high.

<u>Finish</u>

The important factor regarding the dip is its timing. If athlete dip early, he will slow down. It is important not to stick you head out, as this has the effect of pushing the chest backwards. Technique of the athlete should be correct. One cannot practice the dip without race conditions.

There are many sprinters who lose the race because they do not know properly that when and how they have to dip. There is not any set formula or pattern which can be used by all the sprinters, but the sprinter has to understand and learn from his personal experience the right way and manner to dip.

Rules

Track Measurements

The running track shall be of 400m in length which should consist of two parallel straights and two bend lines of equal radii. If it is not a grass track there should be a boarder of suitable material which should be maximum of 5cm in height and minimum of 5cm in width. A white line of 5cm wide and by plastic cones or flags of height not less than 20cm should be placed if the kerb has to remove temporarily at intervals not more than 4m.

30cm outward from the kerb and in case of no kerb 20cm from line marking inside the track should be the place from where measurement is to be made. In all races up to and including 400m, each competitor shall have a separate lane, with a minimum width of 1.22m and a maximum width of 1.25m to be marked by lines 5cm in width.

The distance of the race shall be measured from the edge of the start line farther from the finish, to the edge of the finish line nearer to the start. Lateral inclination of tracks is allowed up to 1:100 and the overall inclination in running direction upto 1:1000 downwards.

Drainage

The nature and extent of the problem of drainage is dependent almost entirely upon local conditions of soil and weather during the track season.

Normally, full excavation of from 21 to 24 inches with rough and medium filling, as indicated later,, will take care of all requirements. Where drainage tile is required, only an engineer can decide just how much and where to put it. Since the track is built 4 feet above the infield, both the subsoil and surface layers are pitched to the inside.

Rough Fill

There is general agreement throughout the country on the use of either heavy clinkers or 3-to-4-inch stone, either crushed or in the form of gravel, for the initial coarse layer. Local conditions will determine its depth, although about 20 inches is usually considered adequate.

To hurry settling and provide an early even top surface, this layer is usually rolled thoroughly. However, such rolling is dangerous to tile and sometimes crushes coarse cinders.

Top Dressing

A mixture of 1 part clay or clay loam to 2 parts "front" or "head-end" cinders is suggested. These latter were the hard little cinder pellets that were caught by the locomotive stack screen and dropped back into the head-end of the fire box to be shovelled out at the roundhouse.

Unfortunately, the use of softer coals and the expense of saving such material has made good head-end cinders almost unavailable. Ordinary boiler cinders crush easily and either turn to dust and blow away or, worse, remain in the track to form an impervious hardpan when dry and mud when wet.

Much care should therefore be taken in selecting cinders, for they can easily negate much of the expense and care of building the track. Without doubt, American coaches should be turning to science and research for the discovery of better materials for top dressing on their running tracks. Actually, our knowledge of what is best for fast running as well as best for maintenance is quite uncertain and based almost entirely upon opinion.

In writing of Stanford's new track, the engineer, J.H. McDonald, stated that "every track in order to have a 'jarless', yet firm surface must be cushioned". The builders therefore very carefully placed 1½ inches of redwood bark 12 inches below the surface, under cinders, clay, and crushed rock, to provide a "cushion" against too solid a foundation. How really effective was this procedure? One of the virtues claimed for cinder tracks generally is that they are easier on the legs in both practice and meets than harder and less buoyant surfaces. Yet teams working on indoor wooden tracks or on the surfaces at the Chicago, Michigan State, or Purdue fieldhouses certainly have no more "shin splints" or sore muscles, and possibly fewer, than where tracks are softer and tend to give with each sprinting stride.

It seems clear that we actually know very little on this and related subjects and that careful research in the future is needed to establish the facts of the case and the best materials to use for both track and field facilities. Greater differences of opinion concerning the right materials and right proportions for top dressing were found by the 1952 Athletic Journal survey than on any other subject. The average opinion was given as 3 parts of cinders to 1 of clay, but at least a dozen alternatives were suggested, several of which had many adherents.

Proportions of 4:1, 3:1, 2:1, 1:1, 1:2, and 1:3 of cinders and clay all had their advocates. Brick dust and clay was suggested by five coaches. The addition of peat moss and sawdust was mentioned as helping to hold moisture in the track.

In the West, where oil-burning makes cinders almost nonexistent, experiments with "decomposed" granite and clay, sifted carbon with clay, decomposed lava ash, or crushed limestone have been tried and have their supporters.

Middle Layer

On top of the rough fill, it is common practice to place about 6 inches of coarse cinders such as would be retained on a ¾"-mesh screen.

Curb

Opinion is almost unanimous that concrete curbing provides the best and most permanent material. Present rules suggest a curb that rise 4 inches above the track, and common practice makes it 4 inches wide. Its depth in the ground is determined by the frost line and should be established so that no heaving during the winter months can possibly occur.

Wood that has been well creosoted has often been used, but at best it provides only a dozen years of use. Old railroad rails have also been used, but one would have difficulty in finding such material available today. Undoubtedly the most unique and spectacular of all curbing was a hollow plastic tube, with fluorescent lighting, which was used at the indoor Purdue relays.

Starting Blocks

In all races including 400m races starting block shall be used, but start line or another lane should not be overlapped by it.

Under mentioned general specification should be complied by Starting blocks:—

Own starting blocks may be used by any player but they should not interfere with other athletes. To avoid any kind of damage to track there should be a number of pints to attach it to the track. There should be provision permit quick removal of starting blocks. Quantity and quality of pins to be used depends in the manner in track is constructed and there should not be any movement during actual start.

They should be rigidly constructed and should not permit any kind of benefit to the participant. In addition to above mentioned specifications the following should also be comply when starting blocks are provided by the Organising Committee:

-There should be 2 foot plates against which in starting position athlete's feet should be pressed.

-Starting blocks should be linked to an IAAF approved false start apparatus in competitions.

In order to hear the acoustic signal clearly starter should wear headphones when the apparatus detects a false start, in other words when reaction time is less than 100/1000ths of a second. In order to confirm which athlete is responsible for false start Starter should examine immediately after recall the reaction times on false start apparatus as soon as he hear the acoustic signal.

Starting

No race can start without the gun is fired upward by the starter. "On your marks" "Set" shall be the commands of the starter in his own language in races upto and including 400m and when all competitors are "Set", the gun shall be fired or any approved apparatus.

However, In races longer than 400m, the commands

shall be "On your marks" and when all competitors are steady, the gun shall be fired, or approved starting apparatus activated. No competitor is allowed to touch the ground with his hand. For all races run in lanes the start will be denoted by a white line which is 5cm wide, whereas in races not run in lanes in order to ensure that all runners from equal distance from finish the start line shall be curved.

Starter shall order all competitors to withdraw from their marks and place them on assembly line again if for any reason he is not satisfied that all is ready for the start to proceed after the competitors are on their marks. Use of starting block and a crouch is compulsory in all races up to and including 400m including the first leg of the 4×200m and 4×400m.

Competitor should approach the start line and take his position after hearing the command of starter. He will take position in such a way that both hands and one knee shall be in contact with the ground and both feet in contact with the starting blocks.

No competitor is allowed to touch either start line or ground in front of with his hands. It is the duty of competitor to take without delay his final position after the command from starter. If within a reasonably time they do not comply with his duty it will be a false start.

Competitors can be divided into two groups if competitors are more than 12 in number, one having more than half of competitors on regular arced start line and other on a separate arced start line. The separate arced start line shall be marked in such a way that all the competitors shall run the same distance. Start will be considered to be false if a competitor commences his starting motion after assuming his full and final set position, and before the report of the gun, or approved starting apparatus.

Competitor can be disqualified from game if he commit

more than 2 false start. The track shall be marked with a mark of 5cm×5cm at the entrance to the finish straight for group starts in 1000m, 3000m and 5000m to indicate where athletes starting in the outer group may join the runners using the regular start.

Race

Running in Lanes

Each competitor shall keep within his allocated lane from start to finish in all races run in lanes. This shall also apply to any portion of a race run in lanes. A competitor can be disqualified if referee is satisfied that a competitor has run outside his lane, but a competitor shall not be disqualified if he is pushed or forced by another person to run outside his lane, and if no material advantage is gained.

Rules for Leaving the Track

A competitor is allowed to leave the track at his will but after that he cannot rejoin the field.

Obstruction on the Track

A competitor who obstructs another competitor to impede his progress can be disqualified from the event and this authority rests with the referee who can order to re-held the race in which disqualified competitor will not include.

Rules for Race if an Athlete Runs Outside His Lane or Outer Line of his Lane

In the following conditions athlete will not be disqualified from play:

a. If he runs outside his lane but not intentionally; or

b. With no material advantage he runs outside he outer line of his lane on the bend and no other runner is being obstructed by him.

Check-Marks

Competitors may not make check-marks or place objects or alongside the running track for their assistance in races except in relay races run in lanes.

The Finish

A 5cm wide line of white colour is used to denote the finish. The competitors should be placed in the order in which any part of their bodies reaches the vertical plane of the nearer edge of the finish line.

The intersection of the lanes lines and the finish line should be painted with black colour in a suitable design in order to facilitate the reading of Photo Finish Film. It is the duty of starter to fire the gun exactly one minute before from finish of race to warn competitors and judges that race is going to be finish. Chief Timekeeper will direct the Starter to signal the end of race by firing the gun.

In order to mark the exact spot where each competitor touched the track for last time before or at the time of firing of the gun some judges will be appointed for this purpose only. The distance achieved shall be measured to the nearest metre behind this mark.

RUNNING

Of various events of athletics, running is the most natural event. Before the first workout, only two important points should be stressed to the beginners. These two are keeping themselves relaxed throughout the running and keeping the body straight.

In running, it can be said that any drill and activity which makes a runner tire or put more burden on him is not proper and desirable. Like this, any activity which decreases the efficiency of a runner should not be used.

It does not implies that there is not anything else to the running technique. Coach's duty is to tell the runner these basic points and continuously keep a watch on their performance and pinpoint their faults. There is no point in coaching something individuals already do naturally. It becomes difficult for them to relax if you make them think more and more. The right approach is to continuously pinpoint their faults.

Sometimes pointing out a fault and stressing proper techniques is all that is needed, but if coach thinks that runner needs more than this, he should deal with the runner personally and find out his faults. Coach should provide the runners to run freely, without any limitation or burden.

Today, the running has become very popular event in many nations of the world, which is reflected by the fact that many national and international events are being organised throughout the world. Basically, two kinds of events are organised under this head which are:

Middle Distance Running,

Long-Distance Running.

There exist other events also, which we will mention under other headings later.

Middle Distance Running

Middle distance races include the 800-metre, 1500-metre and mile races. Long distance races include the 3000 metre steeplechase, 5000-metre, 10,000-metre, and marathon races. People of both the sexes participate in such races. For this event it can be said that a middle distance race is one in which full out effort cannot be maintained throughout the race, because the athlete has to replace the sugars from which he mainly derives his energy whilst he is still running. Those who can do this most efficiently whilst running the fastest pace are the best runners.

People generally consider the middle distance running to be the least complicated form of track and field athletics. There is no aerodynamic equipment necessary, as in the throwing events; no resorting to clandestine use of anabolic steroids in order to develop a grotesque, bulky body; no preoccupation with the technique practice as in the jumps events. In fact, it might seem that, all a distance runner needs to do to improve is simply run, run and run more. This is not the reality.

However, now the face of this event has gone to a dramatic change. Today, running event has become very important and widely popular event in the world and now its modern face is very complicated for which the runner has to learn various skills.

Endurance is considered an important and primary factor in such a kind of running. Today, this event has gained worldwide popularity and standard of performance of runners has improved considerably.

In middle distance running, the speed of the runner is reduced, his stride length becomes shorter and his body is more erect as compared to sprint racing. The foot also strikes more on the heel on landing .

There exist a difference between such running and Sprinting. In the case of Sprinting, athlete has to undergo anaerobic running, i.e., he has to run under oxygen debit, whereas in this event runner undergoes aerobic running. Runner not only use his ability to run under oxygen debt, but also has to make use of all three tempos.

There are not any particular criterions for a middle distance runners, but it can be said that they should be preferably slim in physique, and should possess the ability to run with long steps.

Skills and Techniques

The main characteristics of distance runner's technique is upright body position. In shorter distances, stride length increases whereas it decreases in races of shorter distances. While changing the speed of his running, runner can change the stride length.

Knee lift and leg drive depend upon the distance and the phase of the race. During sprinting phases, the knee lift will be high; during non-sprinting phases, knee lift is minimal. The arm action must balance that of the legs; arm action should be vigorous and powerful during the sprinting phases and moderate to minimal during the non-sprinting phases.

Training the Runners

There is a lot of difference between technique of other events and middle distance running. If an athlete can run in an economical style for once, a lot of care should be given on his body conditioning. Initially, this ability of runner improves, but with passage of time, there comes an declining in his improvement rate. To run a middle distance race well, requires practice over a long period, and in this event, there are always people to train with, as middle distance running is very popular.

It is to be kept in mind that, like all the other events, training is necessary for this event also. Athlete should not think that this event involves only running, running, and only running and they do not have need of any kind of training.

For training, athlete should keep in his mind the following important points:

-It should be regular;

-It should increase in difficulty as time goes on.

-It should be interesting and he should vary his work;

-It should be for a specific object.

-It should be kept up over a period of months.

Strength, stamina and speed are inter-related and one effects the other. It is often a question of emphasis.

Rules

Lanes

All the individual races shorter than 800 m are run completely in lanes. Also run in lanes are the first bend of the 800m and the first three units of the 4 × 400m relay. Lanes are decided by lot.

Any competitor who leaves his lane shall be disqualified, with the following three exceptions, if in these cases he does not gain advantage or obstruct another competitor:

-If a competitor runs out of his lane in a straight;

-If a competitor is forced out of his lane;

-If a competitor runs outside the outer line.

Marks may be placed on or beside the track only for relay races.

Obstruction on Track

Any competitor runner who jostles or obstructs another competition so as to impede his progress shall be liable to disqualification from that event.

If in any race a competitor is disqualified for any of these reasons, the Referee shall have the authority to order the race to be re-held excluding the disqualified competitor or, in the case of a heat, or permit any competitor affected by the act resulting in disqualification, to compete in a subsequent round of the race.

Round and Heats

Preliminary rounds shall be held in running events in which the number of competitors is too large to allow the competition to be conducted satisfactorily in a single round.

Where preliminary rounds are held, all competitors must compete in, and qualify through, all such rounds. The heats, quarter-finals and semi-finals shall be arranged by the Organising Committee together with the appointed Technical Delegates, where appropriate. After the first round, it is recommended that the competitors be placed in the heats of subsequent rounds.

A competitor shall not be allowed to compete in a heat other than the one in which his name appears, except in circumstances which, in the opinion of the Referee, just an alteration. In all preliminary rounds, at least the first and second in each heat shall qualify for the next round and it is recommended that, where possible, at least three in each heat should qualify.

A competitor after voluntarily leaving the track or course shall not be allowed to continue in the race.

Long Distance Running

As the name implies, races of long distances are included in such kind of event. Usually races having distance between 3000m to 10,000 m are included in this event. Like Middle Distance Running, people of both sexes participate in such kind of races.

On the basis of distance of the run, it is decided that which race will be done by males and which by females. In this connection it is important to mention the following facts:

In 3000m events only female competitors may participate in it.

For 5,000 m. events no female candidates can participate in it.

For 10,000m events both men and women may participate in it. In this type of running , stamina is of greater importance though speed is also essential.

In these races, athlete is required to establish his position, however, to cover the last laps and reach the final line, he is also required to conserve his energy. Runner should possess the ability to accelerate his speed.

In comparison to Middle Distance Running, in this event the need of aerobic endurance increases. To run for long distances, runner is required to have more supply of energy, for which runner's heart, lungs and circulatory system have to bear extra strain.

A long distance runner require sprint action throughout his running, which needs anaerobic endurance, which implies use of stored oxygen. For utilising the stored oxygen, runner's muscles should be strong, for which he should run at shorter distances.

The need for anaerobic endurance increases with the increase in the distance of the race. Will power of a long distance runner should be strong. Strong determination and self confidence should be his personal characteristics. Physically, he should not be very flat, but should be built slightly. If his body's size is short, it will be a positive quality for him. Slow heartbeat will increase his positive points.

Secondary muscles of a long distance runner should be strong, as this helps him in achieving his goal successfully. Long distance runners are advised to run with a particular rhythm. He should keep him rhythm constant, inspite of varying it from time to time. By this, he can run at a higher speed. However, in necessary conditions, he should be able to increase his speed.

As a long distance runner has to cover a long distance, he should be able to distribute his energy equally over the whole distance, for which can do changes in his speed. As it is a long race, some athletes feel bored or monotonous and experience tiredness. To avoid this, they are advised to change their speed.

Feeling of relaxation plays a very important and supporting role for such kind of runners. He should not waste any motion, for which his arm swing should be low. While running, he should feel no kind of burden. His arm action should not hinder his stride. He should have a comfortable stride length. They land slow on the ball of the foot. Then they drop down on the heel, and at last push off the toes.

Proper Technique of a Runner

An uneconomical technique of running must be cured by the coach, but it is stressed that there is no ideal method of running. Basically, the most important criterion is comfort.

If an athlete's natural style is mechanically inefficient, causing him to expend extra energy, then the coach will modify the style; otherwise, there need be no interference. Breathing should be through the mouth and nose, there should be no attempt to lengthen the stride, and there should be a minimum of tension especially in the face and neck muscles. Towards the end of a race, the style will necessarily change, the knees coming through higher and the arms driving more.

It is true that there is an ideal form of style for each event, however, this varies from athlete to athlete. A runner can choose his own style in which he can perform comfortably.

With age and experience style of a runner changes, however, it takes a considerable amount of time. With changes in ability of a runner to run, his style also gets changed. Even, styles of a runner for different distance run can vary, i.e., a runner will run differently in half-mile, differently in a mile and differently in two-mile distance run. There is not any particular criterion with which a proper style can be judged, however one can evaluate his style with respect to the following factors:

-Arm swing;

-Body angle;

-Foot placement;

-Rear-leg lift;

-Length of stride; and

-Over-all action.

Arm swing

While running, runner should keep his arms relaxed. The main considerations for coaches should be balance and rhythm. With speed, arm movement of the runner will increase and become more energetic. Not at any speed, runner should lost the relaxation and smoothness of his arms. For proper arm movement, a coach can give the following instructions to the runners:

-Place the thumbs and forefingers together;

-Drop the hands to side and relax them completely;

-Keeping the hands relaxed, lift the hands to a level equal or below the hips;

-Keep the angle of the forearm with the upper arm same throughout and do not swing the hands high or near the face instead, keep them relaxed and low.

-As arms of a doll might swing on a pin through the

shoulders, let the arms swing from the shoulder girdle, do not drive them and let them go of their own weight and inertia and relax;

Once a runner has successfully brought his arms in proper swinging position, he is not required to work on them more. He should drop them and shake them if they have become heavy and tired while running. For this, in the beginning, runner should perform easy and simple arm action and then perform some exercises of arms.

Body angle

Generally, with speed, body of the runner begins to lean forward. All human movement is a process of falling with balance, a constant loss and recovery of balance. Because of this, one cannot prevent the increased angle of speed running.

Runner usually faces with the problem of keeping the body straight. For this, he should keep his eyes properly on the ground. Body will come in proper angle if runner places his eyes on the ground ahead and head properly on the ground. This point on which runner will focus his eyes depends on the style of runner and the pace with which he runs.

Foot placement

Foot placement of a runner varies according to the style of running and speed and distance of run. Better utilisation of effort is the primary consideration, but where speed is increasingly important, length and springiness of stride should be carefully coached and practised.

Runner should drop the weight lightly on the heel in long distance running. Body weight of the runner will shift forward.

Length of stride

These days, many runners are using high-toed, bouncing and long-striding action of sprinters. Runner has to correct this wasteful stride. Matter of length of stride is very important and with increase in distance of race, stride will decrease.

Rear-leg lift

Now-a-days it is suggested to the runners that lift of rear lower is of no use, thus importance is being placed on full forward-reaching stride and knee lift. Runner should swing rear foot upward and backward as soon as the leg starts forward, by this, lower leg and heel swings near the upper biceps. This decreases the weight arm of the leg level and length of pendulum

Lower leg falls easily as soon as upper leg swings forward. To permit the foot to clear the ground, knee swings in forward and upward direction. Runner should not attempt to length the stride, no forward reaching or pointing of toes because this results in tension and waste of energy. This rear-leg lift is not a deliberate backward throw a kick, whereas, it is a relaxed follow-through and follow-up of push of the rear foot from the ground. Runner should specifically concentrate on relaxation, naturalness, and rhythm of the total action.

The over-all action

There is not any particular criterion for over-all action, only it should be efficient, smooth and relaxed. Runner should swing his arms and legs in a rhythm and smoothly. Basically, all the parts of the body should be in a balanced position and in a line.

Important Training for Runners (For Middle Distance and Long Distance Runners)

Basically, two kinds of training a runner should get:

-Anaerobic Training, and

-Aerobic Training.

Anaerobic Training

Such kind of training helps in improving the ability of runner's body to run under the conditions when oxygen debt. This training involves a number of short distance races at a given pace. To develop race rhythm in the athlete and to sharpen his speed, this kind of training is used.

Aerobic Training

Improving the runner's stamina is the main objective of this training. In reality, this training increases the ability of runner to take the oxygen and utilize it properly, which affect his stamina.

This kind of training consists of runs of three to ten miles, however this distance can be increased. An easy tempo involves relaxed recovery running a brisk temp involves running at steady state or oxygen balance, and running beyond steady state is involved in hard tempo.

In the beginning, easy and brisk tempo runs should be included in this kind of training.

Inspite of these training, there are other training methods which are being used today by coaches throughout the world. Some of these activities have been mentioned below. Any activity coach can use. While doing this, he should keep in his mind the objective which he has to attain from the activity.

Resistance Running

When athlete is making running difficult for him, he should use this training. All those drills which help in building the strength and endurance forms a part of this training.

Interval Training

Adapting the heart to stress of running in endurance events is the main objective of this kind of training. It is found that when middle distance runners get training over distances in region of hundred, two hundred and four hundred m, their heart become strong and around the muscles, blood pump in greater volume. Heart fills with blood after a fast run of 200 m. Amount of blood arriving at the heart decreases if athlete jogs slowly for a period of 45 seconds. Again and again athlete should repeat this sequence, however, with intervals of sprinting followed by intervals of slow jogging.

However, this method has some disadvantages. The first of which is that an athlete become too much dependent on stop watch. Some athletes think that it is a boring drill.

Fartlek

This kind of training consists of running over different types of country at different and changing speeds. Basically, the objective of this training is to improve the stamina of athlete, which is generally affected by the kind of drills included. In the beginning, proper guidance and instruction is required for the athlete, however, with experience, athlete will be able to do the drills independently and will include fast running than the slower ones.

As the speed of races in this training goes on changing, thus athlete does not feel bore while using this. A typical course might include speed running on the flat road or on the grass, jogging, through the woods, dodging quickly in and out of trees, fast walking, a short race, on the road section or from the bottom to the top of a hillock and back, running through sand, soft soil, along a path across the track.

Tempo Running

Fatigue in arms, shoulders and leg muscles are very important for an athlete at the end of the race. The objective of this kind of training is to develop this fatigue in the athlete. In this training, fast running with short intervals is included. In this way, athlete is expected to perform with great amounts of lactic acid in the muscle incurring what is known as oxygen debt.

Paarlauf

Two teams are included in this kind of running. One man from each team comes and tries to cover a maximum distance in a fixed time. Thus, this kind of running helps in determining that in a particular time, how much distance can be covered by the athlete.

Timed Running

Fast running involving rest periods are included in this kind of running. By changing any of the following factors, one can change the results of this running:

-Speed of the fast running;

-Length and speed of the resting period;

-The number of periods done; and

-The length of fast part.

With short resting section, athlete's body learns to re-adjust himself. In the runs of shorter distances, number and interval of resting period is less or short, which on the contrary in runs of long distances, the intervals increases.

In middle distance training, length of the fast running period is nearly always less than the length of the actual race distance. In any running practice, one should make such a plan that to run shorter distances at faster speed than race speed, and perform several short distances, which once put altogether, would result more and greater than race distance.

Circuit Training

A distance runner need speed and stamina. To provide these, these days circuit training is being used by coaches in a large number throughout the world. Stride Jumps, Dips on the Bar and Sit Ups are included in this kind of training.

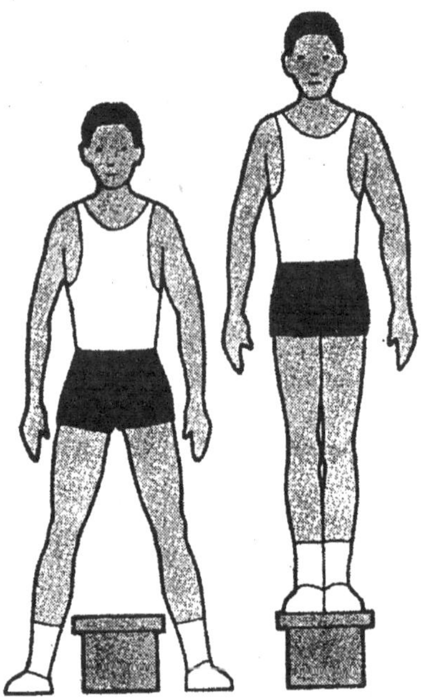

Power and Resistance Training

During the off-season pre-competitive period, this kind of training occurs. Development of muscular power in the athlete and not the useless muscular bulk is the main objective of this training.

Light weight training can be included in such type of training. Running in sand, up hills in snow can be also a part of such training. For distance runners, deep water running is generally preferred. Using flotation devices and keeping their bodies upright, distance runners literally run circuits in the deep end of the pool. However, athletes are not allowed to touch the bottom of the pool.

Rules

Obstruction

A competitor who jostles, runs across, or otherwise obstructs another competitor is liable to disqualification. After a disqualification the referee may order the race to be re-run or, in the case of a heat, permit any affected competitor to compete in the next round.

Leaving the Track

Any competitor who voluntarily leaves the track or course may not then continue running in a race.

Assistance

No person except an official timekeeper shall indicate intermediate times to a competitor. Track competitors will be disqualified for receiving any other assistance from persons within the area, but coaching may be given from the spectating area.

Timing

Fully automatic timekeeping equipment is used for the Olympic Games and most other major meetings. Otherwise timing by timekeepers using stopwatches.

Times are taken from the flash of the pistol to the moment when the competitor's torso reaches the finish.

Finish

Competitors are placed in the order in which any part of their torso (as distinguished from the head, neck, arms, legs, hands or feet) reaches the vertical plane of the edge of the finish line nearest to the start.

STEEPLECHASE

The Olympic Steeplechase is a men's event run over 3000m. It comprises 28 hurdle jumps and 7 water jumps. Competitors may jump, vault, or stand on the hurdles. The hurdles numbered (3) and (4) are positioned after the competitors have passed by on the first lap.

Competitors run outside the water jump on the first lap. Steeplechase, which is derived from cross-country running and obstacle course races, is a combination of distance running, hurdling, and water jumps and as such combines the training necessary for the distance runner and the hurdler. At present steeplechase is a track event for males only.

The laws of the event allow the athlete to jump on and off the water-jump barrier and to use the same technique in clearing the steeplechase hurdles. The athlete is also permitted to vault over the barriers, although this method is seldom used because it is extremely inefficient. The hurdles and the water jump barrier used in the steeplechase are solid, heavy barriers designed to support the weight of several athletes at the same time.

Steeple chase involves distance running, hurdling and water jumps. As such proficiency in steeple chase requires efficiency in all these in all these three types of events. He must be strong enough and should have good stamina.

Skills and Technique

How to cross the obstacles, the knowledge of this is must for everyone who wants to become a steeplechaser. Steeplechasers are always trying to get their time for the race as near as they can to their flat race time for the distance. Crossing the obstacles adds on the seconds.

In the beginning, runners may find himself vaulting some of hurdles, but because of their heaviness, feel tiresome. Thus, it be said that this event requires much, much energy and exertion from runners. Another problem generally faced by the athlete is to cross to perform the water jump, where he has to put his foot on the hurdle to drive himself over.

Water jump posses a barrier having a height of 91.4 cm and a water pit of 3.66 m. Following guidelines should be kept by the athlete while performing this event:

-while coming to the hurdle, athlete should move a little faster. Top of the hurdle is 5 in. in width;

-should put a check mark on the back so that he can perform with confidence and can hit his take off point with same foot every time;

-over the hurdle, keep himself low, he should roll over his foot, however, should not take lot of weight on it;

-rather than upward should drive onwards;

-to move forward should land;

-To bring the rear leg through and up ready to go into the next stride;

Technique of jumping off steeplechase hurdles is used while performing this part. Two types of obstacles differ in that the water jump not only has a barrier but also a 3.66-metre water pit, which the athlete must jump across or run through.

It is advised to jump up onto a barrier of 91.4 cm with one leg and drive across the water with this leg. An athlete will jump from the barrier and totally clear the water, but most athletes land with 1 foot in the water and step out with the other.

Athlete should make a lot of practice before actually performing this particular act. Before using the water jump, he should use other hurdles and on track should mark 12 feet from it in order to stimulate the far edge of the water.

Athlete should run at this hurdle, where he should put his foot up on the rail and push off landing on his other foot about 10 feet away and then run on. In this manner, he can:

a. Practise pushing off and keeping low;

b. Practise the smooth transition from landing into the next stride;

c. Get some idea of where his check mark will come;

d. Decide on the take-off foot.

After doing this, now the athlete can perform actual water jump. To avoid any kind of injury, landing area should be made in such a way that athlete does not injure from it.

Thus, it can be summarise that at about 10 to 15 metres prior to the water jump, the athlete accelerates in order to jump up onto the barrier and then clear the water. Prior to barrier, takeoff occurs around 1.5 to 2 metres. Upper body of runner leans forward and he flex his free leg in order to place his instep on the barrier.

After reaching on the barrier, support leg of the runner should be flex at an angle of around 90° and he should keep his upper body low with which he can passes low over the barrier, instead of jumping in upward direction.

Once the body of athlete has crossed the supporting leg, he should spikes grip the forward edge of the barrier as an preparation for drive over the water. With the leading leg, athlete drives forward and downward with an aim of landing around 30 to 40 cm prior to end of the water jump. While landing, athlete should extend his arms. Such extension of arms help the athlete keeping himself in balance position.

Learning Steeplechase

Only a physically sound person can become an outstanding steeplechaser. Such person should have developed a good hurdling technique over a barrier of 3 ft. height, which will be result of his experience. Because water jump is quite difficult to perform properly, coach should give more time and attention to it, which should be done by running, switching on to the steeplechase hurdle, and then continuously performing the runs of short distances. To drive forward far away from the hurdle, effort should be applied on top of the hurdle.

Once the athlete has become perfect in driving off a steeplechase hurt, then the same action he should do on the water jump hurdle. However, during coaching, no water should be used in the water jump. At a short distance from the water jump, athlete should make use of a check mark. This helps the athlete in arranging his feet in such a manner that he can run faster even at the water jump hurdle. Finally, comes the point at which the athlete must be able to run laps, in each of which, hurdles and a water jump are included.

The face of this event has undergone many changes. Wide water jump and prickly bramble fences are now not used. Not only this, distance has become more standardised to two miles from previously three quarters.

To become a successful steeplechaser, one should be a good distance runner as well as an outstanding hurdler. To surmount all the obstacles in an economical way, this event should be learn.

It is found that in various different manners, beginners tackle the obstacles. Some climb to the top of the edge in an hope of being able to make a standing jump by which they will carry right over the water. Some increase their speed while approaching the hedge in front of water and use much strength in great spring which help them in carrying t far edge of river. However, all these ways do not give the desired results.

Experienced athletes lope easily over the hedge and drop lightly into the water with one foot a little in advance of the other, and land in such a manner that without breaking the rhythm of run, they can stride through the stream straight on to the dry land.

A two miles steeplechase should be trained on the flat at four miles, while three quarter mile steeplechase should be son two miles.

Rules

Some important rules of the event have been described below:

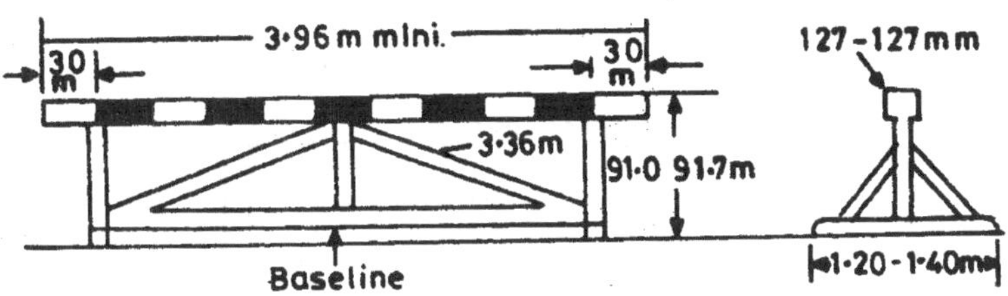

The hurdles shall be 0.914m high with a tolerance of 3mm above or below this height and shall be at least 3.96m in width. The section of the top bar of the huddles, and the hurdle at the water jump, shall be 127 mm square. The standard distance shall be 2000m and 3000m.

There shall be 28 hurdle jumps and 7 water jumps included in the 3000 m event. For both races the water jump shall be the fourth jump in each lap. If unnecessary the finish line shall be moved to another part of the tracks. It is recommended that, in the 2000m, the water jump be the second of the first lap, and thereafter the fourth jump.

In the 3000m steeple chase, the distance from the start to the beginning of the first lap shall not include any jumps, the hurdles being removed until the competitors have entered the first lap. The water jump, including the hurdle, shall be 3.66m in length and width.

The water shall be level with the track surface and at the hurdle and shall be 0.7 metres deep for a space of around 0.3 metres. From this point, the bottom shall have a regular slope upwards to the level of the tracks at the further end of the water jump.

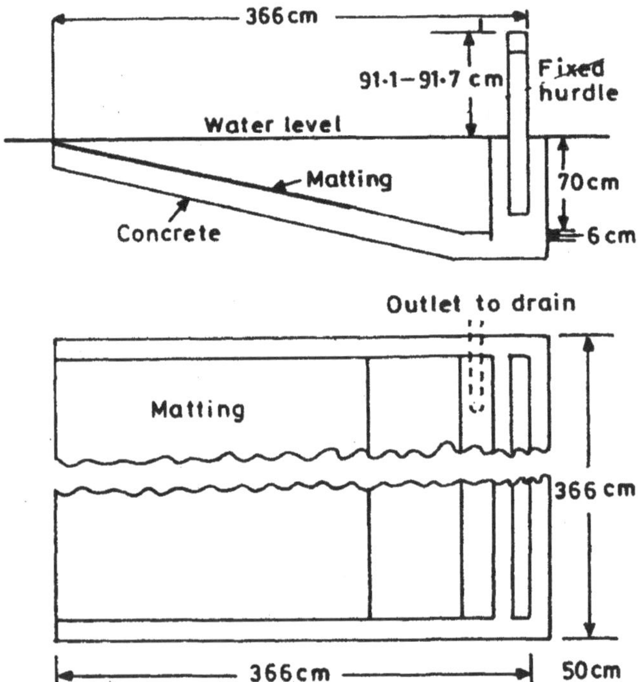

Water jump

The hurdle at the water jump shall be firmly fixed in front of the water and be of the same height as the others in the competition.

Each and every competitor is required to go through the water, and anyone who steps on the one side or the other of the jump or trails his foot or leg below the horizontal plane of the top of any hurdle at the instant of clearance shall be disqualified. Assistance by pushing off by other method will cause disqualification.

The Water jump is the fourth jump in each lap. The water jump hurdle stands the same height as the other hurdles, but is sunk into the ground.

A steeplechaser will be disqualified if,

-he steps to either side of the jump;

-fails to go over or through the water; or

-trails his foot or leg below the horizontal plane of the top of the hurdle.

To ensure safe landing of the competitors, the bottom of the water jump shall be covered at the further end with suitable material at least 366 cm wide and 250 cm long. The thickness of which should not exceed approximately 25 mm.

CROSS-COUNTRY RACES

It was in 1883 that English Cross-Country Union was founded, after which it grew steadily. In 1973, this UCCU came under the wing of Amateur Athletic Federation. After which, Federation worked a lot in making the event popular and provided all the necessary things and services.

It has been rather difficult to define what exactly constitutes cross country running . The problem arises because of varying climatic conditions, seasons, and distances.

According to IAAF's rules, in the international events and championships, race shall be organised over a confined course, to open country, fields and grasslands. A limited amount of ploughed land may be included. If the course passes through woodland without any clearly defined path or track, it must be clearly marked or the runners. In this event, performance of athletes can be measured accurately and efficiently.

85
379
1305

The exact distances even on the same courses may vary year to year, according to the laces where the flags are placed. Because of difference in magnitude of mud uneven ground and long grass, time taken in completing the race can differ.

Actually, this event is a winter sport in which runners compete with each other over courses. Like in other events, athlete completing the race first is considered the winner. It can be said that this event is a game of stamina and strength of an athlete. It demands different kinds of running.

For this event, an athlete should be stocky, tall and thin, however, he should be built slightly. It is very important for an athlete to protect his legs or fit from injury as he runs in fields or on grassland. He should also be particular in his foot placement while running. It is, therefore, important for him to wear spiked or saddled shoes. These usually have a flat rubber heel. This prevents ankle turns and heel bruises.

However, the athlete competing in this event should not make use of ordinary track shoes. It is generally found in cross country runners that they suffer from blisters on their feet, which is the result of friction. Therefore, it is advisable for such runners to use soap on his feet.

Rules

Distances

The recommended international distances are: Senior men: 12km; Junior men: 8km; Senior Women: 6km; Junior women: 4km. Distances may vary in national and local races.

Courses

For major events the courses should be confined to open country, fields, and grassland. A limited amount of plowed land is allowed. Woodland sections must be clearly marked. Roads should be kept to a minimum. There should be no high obstacles, deep ditches, dangerous ascents or descents, thick undergrowth or any other excessively difficult obstacle.

Markings

The course should be clearly marked with red flags on the left and white flags on the right. Flags should be visible from 125m.

Competitors

For local and national races runners may compete individually or in a team; a race may include both competitions. For international events runners must enter as part of a team.

Teams

The regulations for teams, reserves and number of runners to score can differ. The IAAF cross country team championship ruling, which may be a standard guide is as follows:

For men's races teams of not more than 12 competitors can be entered.

Not less than 6 nor more than 9 of these shall be allowed to start, of whom 6 will score for the team.

For women's races, junior men's and junior women's, teams of not more than 8 competitors and not less than 4 can be entered.

Start

Races are started with a pistol shot. A 5-minute warning may be given, if there is a large number of competitors. Stations are provided and the members of each team line up behind each other at the start of the race.

Officials

For major events include: a referee, a judge, a timekeeper, a starter, clerks of the course, pointsmen, umpires, funnel judges and funnel controllers, result recorders and assistants.

Scoring

After the race the placings of the scoring members of each team are added together. The team with the lowest aggregate is the winner. If there is a tie, the team whose last scoring runner finished before the other team's last scoring runner is award the higher place.

i. The finishing places of each eligible scoring competitor for each team are added together and the team with the lowest aggregate is declared the winner.

ii. In case of a tie score, it will be resolved in favour of the team whose last scoring member finishes nearer first place.

Safety

The Organising Committee of road races must ensure the safety of competitors. Organizing Committee should, where possible, ensure that the roads used for the competition are closed in both directions, that is not open to motorised traffic.

Refreshments

The rules laid down permit some kind of refreshment to the athletes, which is called the Approved refreshment. There can be made refreshment stations on the various places of race. These stations can be made at distances of about 11km and then at every 5km.

Other than these approved refreshments, no other refreshment can be provided to athletes. Additional sponging points, supplying water only, are provided midway between the refreshment stations.

At the beginning and finish of all races, approved refreshment should be provided to the athletes. There should be a gap of atleast 2 to 3 km. between the refreshment stations in races of 10 km distance. This depends on the condition of weather.

Refreshments, which may be provided either by the Organizing Committee, or the athletes, shall be made available at the stations nominated by the competitors. They shall be placed so that they are easily accessible to, or may be put by authorised persons into the hands of the competitors. A competitor who takes refreshment as a place other than the refreshment stations render himself liable to disqualification.

WALKING

Race walking appears to be the most simple and easiest event, however, this is not the reality. Today, it has become very complicated. For men the distance of such races are 20,000m and 50,000m, however for women it is set to be 5,000 and 10,000 m. Generally, events of 20km and 50km of road walks for man, while 10km road for women are included in the international competitions.

For this event, it can be said that it is a mid way between the ordinary walking and running. Although, the horizontal forces at right- angles to the direction of movement do not reveal this tidy progression.

While in normal walking and running events, sporting leg's knee remains bent while passing through the vertical position, whereas in this event, in vertical position, knee of the leg remains the straight, which implies that the athlete's remaining body has to take compensatory movements in order to maintain path of the centre of mass on the efficient line.

For around one and an half hour, the 20 km. event lasts. It is very difficult to judge a fast walk as it is not possible to whether a walker has a foot on the ground at all times or that the knee is straight through the vertical for it takes only a fraction of a second to pass through the position.

In reality, unlike simple running and walking, race walking is an artificial skill. The basic essentials of a run walk are stride length and stride frequency. While sprinting the walker will be limited by a stride frequency, which will not respond much to training after the skill is competent enough. On the athlete's inherited muscles, this frequency will greatly depend.

Like other athletic events, a run walker should have flexibility and hip mobility. Race walking, involves a rapid leg cadence and if the arms too are to maintain their synchronous swing they have to be bent at the elbows to reduce their moments of inertia as in running. Although, more concern or importance is given to arms and shoulder action in this event. Not only this, athlete counterbalance his leg action, aid the forward drive with their swinging the strong upward swing of both arms and through driving the leg evokes more forces from the ground.

Skills and Techniques

Technique involve the placement of feet on either side of a straight line results a wasted sideways component of force. Down a straight line, if the feet are moved, the action becomes more accurate and efficient. Walkers should be break the contact with tne ground. So, before advancing foot has made contact, rear foot should not leave the ground. While the food is on the ground, he should keep his leg momentarily straightened.

Rules

Disqualification

A competitor is entitled to one caution, signalled with a white flag, before being disqualified, signalled with a red flag. Action is taken against a competitor after the independent recommendation of three judges, or two judges if one is the chief judge.

Refreshments

Approved refreshments may be taken at official refreshment stations in walking races exceeding 20km. Stations are sited at 10km and then every 5km. No other refreshments are allowed. Additional sponging points, supplying water only, may be provided at points after 20km.

DECATHLON AND HEPTATHLON

Combined events competition is are made up of a number of events.

The decathlon is a men's competition of ten events and the heptathlon a women's competition of 7 seventh. Competitors score points for their performance in each event

Decathlon

The Olympic decathlon was first contested at the Games in Sweden in 1912. The competition was held to discover who were the greatest all round athletes in the world. In decathlon, competitors have to prove their skill and strength in ten gruelling events held over two days. On day one, the athletes compete in the 100m, long jump, shot put, high jump and the 400 m hurdles. The second day begins with the 110 m hurdles and goes on to the discus, pole-vault, javelin and finally the 1500 m.

Points are awarded for each event and the athlete with the highest number at the end of the all ten is the winner.

Heptathlon

The heptathlon is an all round track event for women that takes place over two long and gruelling days. Day one consists of the 100 m hurdles, the high jump, shot and the 200 m. During day two, the women compete in the long jump, javelin and the 800 m. Points are awarded for each of the seven events and the winner is the athlete who finishes with the highest number of points.

The heptathlon was first included in the Olympic Games in Los Angeles in 1984. Before that, many people believed that women could run, jump, hurdle and throw in the five event pentathlon, but no way could they cope over seven events. Heptathletes in particular, have since proved just how wrong they had been.

Today, both these events have been become world famous which can be seen from the fact that they are important parts of the Olympic today.

11

Field Events

Field Events, second part of Athletics event, is as valuable and important as the first one. For these again it can be said that field event is not any particular event, but is a group of some events which are being played or performed on the field. For these events, no particular track is prepared, but various preparations are done on the field itself.

Basically, the events of Throwing and Jumping are included in these events. Now again, these two events, namely the Throwing and Jumping are not any particular event, but consists of various events in them.

When we say Throwing Events, it comprises of the following events:

1. Discus Throw,
2. Shot-Put Throw,
3. Javelin Throw, and
4. Hammer Throw.

In the same manner, when we talk about Jumping Events, it comprises of the following events:

1. Long Jump,
2. High Jump.

Here in this section, we will go through all these events in detail. As in the previous chapter, here we will first give the introduction in brief, then its skills and the latest rules being used these days in various competitions.

DISCUS THROW

The event of Discus Throwing is considered the Classic of all other athletic events. It is believed to be the oldest event of the all the field events. Description of this event has been found in the history of ancient Greek cultures.

This event possessed an important place in the Olympic Games held in ancient Greece. At the first modern Games in 1896, the event was a close contest between a Greek, Panagiotis Paraskevopoulos, and an American, Bob Garrett.

Garrett had been practising before the Games with a much heavier discus, so he was pleasantly surprised with the competition 2 kg discus. He won the gold medal with a third round throw of 29.15m.

The first winner of the women's discus competition, held in Amsterdam in 1928, was Halina Konopacka of Poland. She set a new world and Olympic record of 39.62 m.

Today the discus throwing event has become an important part of Olympics. It is a part of Decathlon, however not of Hepathalone. Today the technique and skill of throwing the discus has improved manifold. Today, athletes use a common technique of throwing, and little variation is seen from one thrower to the next.

Basic purpose of today's discus technique is just to stimulate a rotary cracking of a whip, with the whip swung around the side of the body. Across the ring, thrower runs, twist his legs and hips ahead of the upper body as winding up a coiled spring. After arriving in the throwing position, player unwinds the spring and then crack the whip.

Skills and Techniques

The first step in teaching any of the throwing events should be a classroom session where the simple basic principles of the event are presented to the prospective candidates. It is essential that the young athletes have a basic understanding of the event if the teaching process is to have any meaning. The main objective of organising such kinds of classrooms is to divide the whole process or procedure in various parts and according to that give the coaching or knowledge of each part one by one. By this technique, it becomes easy and simple to learn the whole event in less time and effort.

The discus throw is probably the most difficult and dangerous of the throwing events. However, if introduced correctly it can be performed in complete safety and in such a way that the novice is inspired to practice the event. For complete safety the event should be performed from within a cage, with all observers positioned outside.

The unusual difficulty of maintaining balance while in the turn and of controlling the scale of the discus forces a special approach to this event and a much greater stress upon part learning of each phase than is normally necessary.

For teaching the Discus Throw, it is a good idea to begin the presentation with some loop films of the greats in action in order to allow the beginners the opportunity to see what the event looks like when performed correctly.

Coach should emphasize the following major factors that make any implement go farther:

-the force with which the discus leaves the hand,

-the angle of delivery, roughly 35 to 40°; and

-the factor known as Aerodynamics.

Following are the parts or groups in which the procedure to teach this event is divided:

a. Firstly the coach should tell the players how to hold the discus in their hands so that it go to the maximum distance and how to move the hands while holding the discus.

b. In order to throw the discus at far more distance, player has to rotate his body by which he gets the energy to do it successfully. Coach should tell him how they have to do this in order to get their objective.

c. Then, in last he should tell him that how his body should be while throwing the discus.

All these steps or things should be told by coach to the player so that he can fulfil the objective successfully.

<u>Holding the Discus</u>

As mentioned above that the discus throwing is one of the very dangerous and risky event, but this risk or dangerous can be avoided to a great extent by holding the discus properly, because if thrower hold the discus in wrong manner, it will flight in wrong direction, which can cause a lot of damage and prove destructive.

should follow a sequence of movements. He should rotate his body with discus held at arm's length, which will provide him the forward acceleration. To achieve this end, several methods can be used, however, two methods are generally and commonly used which are Pivot Rotation and Jump Rotation.

Preliminary Swings

Thrower should be placed at the rear of the circle, back to the general line of direction. While training, coach can make such a line himself across the circle from back to front along the line of direction of the throw. Athlete should take not more than two or three preliminary swings.

So that the arm and discus go well behind the right shoulder, discus should be flat and facing downwards and arm swung at shoulder height, while on the other hand, across the chest, left arm holds with ease. While swinging the discus forward, again, it should be kept flat and within the shoulders.

Some throwers like to supinate the hand on the back swing. This they do in order to avoid from being fallen. While taking swings, athlete should keep his trunk erect and move in such a manner that he can easily shift his weight from one foot to other. Behind the shoulder as the discus swings to the right, weight of the thrower should be distributed over his right leg while at the knee, his left leg will flex and heel should be raised. While doing this, he should not bent his right leg.

Step Forward

This action can be considered an extented form of throwing from a stand and also an important step towards learning the rhythm of the turn. Thrower swings the discus while facing the direction of his throw. As it reaches the extreme left position over or close to the left shoulder, the thrower takes a short step about 15 inches forward with the right foot, smoothly pivoting and accompanying the discus to an extreme right position identical to that taken when throwing from a stand. This is from this points that throw is being made.

Such an action provide force to the athlete which add about ten to twenty feet to the throw. A good opportunity to practice natura recoil and bounce from extreme position to the right is provided by this method. In throwing position, backward turn to the right should be supplemented by a very short twisting hop. With this hop, momentum increases and it also effects the bounce to a greater extent.

Throw

After taking sufficiently swings, now the thrower is ready to throw. While doing this, he, very powerfully should extends his legs and towards the direction of the throw should drive the hips. Like hip, he should drive his chest and throwing arm.

While throwing the discus, by reversing the feet, athlete should arrest the forward movement of the body, against the inner edge of the rim of the circle should bring the rear leg forward.

Taking the Turn

Taking the turn is considered to be the most difficult phase of this event. Athlete faces with two problems. Firstly, how to learn the correct form, balance and momentum and second that how to learn them in short period of time. The great majority of coaches attack the problem very cautiously and take each phase step by step.

It should be kept in mind that discus throwers do not take thousands of turns. Discus thrower should work like a ballet dancer, who perform perfectly without taking too much turnings.

To do this, various methods are being used one of which is the Fox style. While using this method, athlete should let the discus go when you call throw. Athlete should not care that in which direction the discus will go. Thrower should neither try for speed nor to hold back either. He should keep his eyes on the horizontal, hold right shoulder, discus just a little and perform confidently.

There is another method called the Fitch style which is used by throwers for this purpose. While using this method, one should keep the following things in the mind:

First, the Fitch leads not only with the hips but with

the entire upper body. Discus and the discus arm are held back. The momentum established is thereby increased beyond what can be secured from a more simple hip lead.

Second, Fitch used a very fast forward throw of the right shoulder, making the reverse somewhat more a part of the throw and landing rather hard on the right leg. However, Fitch did use the left leg as a brace by which athlete can accelerate the lower body momentum and to the upper body, right arm and hand can transfer it.

All the skills mentioned above possess great value and one should learn all these to become a good discus thrower.

Rules

Discus

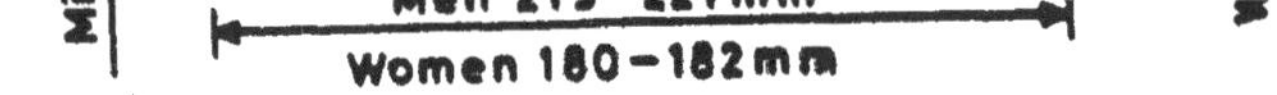

Following are the general qualities of discus which should be used in the event:

-Discus can be of wood or any other material but it should be solid and should be circular in shape.

-There should be a metal rim.

-The cross section of the edge shall be rounded in a true circle having a radius of approximately 6mm.

-There may be circular plates set flush into the centre of the sides.

Sometimes, there may not be any metal plates but it is necessary that equivalent area should be flat.

Discus Cage

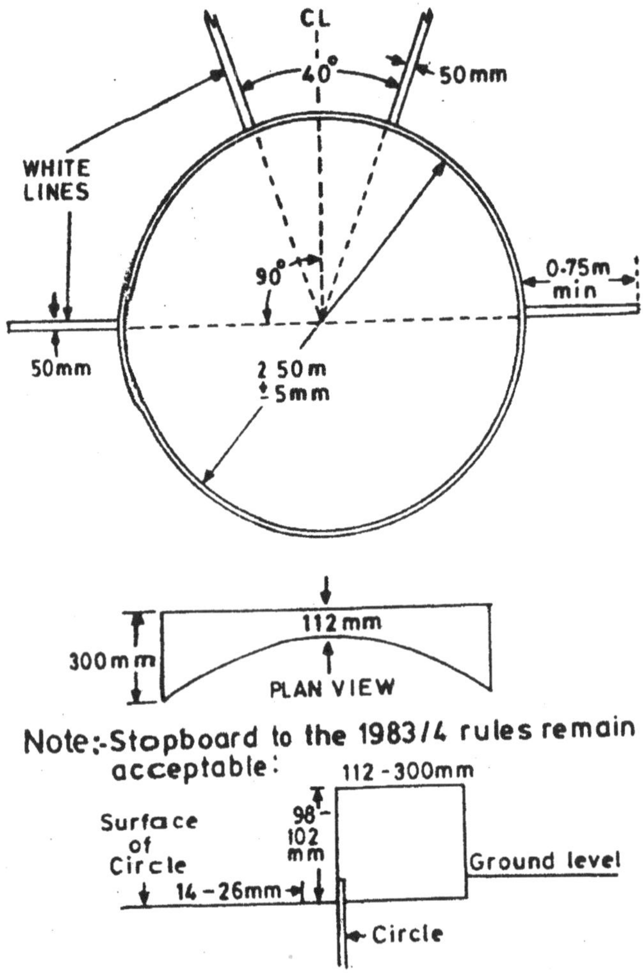

In order to make it safe for spectators, officials and competitors discus is thrown from an enclosure or a cage. In major stadium with spectators all the way round the outside of the arena and where other events are taking place there must be such kind of cage. The cage should be capable of stopping a 2kg discus which is moving at a speed of upto 25m per second. The arrangement should be such that there is no danger of ricocheting or rebounding back towards the athlete or over the top of the cage.

The width of the mouth should be 6m, positioned 5m in front of the centre of the throwing circle. The height of the netting panels should be at least 4m. Cage should be U-shaped.

To prevent a discus forcing its way through any joints in the cage or the netting or underneath the netting panels provision should be made in the construction of cage. There will be a net for cage which can be of any suitable natural or synthetic fibre cord or from mild or high tensile steel wire. 50mm and 44m should be the maximum size of mesh for steel wire and for cord netting respectively.

Minimum breaking strength of the wire should be 40kg however minimum size depends on construction of the cage. In order to ensure the continued safety of the cage, the steel netting should be inspected at least every 12 months. Visual inspection is not sufficient for fibre cord. Instead, several sample lengths of the standard cord should be worked into the netting by the manufacturer. To test the strength of netting, one of these can be removed every 12 months and tested.

Discus is also thrown from a circle and must land within the marked sector. If there are fewer than eight competitors, each one generally has six trials. Otherwise, competitors generally have three trials and then the best eight competitors have a further three. The winner is the competitor with the best distance in his six trial.

Holding the Discus

In holding the discus it should be kept in mind that the fingers should not be tapped together.

Throwing Action

The throw is begin from a stationary position. It is on the wish of the competitor to use any throwing technique.

If he touches any part of his body either the top of the ring bounding the circle or the ground beyond it, the throw becomes a foul. After throw the competitor must from a standing position, leave the circle from behind the dividing line.

Measurement

A throw is measured from the nearest mark made by the discus to the inner edge of the ring bounding the circle. Measurement is along a line from the mark and through the centre of the circle.

SHOT PUT

It is believed that this event came into existence many years ago. It is estimated that before 1896 people started involving in this event. From that period till now, many changes in techniques and in manner of performing has been come. It can be said that with the help of experiments, the technique of throwing the shot put has developed.

For this event it is said that earlier men used it as a means of testing and measuring their physical strength and stamina. This event is considered the domain of the big, strong person. This event can be enjoyed at a low skill level provided there is high passed strength level.

Athlete has to push a round, cannonball shaped object in this event. Weight of this object is not same for all people. According to sex and age of the athlete, this keeps on changing. For female athletes, lighter shot in comparison to one used by male athletes is used, in the same way for younger athletes, light weight shot is used, which is heavier for the experienced athletes. To throw the shot to maximum distance, thrower should keep it near to his neck and in front of his shoulder. While doing this, thrower has to follow some rules and regulations. If he disobeys the rules, his throw is not considered proper for which he can be disqualified from the event.

From a circle, shot is being put which must land within the marked sector. All the athletes get six trials if they are less than eight in numbers. If number of athletes exceeds eight, each of the athlete gets three trials out of which eight athletes performing best are chosen and provided further three trials. Athlete performing well in his six trials is declared the winner.

Skills and Techniques

Although it is said before that shot put was used as a means of measuring the strength and physical stamina of a person, however, today through experiments, its objective as well as its real face has changed. Now, it has become a well reputed and recognized event in all the international Events as also in the most reputed event, i.e., Olympics. Now many rules and regulations have been made to which all the throwers has to follow.

In many countries of the world, this event has become very popular and every nation is trying to grow more and more excellent and outstanding shot putters. Now the event is not so simple, but turned out to be a very complicated and difficult event. There are various fundamental and advanced skills of the events, to which without learning, one cannot even think of becoming a shot putter.

To throw the shot put to the greater distance, it is very important that thrower should hold the shot put properly, remain in the proper balancing state and then throw it. All these we will learn step by step.

Grip

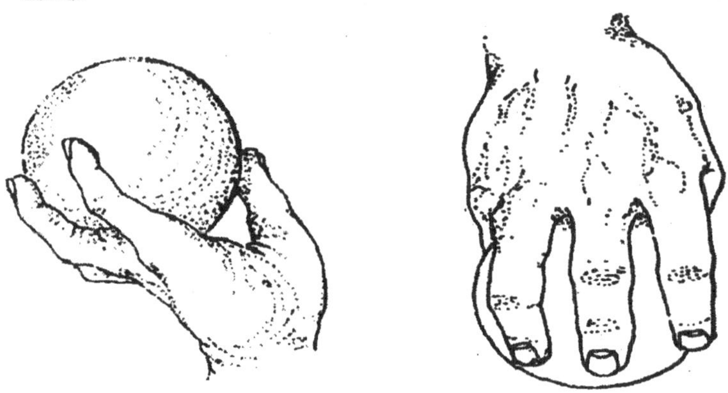

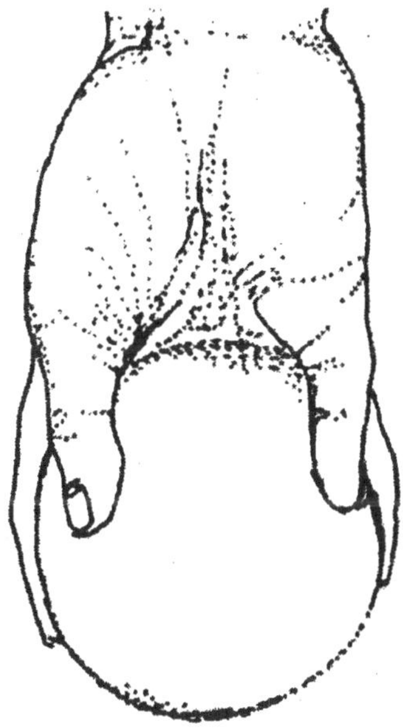

The place where the finger meets the palm of the hand, athlete should keep weight of the shot. Shot should be supported and guided by the thumb and little finger. As a power source, three middle fingers are used.

On the basis of spreading of the fingers, three kind of grips are used which are as follows:

In first method, on the back of the shot, thrower put his first, second and third fingers. In maintaining lateral support, little finger is bent and aids the thumb.

In the second method, athlete spread his three fingers are likewise back of the shot and thumb prevents sideward movement of the missile. There is not a very wide difference exist between this method and above mentioned method, however, in this method little finger contribute force to forward and upward propulsion in addition to maintaining balancing.

Until the musculature of the hand is properly developed, novices should carry the shot lower down in the palm. While doing this, finger development is very important.

The third and last method of gripping the shot is generally employed by throwers of smaller fingers and hands. In this method, fingers are spread wider. Farther back of the shot, the little finger is placed. This helps in adding impetus to the put. Lateral balance is being maintained by the thumb. This kind of grip helps in carrying the shot farther down in the palm of hand.

While teaching the grip, it should be emphasized that you pick up the shot in the left hand and place it against the first three fingers of the throwing hand, using the thumb and little finger as guides.

Placing the Shot

Under the jaw bone underneath the ear, the shot is being held. While doing this, important point to be kept in mind is to place the shot securely in the neck. Keep the little finger at the ear lobe and the thumb at the clavicle, with the front edge of the shot bisecting the middle of the chin.

However, this is not the proper position for every thrower. The exact location of the shot in the neck will vary from athlete to athlete as the physique of all the athletes is not same. The key is to be sure it is securely in the neck.

Starting Position

The putter stands at the back of the circle with the right foot in the 11 o'clock position on the line of direction. The putter keeps the eyes focused on a focal point in the back of the circle, with the non throwing arm and shoulder kept square and held back.

Leg Swing

The most important factor is the speed of release, but if the shot leaves the hand in such a way that is presents a large surface to the air, then the true value of the throw will be lost because of the air resistance considerably reducing the effect of release speed. The expert shot putter first of all puts a high speed in his own body, and hence the shot, by using some form of running rotational movement across the circle, and then adding to this initial speed by performing a powerful long arm, slinging movement.

For the purpose of securing balance for the shift, the putter performs three preliminary leg swing. These swings may be executed by swinging the left leg forward and backward in line with the right leg; or forward and backward in front of the right leg; or forward and backward to the rear of the right leg.

The type of preliminary swing employed rests with the putter. As the left foot reaches the farthermost point back in the last swing, the shift begins, the swinging leg contributing momentum thereto.

Glide

As the swinging end, the glide begins. From the beginning position, body weight shift down over the right leg and raising the left leg. Toward the throwing direction, left leg makes an easy swinging motion. Simultaneously, across the circle, right leg begins its pushing action. This is a ball to heel motion jumping movement.

When the body weight shifts toward front of the circle, underneath the thrower, right leg snaps to centre of the circle in a position similar to 9 o'clock. In the 5 o'clock position, left leg lands simultaneously to left side of the line of direction.

In the beginning of shift, athlete shift his body weight on his right foot and keep the right knee bent. When left foot approaches the forward point in swinging, he straighten his right leg, push right thigh, leg and foot.

To maintain balance, during the shift, trunk is carried. In relation to the body, position of shot does not change. At the conclusion of the hop on the right foot, the left foot is from 6 to 10 inches from the ground. When left foot comes down, trunk and shot do not stop their movement while legs and trunk gather for the delivery.

Throwing

The position which thrower makes while throwing the shot is called the Power Position. The success and failure of a thrower depends on this position.

The total of all the forces generated in the shift and the delivery has been transmitted to the wrist and fingers. Added to these factors is an instantaneous forward snap of the wrist and flip of the fingers which provides added impetus to the shot.

Keeping the force directly behind the centre of the shot in the line of flight is important for good form as it provides a slight backward rotation to the missile. Velocity with which shot leaves the athlete's hand is an important factor in determining the angle for the release. Generally this angle ranges between 37 to 42 degrees.

Because of difference in direction of the follow through, the action of the right arm at the release varies from athlete to athlete. Athletes employing crossfire style give more importance or attention on trunk twist and a

rapid cross body action of the arm. This kind of release led the missile fall to left side of the line which is drawn through centre of both the circle.

There is another method which can be used to release the shot. By this method, shot leaves the hand of the thrower from a point above and directly in front of the right shoulder. Generally, with this method to the right side of the centre line, shot lands.

While throwing the shot, thrower should have such position:

-should stand in direction of the throw and turn so that you are facing 90° sideways to the direction of throw;

-36 inches apart should spread the legs. This is not the particular distance, as this distance can vary from athlete to athlete;

-on a line through centre of the circle, should place the toes of both feet. In the direction of the flight, line should locate. Move of the toes of the left foot back 6 inches to the left of the centre line;

-take the right foot about 45 degrees far fro the direction of flight, with which rear foot will be put at an angle of 135 degree to the direction of flight;

-the weight should be on the ball of the right foot with the left heel up and only the toes of the left foot in contact with the ground for balance;

-the head and shoulders should be facing directly to the rear with the left arm reaching beyond and slightly below the right knee. The right hand is holding the shot securely in the neck;

-at about one quarter squat position, both legs should be bent. Knees should be kept in direct line with the toes;

-keep the trunk erect, head up and back straight. Over the rear leg, trunk should be kept.

Thus, in order to throw the put to far distance, keep the above mentioned points in mind while delivering it.

Follow Throw

Follow throw is not a part of the throw itself, although it does play an extremely vital role in the entire process. Following through too soon may well be the most common fault for beginners in all the throwing events, especially in the shot put. This is because of the reason that it is so prevalent, a basic understanding of principles behind the following through must be made clear before the athlete begins to develop technique.

The first thing to impress upon the players is that the follow through takes after the implements leaves the hand and never before the delivery is completed. If an athlete is right handed, the throw is always made off the left leg. A left handed athlete will always throw off the right leg.

Now the question arises that when follow through is not a part of throwing the shot, why is it important for a thrower. This can be explained by an instance of hitting a ball. Once contact is made and ball leaves the bat, there is nothing further we can do to add distance, the latter has already been determined. Why then not stop the swing as soon as the ball leaves the bat. The answer is that if you were swing the bat at maximum velocity, when contact with the ball was made, then stopped abruptly, you would break your arms

In the same manner, the follow through is necessary simply to give you time to slow the swing down after striking the ball at maximum velocity. The same principle is true in throwing and analogy of hitting the ball makes this much easier to understand.

It should be impressed upon the athlete that if he throw without following through, he is holding back and not throwing with the full force of the body. Follow through is necessary because all throwing events must take place within a legally established limit. The shot is throw within a circle. The follow through also serves the very vital function of preventing fouling.

Rules

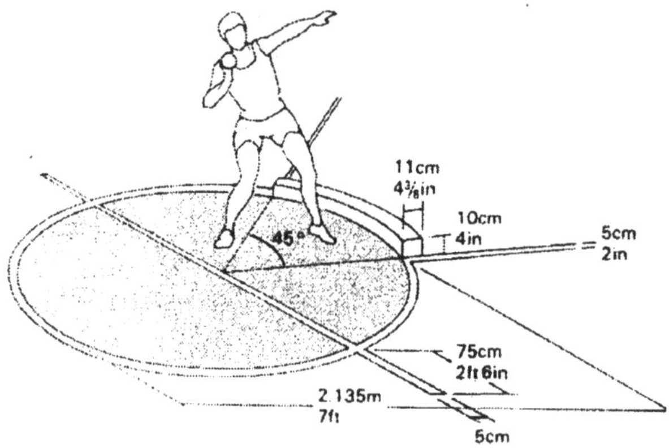

The shot put is one of the throwing event. It is put from a circle and must land within the marked sector. Generally competitors have three trials but if the number of competitors is fewer than eight each one can have six trials. The best eight competitors are given further three trials. The competitor with the best distance in his six trials will be the winner.

Throwing the Shot Put

The Shot

Construction: It should be of spherical shape made of solid iron, brass or any other metal but which should not be softer than brass.

There are different weights for men and women of a shot. For men the weight of shot should be 7.26kg and for women it should be 4kg.

Putting the Shot

One hand is used to put the shot. It should be put

from shoulder and should not go behind the shoulder line. At the time the competitor takes a stance in the circle to commence a put, the shot shall touch or be in close proximity to the neck or the chin and the hand shall not be dropped below this position during the action of putting.

Circle: It is bounded by a white-painted band of iron, steel or wood. There is a raised stopboard for this event.

<u>The Stop Board</u>

Construction: The board can be of wood or any other suitable material which should be in an arc shape and have a white colour. In order to firmly fixed to the ground it should placed midway between sector lines.

The width of board can vary between 11.2cm to 30cm and should have a length of 1.22m.

<u>Measurement</u>

After each trial measurement takes place. Measurement is along a line from the mark and through the centre of the circle.

JAVELIN THROW

In the Pentathlon of the ancient Olympic Games, event of Javelin Throw possessed an important place. It remained a regular event in most sports competition from very early times. In ancient days, it was not only used as a sport event, but also used in wars as a weapon. The history of modern javelin throwing, from the combined standpoints of the development of style, of championships won, and of world's records, is an almost exclusively Scandinavian story.

Evidence shows that for the first time in 1886 the javelin was thrown in modern era of Athletics. The man who used it first was Swede named A. Wighert. However, it was in 1906 that it was included in Olympic Games for the first time at Athens.

It was in 1934 when the Jarvinen first caught world attention. In 1909 it appeared for the first time in National AAU Championships, however it was not earlier than 1922 that it adopted into the ICAAA Program. Because it was quite risky and can prove dangerous for the thrower as well as for other persons if done carelessly, no school included it in its program.

From other athletes, javelin throwers are different as they do not have to compete during the long indoor season. A javelin thrower cannot participate or perform any other field event as throwers of other events can. Like, for example, discus men can put the shot, and hammer man 35 pound weight, however, this is not the case with javelin throwers.

This event is considered totally different from other events for a number of reasons. Javelin thrower should not be heavy weighted like other throwers. He can be a person slenderly built. The javelin thrower, has a completely different personality from the heavy thrower and could be placed in a category alongside the other athletes.

Skills and Techniques

Not same kind of javelin is used for all the throwers. Dimension and weight of javelin changes according to age and sex of thrower. Usually javelin of 800 gm is used for male throwers, while of 600 gms for women.

In technical terms the performer is concerned with three fundamental mechanical principles. They are:

The speed of release,

the angle of release and

aerodynamics factor mainly associated with flight stability.

Speed of release is very important factor. Flight range changes to a great extent by mere changing the angle of release to little extent. A six feet improvement in flight range can be brought by increasing the speed of release of one foot per second.

Throw require calls for the performer to put a high speed in the body by executing a preliminary approach run, and then with a final flinging action, adding to this speed. Split second timing and co-ordination is required to blend together all of the facets of the approach run. Fast arm is very important or very necessity of javelin thrower.

Holding the Javelin

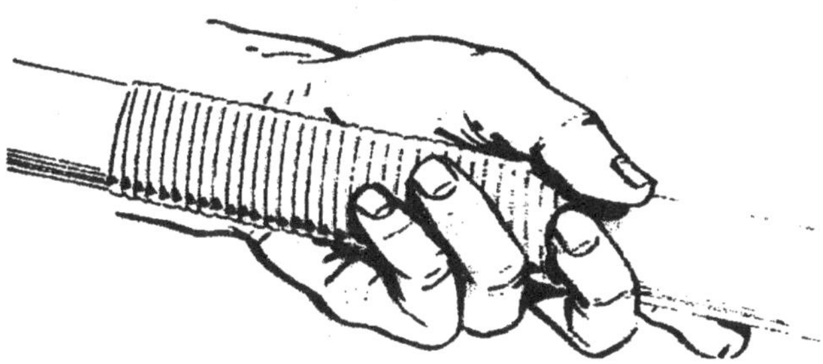

As in every throwing event, it is very important to hold and javelin properly in order to throw it to a long distance. Athletes should place the binding in the V of the palm of the hand with the second finger gripping the binding edge.

First finger grip should not be used as it proves to non-efficient. Beginners are expected to commit this mistake and they will become habitual of it if coach does not find their fault in time.

Fork Grip is an important and commonly used method for holding the javelin. Generally this grip is used by a coach to teach the beginners. In order to avoid confusion, coach should start all the beginners off with the same grip. However, if coach thinks that any other method can be used for any athlete, he can employ that.

It can be said that reliable grip is one in which fingers of the thrower is placed behind the ledge which is being formed by binding. This is for the reason that when power is put to the javelin, none of it is lost in fraction should hand slip down the shaft.

Thus, it can be concluded that firmness of grip is an important feature of the throw. For proper grip, many athletes use a tacky substance, which is generally made from resin which helps them in consolidating their hold on javelin.

Thus, it can be said that there are some particular kinds in which you can hold the javelin. The type of hand-hold which an individual selects depends on the length and strength of the fingers, the size of the javelin shaft, and the athlete's personal choice. Some of these methods have been mentioned below:

One method of holding the javelin is Finnish hold. In this method, athlete grasp the javelin at the rear of the binding so that second finger can encircle the shaft and can make contact with extended thumb. Approximately in line, the first finger rest while around the shaft, wrist and curls.

Hungarian form is another method of holding the javelin. This style is not very different from Finnish style, however, some differences lie. In this method, along the underside of the shaft, first finger is being extended to the rear. Second finger exerts the pull, while lateral support is provided by the thumb.

American Grasp is the third method of holding the javelin. In this method, javelin is held with three fingers encircling the whipcord while along the shaft, thumb rest lightly. In this method, unlike Finnish grasp, first finger exert the pull. At a greater angle to the forearm, the javelin is held.

In all the above mentioned manners, amount of finger tension is quite same, the only difference is that there is only a moderate degree during the approach and at the initial stance, however, at the start of the delivery there exists a high degree of tension.

Carrying the Javelin

As mentioned earlier, there are different methods or styles in which a thrower can hold the javelin, however, the method best suited to him has to be selected by himself. He should measure himself that in which method he can perform comfortably. Which kind suits his physical as well as other qualities.

While coaching carry over, right shoulder of the athlete should be kept above the head about at a distance of three to four inches. Athlete should carry the point slightly downward as this helps in keeping the javelin in line while withdrawing.

Five Step Sequence

The competitor grasps the javelin and assumes a front carry, point down. This phase can the called the five step transition phase. Here we are using the Finnish style with a five step sequence. There is nothing sacred about a five step transition approach, but beginners are most comfortable with this technique.

While learning the five step sequence, the athlete completes the run up on the right and begins the transition steps with the left foot. In teaching this process, walk the beginners through the five steps by the numbers, constantly checking to be sure they are executing properly.

The first two steps involve the withdrawal of the javelin and should not be considered a crossover. Emphasize running by the javelin, not jerking it backward. The key coaching point here is to be sure the athlete keeps the javelin straight. The withdrawal should be complete by the time the right foot strikes the ground on the second step and should be completed with the throwing hand, palm up, at shoulder level with the javelin as close to the body as possible, straight and positioned at an angle running through the hair line, just above the forehead. The left arm is curled across the chest and the throwing arm is straight, but the elbow must not be locked.

Thrower should get into the throwing position on third and fourth steps. This is where the crossover take place. The coaching points to emphasize here are to point the feet 23° to the right, turn the shoulders 90 degrees to the line of flight while keeping the hips as much to the front as possible, and gaining a backward lean. The fifth step begins before the fourth lands and a sort or bounding action results. The rhythm you are looking for is not 1-2-3-4-5, but rather -2-3-45.

While teaching this as a walk through, this point is not important, but the athlete should be made aware of it and as soon as you start to put the process into a run, it should be introduced. The key coaching points on the fifth steps are as follows:

a. the left leg lands heel first with the toe pointing in the direction of the line of flight. The left leg lands straight, but will begin to bend as soon as it makes contact;

b. the right knee and foot should be turned inward and pointing in the direction of the line of flight;

c. as soon as the left heel strikes the ground, drive the right leg and hip vigorously forward, with the head tilted up and slightly to the left with the back arched so that the body forms the classic, and very distinct, Bow position.

Delivery, the Release, and the Recovery

There are different methods which can be used while throwing the javelin some of which arc as follows:

1. The Hop-Step Form of Throw

Generally, this kind of throw is used in developed countries.

Approach

From a point which locates about 80 to 90 feet from the stop board, thrower begins his run. This point is being named as Third Point. At one half effort, a seven stride run is executed from this point. This point is marked the Second Point. From Second Point, the speed is increased so that at the end of six additional strides three-fourths of the best effort is being exerted. Completion of 13 running stride is marked with a point named First Point. There should be atleast a distance of 12 to 15 feet between first point and stop board. All important hop, gather and throw are made in the third segment.

Thrower should not hold the javelin rigidly. Both Over-Shoulder and Under-Arm Carry, javelin position put a kind of restriction on arm in aiding the run. During the run, athlete should tend only the natural body tension, however at the first application of throwing power, spread should be grasped firmly.

Delivery

A hop coupled with a quarter body turn is executed as soon as the right toe strikes the very First Point. He should spread his foot moderately wide and from this position athlete should throw the javelin. At the instant of release, foot should swing the right leg swiftly forward so that near the stop board, foot can land.

Planting of the right foot well forward helps in avoiding fouls. Near to scratch line, athlete should set his right foot. So that left foot can touch the ground in fair territory, sufficient room should be allowed. After the right leg has been planted close to the toe board, left leg should swing backward. Such kind of swinging of left leg provides balance to the athlete. In the beginning of hop, the initiation of the draw-back of the throwing arm causes a quarter body turn. Throwing is drawn well back after placing the right foot.

Now, at this point, weight of the thrower rests on the right foot, however, while carrying the javelin forward, he should shift his weight to the left foot. In its forward progress, right elbow precedes the hand. Sharply in backward direction, the left arm is carried.

Good form in all types of javelin throwing calls for a delivery in which the javelin path is close to the head. In comparison to a side arm swing, action is an over shoulder whip. Above and in front of the right shoulder, release should take place. An angle of 35 degrees should be made while releasing.

2. Finish Form of Throw

<u>Approach</u>

Athlete should begin his run from a point which locates at a distance of around 100 to 110 feet from stop board. This point is called the Scratch Line. A point is set around five stride toward the scratch line. A distance of around eight stride exists between both these points. Greater attention should be given to the distance from first point to the scratch line. This is because of the reason that during last four or five strides, delivery is to be completed. Fifth stride is considered to be the recovery step.

Athlete should carry the javelin to the front while approaching. Thrower keeps on moving the javelin in upward and downward direction, thus synchronize the action of right arm with his left leg. During the approach, neither body nor hand grip is extremely tense.

Competition begin himself for leave as soon as the left foot strikes. The Finnish competitors count 1, 2, 3, 4, and 5 for the five steps involved in the delivery and recovery. Athlete can count silently or audibly.

On the count of 1 the right foot strikes the ground in

the direction of the board.

On count 2, the left foot, pointed to the right, strikes the ground.

On count 3, front cross over step landing is being executed by the right foot which toe point in the right direction and right cross over parallel to the board.

On count 4, athlete takes a long step in such a manner that in direction of the throw, his left foot land. As soon as right foot come in contact with the ground on step preceding the throw, athlete incline his whole body in backward direction at an angle of about 35 to 40 degrees, while in forward direction travelling the centre of weight with the rate of 15 to 25 feet a second.

While the feet become motionless on the ground, centre of weight remain continuously forward which force top of the body to double its forward speed, thus aid the whipping of the javelin arm forward.

At the count 5, near the stopboard, thrower brings his right foot. This he do with a purpose of checking the speed of his body. To remain in balanced position, on the right foot, athlete may hop while keeping the left leg extended in backward and sideward directions.

Rules

Competition

In throwing javelin non-orthodox styles are not permitted. It should be held at grip and thrown over the shoulder or upper part of the throwing arm and should not be hurled. The tip of the metal should touch the ground first before any part of the javelin in order to consider the throw a valid throw.

A competitor may not turn completely around so that his back is towards the throwing arc until the javelin has been discharged into the air. Breaking of javelin while throwing or in the air is considered to be a foul throw but if attempt was made in accordance with Rule and then javelin breaks it will not to be considered as a foul throw. But if because of imbalance of competitor javelin breaks it again will not to be considered as a foul throw.

The Javelin

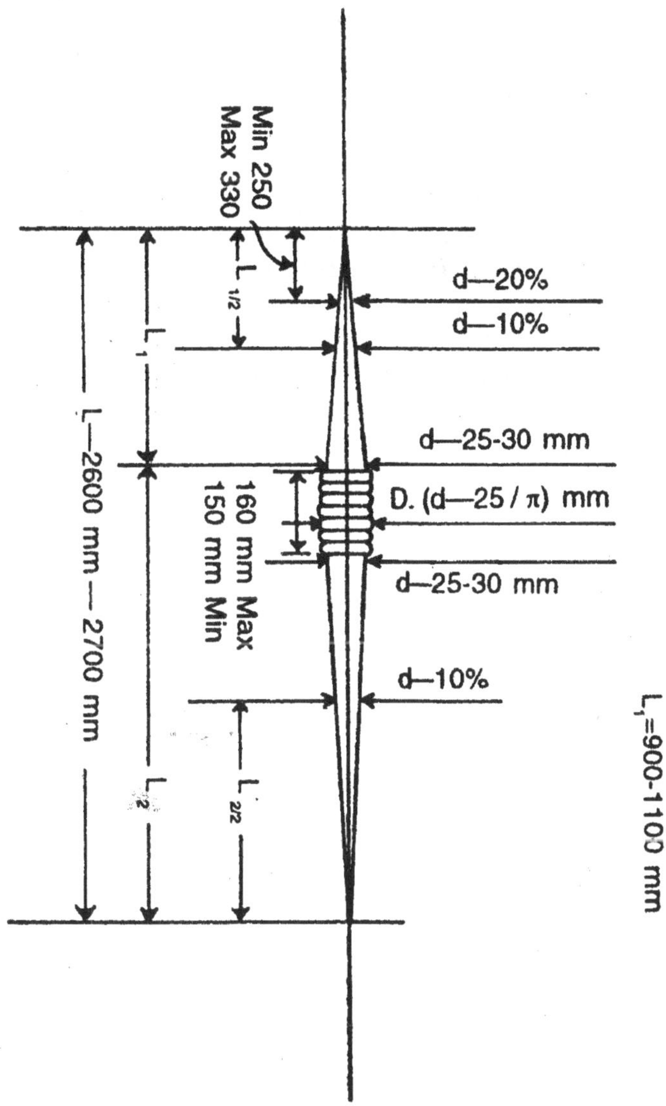

Head, shall and cord grip are three parts of a javelin. The shaft shall be constructed completely of metal, or of another suitable homogeneous material, and shall have fixed to it a metal head terminating in a sharp point, but the surface of shaft should be smooth without any kind of holes or roughness.

The maximum diameter of the shaft shall be immediately in front of the grip. Central portion of the shaft may be cylindrical or slightly tapered towards the rear but diameter should not be allowed to reduce more than 0.25mm from front of the grip to behind of it. Tail should taper at the rear and javelin to the tip at front from the grip. Straight or slightly convex should be the longitudinal profile from grip to tail and to front tip.

Throwing Action

It must be held at grip and should be thrown with one hand only over the shoulder or the upper part of the throwing arm. It must neither slung nor hurled. After preparing to throw and before discharging the javelin a competitor is not allowed to turn his back to the arc.

If a competitor touches with any part of his body the arc or scratch lines or the ground beyond them the throw is considered to be foul. The competitor is now allowed to cross either of the parallel lines forming the runway.

Measurement

A throw is measured from the nearest mark made by the head of the javelin to the inner edge of the circumference of the arc. Measurement is along a line from the mark and through the centre of the radius of the arc.

HAMMER THROW

This event is considered to be new or younger to all the other events included in field events. It has developed from a rural pastime of throwing the hammer only in this case the hammer being of the sledge variety or that used in heavy masonry. In the Court of Henry VIII, this event became popular for the first time.

The credit of developing or introducing this event goes to the people of United States of America. People of this nation set a number of records in this event.

The event of hammer throw is considered to be the most difficult of all the field events. One should possess many qualities to become an outstanding player in this event. The event presents the administrators of the sports with tremendous problems, all of which are constantly threatening the future of the event.

Today, various kinds of facilities are being provided for this event. While dropping from the sky, heavy head of the hammer can bury itself deep in the ground which make a large extent crater and even can damage the turf if done frequently.

The problem increases more with the fact that rapid development in the use of artificial turf surfaces, for major games pitches, can produce a situation, within some time where the central areas of all of our major stadia have such a surface. Certainly, this will lead the hammer throwing banished from main arena.

If the damage to the turf was the only problem affecting the future of the sport, then fewer enthusiasts would express concern. However, with the greater distances being thrown the risk increases. If the performer is fully trained, hammer can be dangerous for person who are being standing at the place where it is likely to land. Thus, in national and international events, this threat can be decreased by not allowing anyone to come near the central area.

In relation to this event, it is said that in comparison to other field events, it is less popular in Olympic Sports, the reason of which is less publicity. It is important to say here that till now only male athletes can participate in this event and female are not allowed to take part. Because of its difficult, this event seems to be unglamorous and unexciting to many people of the world.

Skills and Techniques

It is true to say about this event that it has not gained much popularity as the other events of throwing. However, it does not imply that any person can perform this event, but the reality is the that to perform this event, one should possess much more qualities than performers of the other throwing events. To excel in the hammer, requires technique, which has been described here.

Holding the Hammer

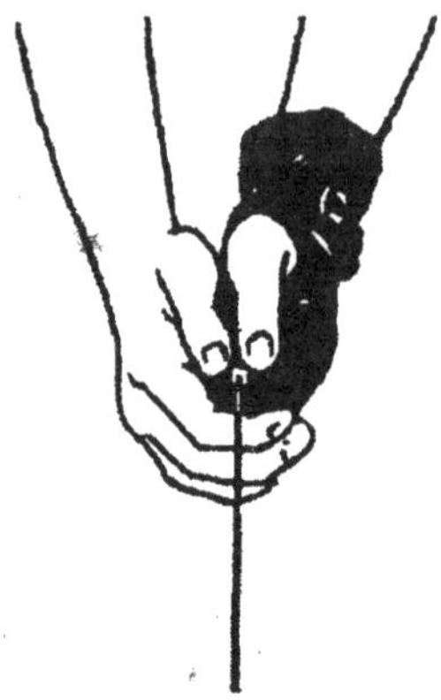

For safety point of view, hammer throwers wear gloves on their left hand. Between the legs, athlete should place the hammer which helps him to get hammer easily. To plane of the hips, length of handle should be placed at an right angle. So that handle can run complete width of the hand and rests on the second joint, gloved left hand should be inserted from left hand side. From the right side, right hand should be inserted, over the left hand should fold and thus in this manner athlete secure its grip.

Preliminary Swings

Each full rotation of the hammer around the body performed prior to the athlete's entering the turns is called a preliminary swing, or simply a swing. Athlete should understand that in this or in any throwing event, swings are foundation of the throw as they speed up the hammer in controlled manner. To build up the hammer head velocity, generally athlete uses two preliminary wind-up, whereas number of these wind-up increases to three for the beginners.

While standing behind the body, thrower let the hammer in motion. As the hammer head is thrown to a position high above the left foot, to a new low point, hammer will begin to drop. As soon as the hammer reaches downward, thrower's arm bend, trunk twist and his weight shifts over to his right foot.

On the lateral movement from the hips, athlete should again perform this activity with faster speed. Hips of the thrower shift to the left side when hammer is positioned in this side, whereas to the right side when hammer is positioned in right side.

Turns

To build up maximum peripheral velocity in hammer head is the basic purpose of the turns. This is done by increasing the turning speed the length of radius through which head of hammer is being swept. If the athlete wants to release the hammer with maximum speed, it should be gradual. Rhythm, balance, strength and quick reflexes are some important factors which help in doing this.

First Turn

When the hammer sweeps high to left side of thrower, and when the weight shifts to his left foot's ball, quickly the right foot is picked up as on the ball of left foot, athlete makes the turn. To keep both the foot parallel to each other, thrower place his right foot to the ground. Athlete should not raise his right foot and near to his left foot should keep it. While doing this, athlete should not bend his knees and keep them flexed. While completing the turn, thrower should get the sensation of turning under the hammer while the hammer is at the high point.

During the turn the right knee if forced across the body to help speed up the turning moment. Athlete should pick up the right foot and should rotate the limb. From the hip joint, he should perform the lifting action.

Successive Turns

To increase the speed of the hammer head, all the successive turns should be performed with comparative speed than the first turn. Right leg should perform quicker to keep the hips ahead of the shoulders. Because of force builds up, countering of this pull becomes more important. This is the result of more force exerted by the hammer on the body of athlete. On each turn, thrower would be pulled up to high point of the hammer if athlete is not able to counter this forces properly.

To counter this tendency to get to a higher point, thrower should sit and hang from the hammer. While doing sit, he should keep his turn erect. Control of left leg knee is very important, thus, while bringing the hammer at high point, over the left leg, weight should poised. After a considerable period athlete should picked up his right leg. While phasing the single contact, with the hips well ahead of the hammer, it should transmit the impulse to the athlete.

Delivery

After taking sufficient turns, now thrower should place his right foot down properly. It is important to mention here that generally three or four turns are considered sufficient for the thrower. Thrower should pull on the hammer in an upward spiral, for which he should lift his chest and extend the legs and his back. While hammer is in front of the body and passing through the low point, athlete's pull on the hammer should occur. While releasing the hammer, athlete should keep his body fully extended while his left shoulder should remain toward direction of throw.

Before the hammer reaches its final low point the back should start to arch. As the hammer is released high over the left shoulder, athlete should lift vertically both his legs. Vertical lifting action of maximum height should be experienced by the thrower.

Transition

Thrower should shift his body weight to left foot while holding the hammer in a position low to the thrower's right and behind the plane of the hips. While doing so, athlete should remain very careful as rushing action can lead the hammer to land in a low position. Till hammer is released, athlete should keep his arms straight out of low point.

As weight start to transfer to the left and towards the thrower's left hand side, hammer rises, his body weight should pivot on his left heel. Athlete should keep his knees bent while trunk erect. As soon as the weight of body shifts to left foot, athlete should begin his first turn. Until the right foot is not picked up from the ground, athlete should not take the turn. While doing this, athlete should perform while keeping control on himself as speedy actions can ruin his whole performance.

Rules

Throwing the Hammer

<u>The Competition</u>

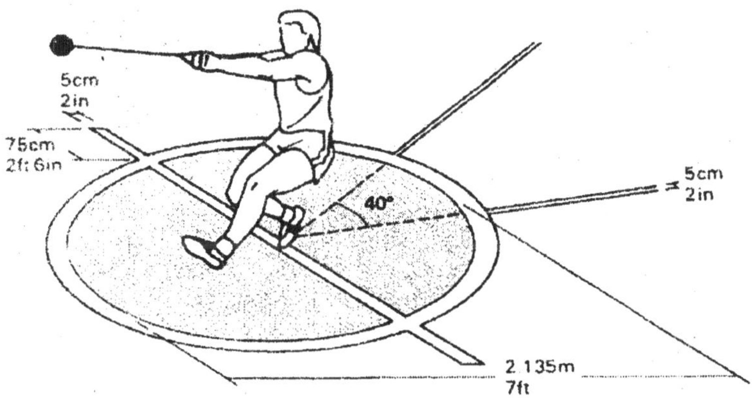

In starting position a competitor is allowed to put the head of hammer on the ground inside or outside the circle. At the time of preliminary swings or turns if head of the hammer touches the ground or top of the iron band it will not considered to be a foul throw, but after having touched the ground he stops throwing to begin the throw again it will considered to be a failure.

Breaking of hammer during throw is considered to be a fault but if attempt was made in accordance with rules it will not to be considered as a fault. Similarly, if hammer breaks because of imbalance of competitor it will not to be considered as a fault.

The hammer is thrown from a circle and must land within the marked sector. As in other throwing events some competitors may be eliminated after three trials. The winner is the competitor with the best distance in his six trials. A tie is decided by the competitor's second-best trials.

The Hammer

Construction: Three parts of the hammer are:
Metal head,
a wire and
grip.

Head—The head should be spherical in shape and its head should be of solid iron or other metal not softer than brass or a shell of such metal, filled with lead or other solid material with a minimum diameter of 110mm for men and 95mm for women.

A filling can be used but it should be kept in mind that while using filling it should be inserted in such a manner that from centre of sphere the centre of gravity should be less than 6mm and it cannot move.

Wire—Wire should be of spring steel which should not be less than 3mm in diameter. It should be such that it cannot be stretch while the hammer is being thrown.

Hammer Cage

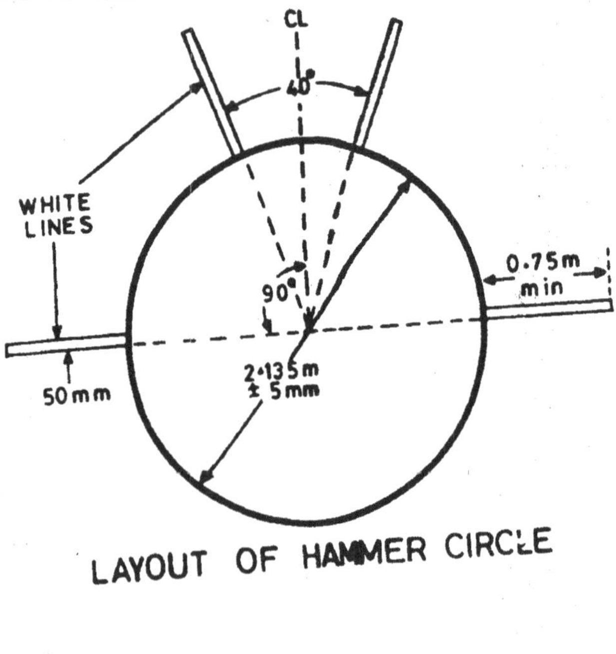

LAYOUT OF HAMMER CIRCLE

To ensure safety of spectators, officials and competitors hammer is thrown from a properly enclosed area or a cage. The major stadium with spectators all way round the outside of the area and in which other events are also taking place should comply with this rule. But in places where space is limited like training areas, it will be satisfactory to have a small cage with simpler construction.

Following are the guidelines for creating the hammer cage:

-The width of the mouth should be 6m, positioned 4.2m in front of the centre of the throwing circle.

-The height of the netting panels shall be at least 7m.

-It should be kept in mind that the cage should be U-shaped. 2 netting panels shall be provided of 2m width at front of the cage but only one out of which shall be operative at a time.

-The cage should be capable of stopping a 7.26kg hammer moving at a speed of 32 metres per second.

-Cage should comply with rules otherwise any form of construction can be used.

-Cage should be designed in such a way as to avoid any kind of danger like rebounding of hammer towards athlete.

-Proper provisions should be there to prevent a hammer forcing its way through any joints in the cage.

<u>Throwing Action</u>

Throw must begin from a stationary position, when the competitor is permitted to rest the head of the hammer on the ground inside or outside the circle.

If after commencing the action, the competitor touches with any part of his body either the top of the ring bounding the circle or the ground beyond it, throw is considered to be foul.

Measurements

From the nearest mark made by the head of the hammer to the inner edge of the ring bounding the circle throw is measured. Measurement is along a line from the mark and through the centre of the circle.

COMMON RULES APPLICABLE TO ALL THE THROWING EVENTS

COMPETITION

No competitor shall be allowed to compete outside his own country unless his amateur status is guaranteed in writing by the recognised governing athletic Association of his country, and he has permission from such body to compete. In all international competitions, such guarantee of the amateur status of an athlete shall be accepted unless any objection as to his status shall be referred to the I.A.A.F.

Competitions under I.A.A.F. are restricted to amateurs in accordance with the I.A.A.F. Rules relating to the eligibility of athletes to compete.

Failure to Participate

At Olympic Games and area or group championships, it is recommended that a competitor be excluded from participation in further events including relays in cases where:

-He or she qualified in preliminaries or heats for further participation in an event but then did not compete further without giving a valid reason.

-A final confirmation was given that the athlete would start in an event but then he or she failed to participate without giving a valid reason, making impracticable the deletion of his/her name from the official list of the starters of that event.

DUTIES AND RESPONSIBILITIES OF VARIOUS OFFICIALS

Referees

The appropriate Referee shall check all final results, shall deal with any disputed points, and, in the case of field events, shall supervise the measurements of record performance. The appropriate Referee shall have authority to change the place of the competition in any field event, if in his opinion the conditions justify it. Such a change shall be made only after a round is completed.

At the conclusion of each event the results card shall be completed immediately, signed by the appropriate Referee and handed to the Recorders. If, in the opinion of the appropriate Referee, circumstances arise at any meeting such that justice demands that any event should be contested again, he shall have authority to declare the event void and it shall be held again, either on the same day or on some future occasion, as he shall decide.

Umpires

It is his duty to indicate any kind of breach of rules by raising a red flag. Umpires are assistants to the Referee without authority to make final decisions.

Starter's Assistants

They must place each competitor in his correct lane or station, assemble the competitors on an assembly line 3 metres behind the starting line and when so placed, they shall signal to the starter that all is ready. When a fresh start is ordered starter's assistants shall assemble the competitors again. When the starter has ordered the competitors to their marks, the starter's assistants must see that no competitor places either finger, hands or feet on the starting or in front of it. If any difficulty arises they should signal immediately to the starter.

The Announcer

The announcer shall announce to the public, the names and numbers of the competitors taking part in each event and all relevant information, such as the composition of the heats, lanes or stations drawn and intermediate times.

The result of each event should be announced at the earliest possible moment after receiving the information from the recorder.

The Recorder

The recorder shall collect the result of each event, together with the times or heights or distances, which shall be furnished to him by the referee, chief time keeper, Chief photo finish judge, and the wind gauge operator.

He shall communicate the information to the announcer as soon as possible and after recording the placings, times, heights or distances, he shall hand over the official result, together with all cards to the manager of the meet.

Lap Scorers

An additional lap scorer shall be appointed to notify to each competitor the number of laps which he still has to complete. He shall notify the final lap by the ringing of a bell or otherwise. The lap scorer shall keep a record of the laps covered by each competitor in races longer than 1500 metres. For races exceeding 5000 metres and for walking events a number of lap scorers shall be appointed and provided with lap scoring cards on which they shall record the times over each lap of the competitors for whom they are responsible. No lap scorer should record for more than four competitors.

Judges

The judges shall judge and record each trial and measure each valid trial of the competitors in all events in which the result is determined by height or distance. In the high jump and pole vault, precise measurements should be made when the bar is raised, particularly if records are being attempted. At least two Judges should keep a record of all trials, checking their recordings at the end of each round.

The appropriate Judge shall indicate the validity or non-validity of a trial by raising a white or red flag, as appropriate.

Timekeepers

The Timekeepers shall be in line with the finish and outside the track. Wherever possible, they should be placed at least five metres from the outside lane of the track. In order that they may all have a good view of the finish line, an elevated stand should be provided. Each Timekeeper shall act independently and without showing his watch to, or discussing his time with, any other person, enter his time on the official form and, after signing it, hand it to the Chief Timekeeper who may examine the watches to verify the reported times.

Timekeepers shall use either stopwatches or manually operated electronic timers with digital read outs. All such timing devices are termed "watches" for the purposes of I.A.A.F. Rules. A sufficient number of timekeepers for the number of competitors entered shall be appointed, one of whom shall be the Chief Timekeeper.

Measurement Judge

A measurement Judge shall be appointed when electronic distance measurement is to be used. Before the start of the meeting, he will meet the technical staff involved and familiarise himself with the equipment. He will report to the Field Event Referee to certify that all the measurements are correct.

Before the start of the meeting, he will meet the technical staff involved and familiarise himself with the equipment. During the competition he will remain in overall charge of the operation.

Clothing

In all events competitors must wear clothing which is clean, designed and worn so as not to be objectionable. The clothing must be made of a material which is non-transparent even if wet. The competitors must not wear clothing which could impede the view of the judges. At all meetings competitors shall participate in the uniform clothing approved by their National Governing Body. At all meetings, competitors shall participate in national uniform clothing or in club clothing officially approved by their National Governing Body.

Shoes

Competitors may compete in bare feet or with footwear on one or both feet. The purpose of shoes for competition is to give protection and stability to the feet and a firm grip on the ground. Such shoes, however, must not be constructed so as to give the competitor any additional assistance, and no spring or device of any kind may be incorporated in the shoes.

Number of Spikes

The sole and heel of the shoes shall be so constructed as to provide for the use of up to 11 spikes. Any number of spike up to 11 may be used but the number of spike positions shall not exceed.

The Sole and the Heel

The sole and or heel may have grooves, ridges, indentations or protuberances provided these features are constructed of the same or similar material to the basic sole itself.

In the high jump, the sole shall have a maximum thickness of 13 mm and the heel shall have a maximum thickness of 19 mm. In all other events the sole and/or heel may be of any thickness.

JUMPING EVENTS

As mentioned earlier, jumping events includes the two events, namely the Long Jump and High Jump. Here we will discuss both of these in detail.

LONG JUMP

The event of Long Jump is one of the oldest events of Field Events. The first recorded long jump dates back to ancient Greece and a Spartan called Chionis. The performance of ancient players was not very different or inferior in any way from our today's jumpers because of the fact that in old days, jumpers used perform short runs while carrying the weights in their hands.

Today, the technique of long jump has undergone

many changes. The first change is in the distance of the jump. Earlier 90 to 100 ft. was the minimum distance of the jump while today this distance has increased to 120 feet. Not only this, various new styles have been introduced in the event which were not used previously

For early periods it is said that pits were very poor in that time and it was not until 1886 that takeoff board was used. Because of lack of facilities and proper training, earlier performers were not able to make various or number of records in this event.

To perform or learn this event, not expensive or special equipments are required which makes it easy to participate in this event. However, it is very important to learn and understand the basic and fundamental skills of this event to become an outstanding player.

Skills and Techniques

There is not any particular criteria on the basis of which one can judge or decide who can become a good long jumper and who cannot, however, there are some qualities or abilities which, if present in one person, can make him a successful long jumper. Good sprinting speed, rhythmic, powerful jumping and consistent stride pattern are some of these qualities.

As has been said earlier that to become an outstanding player, one has to learn the basic and fundamental techniques of this event. The basic technique of the long jump can be broken in several parts which have been mentioned below:

<u>Approach</u>

The objective of each jumper is to cover maximum distance by his jump, for which he jumps according to his physical ability. To do this, before jumping, jumpers run from a particular distance which give them the power, by which they can put them to longer distance.

This run is called the Run Up or Approach.

Generally the total distance of approach varies between 90 feet and 130 feet. The odd number of strides is sometimes used with beginners because they may start the run, hit the check marks and the board all with the same foot. However, many jumpers walk, jog or run on to a starting mark.

With the feet together toeing the starting mark, beginner should start his run. He should step off with his foot with which he wants to hit the board and check marks. While approaching, jumper should get to take off board with a controlled speed and should possess the position to lift. Thus, while approaching, relaxation and consistency of stride length are two important factors.

One stride from take off board, jumper should run twelve to sixteen strides in opposite direction of jumping pit. He should do this till the same foot from which he has to hit the take off board lands on the track. Such kind of movement or action helps the athlete in performing properly. In this direction, jumper perform with four to five run through. This he does till his take off foot does not hit at the same point. Then, at that point, he places the checkmark, stand on stride away and with the take-off foot, hits the mark.

Jumper makes around four to five run through while running toward the jumping pit. This he do until the board is not hitten. As the jump is measured from scratch line, so it is very important for the jumper to perform accurately. So, on the approach run the important words are speed, rhythm, posture and accuracy.

Take-Off

The distance covered by the jumper will depend to a great extent on the take off. In this, jumper tries to transfer his forward momentum to upward and forward momentum.

After taking sufficient run up, the next to last stride is a longer, settling stride preparing for the lift. The last stride is shorter, and the takeoff hits in a heel toe action. The free leg comes through as in a normal running stride.

Before takeoff, during last third or fourths stride, runner settles into a controlled run. For average to good jumpers, the last stride to the toe-board is usually from 4 to 8 inches shorter than the preceding one.

The great sprinter could probably use a longer last stride if he had gained enough forward momentum to carry his body to beyond his foot at the takeoff. This would enable him to keep his foot longer on the board, and therefore exert more force with it.

Athlete should keep his eyes, head and chest in an erect position when board is being strucked by take off foot in a heel-ball toe motion. Athlete should swing his lead leg in forward and upward direction while keeping the knee flexed. To enable the jumper to use the hip swing, he should keep his back arched. The takeoff leg then comes up and body assumes a sitting position in preparation for the landing. To aid in elevating the body, arms are raised at the take off.

By the final two strides a very high speed should be

achieved. The penultimate stride is slightly longer than the preceding ones, with the hips lowering slightly in preparation for the spring off the board. At this stage of the approach the athlete must always think of high hips, even though they do actually sink. The final stride is a shorter stride, where effort is put into take-off. During the final stride the elbow opposite the take-off leg should be driven backward.

Flight

At the time of takeoff, the most important thing jumper should keep in his mind is to get height in his jump. Nothing can increase the distance covered by the jumper, except spot where his feet will land on the landing area. Just before landing, athlete should put his legs out in front, as this will help him in getting the feet in best landing position.

After leaving the ground, jumper cannot do anything which can help him in landing to the farther distance. Although the jumper can leave the board with forward rotation, backward rotation or no rotation at all, generally speaking there will be forward rotation in the body after take-off. If this is allowed to continue, without being slowed prematurely and a consequent loss of distance.

Thus, after leaving the board, the jumper can use one of the three types of techniques in the air, which are:

the hitch kick,

hang, or

the sail.

Hitch Kick—This is done with a run in the air action.

Hang—This is performed by letting the legs hang down, with the hips forward and the upper body back.

Sail—In this technique, the legs are tucked up under

the body.

The purpose of all the above mentioned methods is to prevent forward rotation and to get good leg extension in landing.

After achieving the knee opposite hip position, jumper should allow the free leg to drop down long. Left leg moves in forward direction while bending at the knee, then right leg joins it in order to prepare for landing. Athlete should not achieve hang position very early. Firstly, he should possess the knee opposite hip position and then switch to this so called Hang Position.

Landing

Getting good extension is very important for good landing. So, as landing begins, athlete should hold his feet high. Until the buttocks nearly strike the ground, he should keep his legs fully extended. After this, head, chest and shoulders should thrust in forward direction and when the heels touch the pit, knees should be kept in a relaxed state. Jumper should possess a compact tuck position and should fall onto his hands and knees.

Athlete should have strong abdominal muscle action to keep the feet high. This is the main phase of whole event which requires a lot of practice, for which short run, jumping into a pit of foam rubber or other shot absorbing material proves to be helpful.

Jumper should work through the jump so that he does not sit back, which is done by dropping the chin to chest and by driving the arms forcefully behind the body, i.e., in backward direction.

Rules

The Competition

A competitor is considered to be failed :

-If while jumping he touches the ground beyond the take-off line with any part of his body;

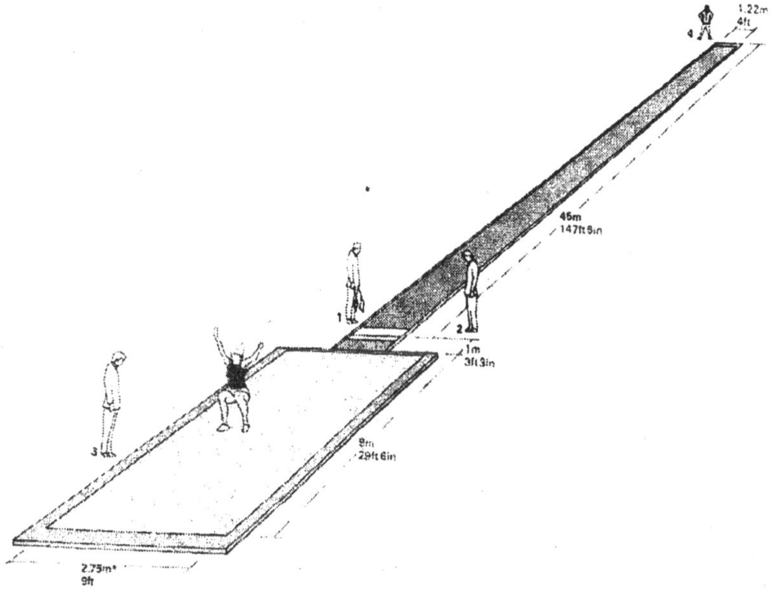

-if he takes off from outside either end of the board, whether beyond or before the extension of the take-off line;

-if he touches the ground outside the landing area nearer to the take-off than the nearest break in the landing area while jumping;

-if he walks back through landing area after jump;

-if he uses any form of somersaulting while running up or in the act of jumping.

The place where competitors body first falls in landing area will be basis for measurement of jumps. It should be measured perpendicular to take-off line.

Take-Off: A failure is counted if a competitor touches with any part of his body the ground beyond the take-off line or take-off line extended. This rule applies whether competitor makes his jump or merely runs up without jumping. Long jumpers may not use weights or grips.

The Take-off Board

A board should be used to mark sunk level with runway and surface of landing area. There will be a take-off line which will be the edge of board nearer to the landing area and beyond which there will be a Plasticine indicator board which will assist the judges. If it is not possible to use the above mentioned apparatus, immediately beyond the take-off line and across the length of it over a width of 10cm the ground should be sprinkled with soft earth or sand, at an angle of 30° horizontally. Minimum distance of 10m should be there between the take-off board and far end of landing area.

The Landing Area

It can have a width of 2.75m but not more than 3m and should be placed in middle of runway. The sand in the landing area should be moistened before the competition begins. It must be raked level with the take-off board before every jump.

Landing

It is a failure if the competitor when landing:

—touches the ground outside the landing area nearer to take-off than the nearest break in the landing area;

—employs any form of somersaulting;

—after a completed jump walks back through the sand.

Judging

There are four judges. One judge watches for failures; he has two flags, one red and one white. Two judges measure the jump after marking it and the fourth judge calls up competitors and clears the runway.

Measurements

A jump is measured from the nearest break in the landing area made by any part of the competitor's body. Measurement is up to the take-off line and at right angles to it. Distances are recorded to the nearest 1cm below the distance jumped.

HIGH JUMP

The earliest records of high Jump competitions date back to Africa. They are also known to have been part of the ancient Greek Olympic Games. The winner of the gold medal in the first modern Olympics in Athens, 1896 was Ellery Clark of the USA.

High jump is a run, jump and lay-out over a bar. Many kinds of changes have come in this event. The improvement in landing areas is one of the principal factors. Earlier, lands with grass were used as landing area. With the invention of the Fosbury flop, soft foam landing areas were used which helped the jumpers from being injured.

In early day, landing areas were not used because of which event proved very dangerous on many occasions. While using the Scissors Style, athlete use to clear the bar in a trunk upright position and gave a lot of notice and consideration to the place where he would land. While clearing, he kept his body above the bar, however, this was not a very efficient or good position. Because some faults were found in this method, a new method or technique was used for this purpose which was called the Eastern Cut Off. This later method gave more efficient layout over the bar in comparison to the previously used method. But, this method was not so successful in providing the efficient bar clearance position. Thus, a new method again replace this method which was the Western Roll. With this new method, jumpers became able to clear the bar efficiently and this also allowed them an angled approach to the bar. After this came the Straddle technique. This was proved to be the most successful technique in this event the evidence of which is the fact that still today this technique is being used by a large number of jumpers even today. However, no one can use this technique without getting prior coaching or training for this technique. One should carefully learn this technique and then only should use it.

In this event, jumpers often have to face problem of converting the forward momentum of the body to a vertical direction. By crouching slightly during last two or three stride and by sticking the take off foot well ahead of the body helps in facing this problem.

A jumper can use any method he likes or in which he feels comfortable, but today, almost all high jumpers use the Flop technique, which is because of the fact that this method offers many advantages. This method is crude, one can learn it easily. However, while using it, athlete should ensure that a soft foam landing area is available, otherwise this can prove to be very dangerous for the athlete.

Skills and Techniques

'Jumping High' and 'Economy of Clearance' are the two important factors which one jumper should keep in his mind while performing. For the sake of correct position, not much attention is paid to factor of 'Jumping High' these days.

The skills and techniques of this event can be broken into the following phases or parts:

Approach

Large number of jumpers use the J approach, which includes run of three, four or five stride straight ahead, after which three, four or five stride run in curve shape. To maintain velocity into the bar, jumper must lean to the inside of the arc. While performing, jumper should keep in his mind that speed is very important for proper approach.

Take Off

Last two or three steps of the run and actions of all body parts of the athlete are considered to be the part of Take Off.

The velocity with which athlete drives his body vertically from it base is considered to be an important factor in judging his efficiency to perform take off. Last three steps should be smooth and quick. Such kind of speedily steps help in bringing the take off ahead of the body weight and force an upward leap. At first, centre gravity of athlete's body lowered well back of take off, by which heel is drive hard into the ground.

Jumpers prefer a heelless track shoe because bracing action involves backward lean with the weight on heel. It also involve Les Steers to construct a special having the no-heel feature of the ordinary track shoe. Lowering of body is necessary for last two steps, which is a natural accompaniment of backward lean. This aids in action described as well as leap into the air.

It can be said that this action put the legs effectively in proper position. Athlete should keep his eyes always in upward direction. Position of eyes should not changed even if the height of bar is less than the athlete. This will aid the backward lean and emphasize the important principle that all jumps should be made as though the bar were higher than one's head.

In a nearly vertical direction, lead leg should be thrown vigorously with straight knees. Athlete's foot should point in straight upward direction and over the bar should start its turning. It is difficult to perform excellently from take off leg. When a distance of around six inches remain between head of the athlete and the bar, athlete should move his head. Athlete should keep this principle in his mind irrespective of the fact that whether the height of bar is higher or lower than his head.

Clearing the Bar

To clear the bar, many methods are used by the jumpers some of which are as follows:

1. Western Roll

From the side next to the bar, clearance in this

technique is made. Here we are describing that how a left foot jumper will perform while using this technique. If jumper is left footed, he will run from his left foot, take off from left foot, run from left foot, clear the bar with left foot and land on his left side. With an angle of 45°, run is generally made.

With the direction of the run, both the planting of take off foot and vigorous swinging of the lead leg is done. In terms of take off and upward propulsion, this straight ahead and vertical throw of right leg seems to be logical. In place of Straddle Form, beginners should use this technique.

While doing this, athlete should keep in his mind the probable change over and with this a form of Western Roll develops. This form so called the Western Roll will be consistent with straddle and involve no or less change in action.

By a vertical hunch of the inside left shoulder and arm, this action should be accompanied. With this action, vertical jump is insured and before completing the jump, it also prevent a premature lay out. During the take-off, athlete should keep his head vertical.

All jumps are advised to assume that the bar is higher than the head and that therefore one must jump up before attempting to lie out. Earlier actions in the take off are main factors on which position of the body while directly over the bar depends. Thus, Western Roll is very famous and used by a large number of jumpers because of its simplicity.

2. Straddle Form

Most perfect technique of performing this event is known as Straddle Form. In terms of economy of clearance of bar, it is considered to be the final form. However, with advantages it has some disadvantages also. It is considered poorest of all forms in its tendency to lessen the effectiveness of the take-off and of all actions related to this event.

To perform the later action in this technique, jumpers lean in toward the bar at take off, take the weight of their body on whole foot inspite on its heel, turn the take off in to the left and toward the body, bend the lead leg, cut its vigorous upward action.

Once athlete has raised his head and shoulders above the bar, he should turn them in downward direction and to left side toward the bar. This whole action should be done very quickly. In achieving a full body twist, this snap of head around and down is considered to be an important factor. With this, left leg of the athlete is pulled over and away from the bar. In this turn, left arm should aid to left side and from its position should be thrown at side or above the head and to its left side.

Movement upward and to left of the left hip, leg and foot is considered to be the last of all movements while clearing the bar. Twisting snap outward and upward of the toe of left foot is considered an effective and good method. Properly done action can move the knee and hip. While landing, body weight will shift on to the right leg, however, the body will roll over to left shoulder and back if the leftward turn has been executed properly. With an unusual jar, this will break the fall.

Thus, the jumper can use any of the above mentioned methods.

Whichever method has been used while there are some points which all the jumpers should keep in mind while clearing the bar. Athlete should keep his lead knee in upward direction. He should keep both the legs at a distance from each other, while the knees should be in a frog position while both feet should be near to each other. Till bar passes along the back and the hips, there should be a laying back of the head and an arching of the back. To fold the body in an L position, athlete should tucked down the chin to the chest.

Rules

The high jump is made over a crossbar between rigid uprights. The crossbar is raised after each round, and competitors remain in the competition until eliminated by three consecutive failures.

The Competition

One foot will be used by the competitor to take off. In the following conditions competitor is considered to be failed:

-If because of action of competitor after the jump, the bar does not remain on the supports; or

-If without clearing the bar he touches with any part of his body the ground including the landing area beyond the plane of the nearer edge of the uprights, either between or outside the uprights.

The Runway and Take-off Area

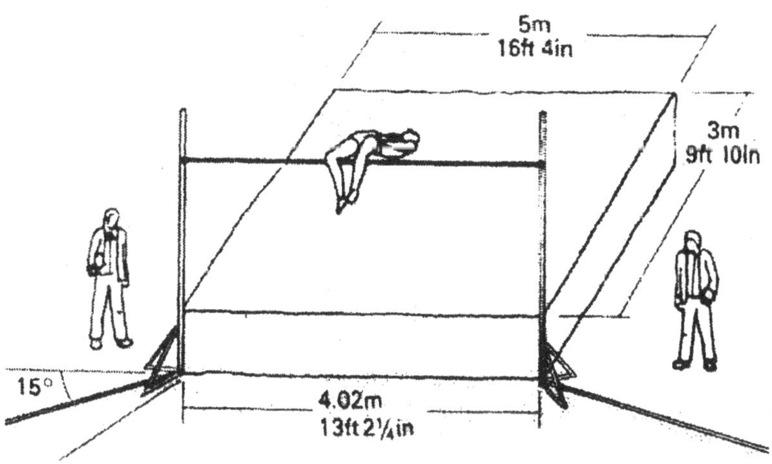

In all competitions runway should not be less than 15m but in competitions held under Rule 12.1(a), (b) and (c) this size increases to 20m, which can be increased to 25m if conditions permit. Overall inclination of runway of area should not exceed 1:250 which should be in the centre of the crossbar.

Landing Area

a. Minimum size of landing area should be 5m×3m.

Important: To avoid displacement of the crossbar the uprights and landing area should also be designed so that there is a clearance of at least 10cm between them when in use.

Crossbar

It should be circular. Crossbar support must face the opposite upright and be flat or rectangular. Each end of the bar will have a flat or concave surface for the purpose of placing the bar on the supports. It must weigh not more than 2kg.

There must be a gap of at least 10mm between the ends of the crossbar and the uprights and the crossbar must rest on the uprights in such a way that, if touched by a competitor, it falls easily forward or backward to the ground. The crossbar must always be replaced with the same surfaces facing upward and forward.

Procedure

Starting heights for each round are announced by the judges before the event begins. The minimum height the bar is raised for each round is 2cm. Competitors may start jumping when they wish and choose whether to attempt any subsequent height. Elimination occurs after three consecutive failures, regardless of the height at which they occur.

Apparatus

Uprights. Uprights should be rigid and can be of any style. Crossbars should be fixed to them properly and should have sufficient height in which crossbar can be raised upto 10cm. At least 4m should be the distance between the uprights but this distance should not exceed more than 4.04m.

Judging

There are 2 or 3 judges who ensure that the apparatus and landing area are in order and that all jumps are correctly made.

Measurements

Perpendicularly from the ground to the lowest part of the upper side of the bar the measurements are made. New heights are measured before jumping begins, and heights are re-measured after jumping if a record is to be established.

12

Awards in Athletics

As we know that in order to encourage the athletes and to honour their good performance, Govt. of India provide various kinds of awards to players related to various events, and thus is the case with Athletes. As we know that various competitions are being organised in which athletes take part and on basis of their performance in these competitions, they are provided with awards. Many kinds of awards are provided to these players, however we have mentioned in this chapter the names of various athletes and the years in which they were provided to the athletes.

Rajiv Gandhi Khel Ratna Award

S.No.	Winner	Year
1.	Smt. Jyotirmoyee Sikdar	1998-99
2.	Mrs. Anju Bobby George	2003

Dronacharya Award

S.No.	Winner	Year
1.	Sh. O.M. Nambiar	1985
2.	Md. Ilyas Babar	1994
3.	Sh. Karan Singh	1995
4.	Sh. Joginder Singh Saini	1997
5.	Sh. Bahadur Singh	1998
6.	Sh. Hargobind Singh Sandhu	1998
7.	Sh. Kenneth Owen Bosen	1999

8.	Ms. Renu Kohli	2002
9.	Shri Jaswant Singh	2002
10.	Sh. Robert Bobby George	2003
11.	Sh. Robert Bobby George	2004

Arjun Award Winners

1.	Sh. G.S. Randhava	1961
2.	Hav. Tarloak Singh	1962
3.	Km. Stephi D' Souza	1963
4.	Sh. Makhan Singh	1964
5.	Sh. K.L. Pawell	1965
6.	Sh. Ajmer Singh	1966
7.	Sh. B.S. Barua	1966
8.	Sh. Parveen Kumar	1967
9.	Sh. Bhim Singh	1967
10.	Capt. Joginder Singh	1968
11.	Km. Manjit Walia	1968
12.	Hav. Karnek Singh	1969
13.	Sh. Mohinder Singh Gill	1970
14.	Sh. Edward Sequeria	1971
15.	Sh. Vijay Singh Chauhan	1972
16.	Hav. Sriram Singh	1973
17.	Sh. T.C. Yohannan	1974
18.	Sh. S.S. Rajput	1974
19.	Km. V. Ansuya Bai	1975
20.	Inspector Hari Chand	1975
21.	Km. Geeta Zutshi	1976

22.	Sh. Bahadur Singh	1976
23.	Sh. Satish Kumar	1977-78
24.	Km. Angle Mary Joseph	1978-79
25.	Sh. Suresh Babu	1978-79
26.	Sh. R. Gyanasekharn	1979-80
27.	Sh. Gopal Saini	1980-81
28.	Sh. Sabir Ali	1981
29.	Sh. Charles Boromeo	1982
30.	Sh. Chand Ram	1982
31.	Sh. M.D. Valsamma	1982
32.	Kin. P.T. Usha	1983
33.	Capt. Suresh Yadav	1983
34.	Km. Shiny K. Abraham	1984
35.	Shri Raj Kumar	1984
36.	Shri R.S. Bal	1985
37.	Km. Asha Agarwal	1985
38.	Sh. A.J. Sumariwalla	1985
39.	Km. Suman Rawat	1986
40.	Sh. Balwinder Singh	1987
41.	Sh. Bagicha Singh	1987
42.	Km. Vandana Rao	1987
43.	Km. Vandana Shanbagh	1987
44.	Km. Ashwini Nachapa	1988
45.	Smt. Mercy Kuttan	1989
46.	Shri Deena Ram	1990
47.	Smt. Bahadur Prasad	1992

48.	Km. K. Saramma	1993
49.	Mr. K.C. Rosa Kutty	1994
50.	Ms. Jyotirimoye Sikdar	1995
51.	Shri Shakti Singh	1995
52.	Shri Ajit Bhaduria	1996
53.	Ms. Padmini Thomas	1996
54.	Smt. Reeth Abraham	1997
55.	Ms. Neelam J. Singh	1998
56.	Ms. Rachita Mistry	1998
57.	Capt. Shri Chand Ram, VSM	1998
58.	Mr. S.D. Eshan	1998
59.	Shri Paramjit Singh	1998
60.	Shri Gulab Chand	1999
61.	Smt. Gurmeet Kaur	1999
62.	Capt. Ris Maj. Parduman Singh	1999
63.	Ms. Sunita Rani	1999
64.	Ms. K.M. Beenamol	2000
65.	Smt. Anju Bobby George	2002
66.	Smt. Saraswati Saha	2002
67.	Km. Soma Biswas	2003
68.	Smt. Madhuri Saxena	2003
69.	Smt. Anju Bobby George	2004

Dhyan Chand Award

1.	Brig. Labh Singh	2004
2.	Sh. Digamber P. Mehendale	2004